A
Town Like
Paris

A Town Like Paris

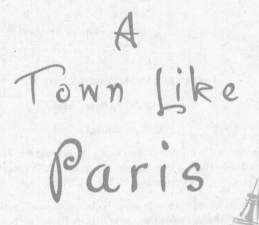

Falling in Love in the City of Light

Bryce Corbett

BROADWAY BOOKS

NEW YORK

PUBLISHED BY BROADWAY BOOKS

Originally published in a slightly different form in Australia and New Zealand as *A Town Called Paris* by Hachette Livre Australia, Sydney, in 2007. This edition published by arrangement with Hachette Livre.

Published in the United States by Broadway Books, an imprint of The Doubleday Broadway Publishing Group, a division of Random House, Inc., New York.

www.broadwaybooks.com

Book design by Caroline Cunningham

Library of Congress Cataloging-in-Publication Data
Corbett, Bryce.
A Town Like Paris : falling in love in the city of light / Bryce Corbett.
p. cm.
1. Paris (France)—Social life and customs. 2. Paris (France)—Description and travel.
3. Love—France—Paris. 4. National characteristics, French. 5. Sex customs—France—Paris. I. Title.

DC715.C77 2008
944'.361084—dc22
2007039138

ISBN 978-0-7679-2817-5

PRINTED IN THE UNITED STATES OF AMERICA

1 3 5 7 9 10 8 6 4 2

First U.S. Edition

For Shay, who inspires me daily.

And for my parents,

who have always been there for me.

"*Writing should be testimony to the vast flow of life through us.*"

—Victor Serge

"*We shall not cease from exploration, and the end of all our exploring will be to arrive where we started and know the place for the first time.*"

—T. S. Eliot

Contents

A
Town Like
Paris

Chapter 1

Are You Sure You've Got
the Right Person?

I N JANUARY 2000 the world was flush with the excitement of a new millennium, and I was crossing a continent on a day-return train ticket to do an interview for a job I wasn't the least bit interested in.

It was a typically gray European winter's day, the kind that makes you wonder when you last felt properly warm and why you left your sun-drenched homeland in the first place. On the tray table in front of me, a collection of barely opened books told the riveting tale of European economic integration. I knew the tale was riveting because I had fallen asleep over it three times in the last hour. Outside the flat, featureless plains of Picardy flashed by in a dark brown blur. I hunkered down in my seat and wondered who the hell I thought I was kidding and what the hell I was doing here in the first place.

It had all started one dull November afternoon in the newsroom of the twenty-four-hour TV news channel for which I worked in London. As a showbiz producer for Sky News, my job consisted of keeping track of the tedious intricacies of the lives of inherently dull, inexplicably famous people. This particular afternoon saw me flicking listlessly through copies of *Hello!*, *OK!*, and other quality celebrity mags under the pretense of doing my job.

Finished with my research, and motivated by the kind of pure boredom that I felt at least seven or eight times an hour in that job, I wandered over to the nearby cluster of desks occupied by the business reporters.

Financial news commanded almost as much importance in the minds of Sky News's editors as entertainment news, occupying the small portion at the end of every news bulletin that was not otherwise dedicated to soccer, royals, or whatever "shock crime wave" they were manufacturing on any given day. As a result, the finance reporters were at least as underutilized as we showbiz reporters, leading to much crossing of the corridor, bored chitchat, and the occasional perusing of one another's magazine collections. While our repository of showbiz and gossip rags were especially prized in the greater newsroom environment—and hence were often stolen—their piles of *The Economist* and *BusinessWeek* were usually left unopened.

It was only out of abject desperation, and some perverse idea that its contents might serve to expand my mind, that I picked up a copy of *The Economist* and started flicking through it. On previous sorties into the dense geopolitical realm of *The Economist*, my sense of the absurd had been piqued by the jobs section. If you've ever had the pleasure of perusing it, you will know that the job advertisements there are weekly exercises in bureaucratic nonsense. *The Economist* is where you advertise any job that should otherwise exist only in a comedy sketch or an Evelyn Waugh novel. For instance, it's where the Ugandan Ministry for Roads might post a half-page advertisement for a new Deputy Director of Road Leveling.

> The successful applicant will have at least five years road-leveling experience at an international level, must be familiar with the latest global standards for gutters, be good with concrete, be a dab hand at dealing with troublesome secessionist rebel soldiers, and be in possession of a license to operate heavy road-leveling machinery. The Ugandan Ministry of Roads is a nonsmoking workplace and an equal opportunity employer.

It's quite common to find within *The Economist*'s job section ads for project directors for far-flung fieldwork in random West African nations, for which, mysteriously, the speaking of fluent Finnish always seems mandatory. In between guffaws and inner monologues on the shocking waste of taxpayers' money that was routinely channeled into the creation of these absurd jobs, I happened upon one advertisement that caught my eye:

> The International Chamber of Commerce (ICC) is seeking a Director of Communications. ICC is the world business organization. The applicant will be responsible for the global communications strategy of the organization. He/she must be familiar with the work of the ICC and have at least five years experience as a PR and communications director of an intergovernmental or nongovernmental organization of similar international stature. He/she must have demonstrated managerial experience and at least ten years experience in an executive role in the private or public sector. The candidate will be experienced in the creation and implementation of effective media and communications strategies. He/she will be fluent in French and English and have excellent writing and organizational skills.

And then, almost apologetically, at the end:

> The successful candidate will be required to relocate to Paris and be expected to undertake regular international travel.

I did a quick mental checklist of my work history and concluded I was hopelessly underqualified for the job. I didn't have any of the experience they were looking for, I knew nothing about international organizations, my French was rusty from years of neglect, and I neither knew nor cared what the ICC was, what it did, or who it represented.

What I did know was that I had always dreamed of living and working in Paris, that I was nothing if not creative when it came to CVs, and that one more month spent in London, doing the daily early morning shuffle out to the industrial park in far west London that Sky News called home was surely going to kill me.

I took to my computer and bashed out a letter of application, making a few judicious changes to my patently unsuitable résumé. A spot of finance reporting here, a sustained period of economic analysis there—anything to make my gossip-columnist past and entertainment-producer present seem less obvious to a bunch of suits in Paris.

Three weeks later an in-depth editorial conversation with colleagues about the new Britney Spears single was interrupted by the shrill ring of my telephone. On the other end of the line was an English gentleman, introducing himself as Lionel from the ICC in Paris, asking if I was available for interview.

"It will require you to come to Paris for the day, I am afraid," he explained. "It seems our secretary-general is very interested in your résumé, and she would like to meet you."

As I frantically tried to recall the extent to which I had embellished my résumé, I found myself agreeing to a rendezvous in Paris in a week's time.

What a hoot! A fully funded day trip to Paris—a chance to escape the office, scarf a few crepes, and sink a carafe of Bordeaux or two in my favorite city in the world. Sure, the hour of the actual interview might prove a little awkward, and the ensuing embarrassment when they discovered that I was a patently underqualified charlatan might be a tad uncomfortable, but for the sake of a free trip to Paris, it was a risk I was willing to take. Besides, it would make for a great story at my next dinner party.

So here I was now, barely an hour out of Paris, cramming for an interview for a job I didn't really want, speed-reading an array of books whose titles I barely understood. I paused to reflect on the improbability of it all.

There was no way in the world a Paris-based international business organization, deeply involved in the cut and thrust of global commerce, was going to employ a former Sydney gossip columnist as its director of communications. Quite apart from the fact that I was spectacularly underqualified and uniquely lacking in relevant work experience, I was twenty-eight years old, single, and possessed of only one purpose in life: to be as drunk as possible for as sustained a period as possible in as many exotic European locations as possible. Surely they would see that and send me packing.

The train made its slow crawl through the outer suburbs of Paris. Graffiti-covered walls, heavy industry warehouses, and nondescript high-rises gradually gave way to lead-roofed apartments, terracotta chimney pots, and glimpses of streets lined with *brasseries, boulangeries,* and *épiceries.*

As we glided up alongside the platform at Gare du Nord, I stared up in wonder at the lattice of glass and iron that formed the massive canopy of the station. Businessmen strode purposefully along the platform in finely cut overcoats and artfully tied scarves. Women in heels and woolen twinsets moved gracefully among the throng. It had all the bustle and movement of your average train station, yet there was something otherworldly about it: as if by crossing the English Channel and entering the Paris city limits, I had been transported to an older, more elegant place in time.

I joined the surge of people alighting from the train and making for the taxi stand. Standing patiently in line, I was bewitched by scenes of Paris café life across the street. A waiter in black tie and wearing a long apron moved officiously among tables, dispensing espressos and handing out croissants. His patrons sipped on their coffees and lazily perused their newspapers, apparently disinclined to interrupt the gentle pace of their morning reverie with anything as troublesome as work. I reflected upon this sudden change in workaday pace as I clambered into the back of a taxi and instructed my driver in broken French to take me to the Place d'Alma in the eighth arrondissement.

Crossing a wide boulevard, I glanced to my right. The Arc de Triomphe stood proudly at the top of the Champs Elysées. The sun had mustered enough strength to cast the massive monument in a bold yellow light. I was gobsmacked. If Edith Piaf or the French national anthem, "La Marseillaise," had suddenly burst forth from the radio, I wouldn't have been the least bit surprised. To my left, the Champs

Elysées, the most famous avenue in the world, unfurled between leafless trees to the Place de la Concorde, ending at the Jardin des Tuileries—and beyond it the Louvre. I was having a pure Paris moment.

The spell was soon broken, however, as we pulled up outside the ICC. Though surrounded on either side by stunning nineteenth-century Haussmannian *hôtels particuliers,* the International Chamber of Commerce was housed inside a squat gray concrete bunker—an architectural carbuncle on the otherwise-picturesque Cours Albert 1er.

From the lobby, I called up to the communications department. As I waited to be met, I ambled nervously about the reception area. Flags of every nation were mounted in the entrance hall. Faded and dusty, they hung limply under wan fluorescent lighting. A collection of ICC publications lined the walls: books with titles I didn't understand, dealing with subjects I neither knew nor very much cared about. I cursed myself for not having better prepared for the interview.

A few minutes later a jovial, late-sixty-something gentleman walked down the stairs and introduced himself as Lionel.

"Welcome, welcome," he said, taking my hand and shaking it rigorously. "It's very good of you to come over. I trust you had a pleasant journey." He was an English gentleman, of the old-school type. After exchanging pleasantries and leaving my coat with the receptionist, we made our way up carpeted stairs to the office of ICC's secretary-general. Lionel gave the door a gentle knock.

"Come in!" barked a voice from the other side.

Pushing open the double doors, Lionel ushered me into the office. A small woman in her early fifties, with short cropped hair and a profusion of gold jewelry, sprang up from behind her desk and charged over to shake my hand.

"How do you do. Maria Cattaui," she offered brusquely, shaking my hand and indicating for Lionel and me to take a seat. I could tell it was not going to be an easy chat about the weather.

Maria had spent the better part of the last twenty years creating and nurturing the development of the hugely successful, high-powered business and political love-in that is the annual World Economic Forum in Davos. Now, sitting across the table from me, she proceeded to hold forth about the ICC, her new pet project—its goals, its objectives, and its need for dedicated, attentive personnel.

I didn't absorb a word. I was too busy being transfixed by the view from her window, taking in as it did a majestic sweep of the Seine and a stunning view of the Eiffel Tower. With an idiot's grimace pasted to my face and the presence of mind to occasionally nod in answer to her questions, I sat and stared at the Bateaux Mouches plying their way up the river. I imagined the route they were about to undertake, past the Louvre, under the Pont Neuf, and around the flying buttresses of Notre Dame. Paris, the old harlot, was already casting her spell, seducing me with coy flashes of her well-worn but timeless beauty.

Fortunately for me, Maria's interviews consisted more of oration than actual conversation. They were little more than an opportunity for her to give rein to her fierce intellect and hold forth on whatever topic of macroeconomic importance had taken her fancy that particular day. More often than not, they were also a chance for her to show off the caliber of her considerably bulging black book. After half an hour of listening to her reminisce about the time Yassir Arafat refused to use the same backstage door at the World Economic Forum as Ehud Barak, I stood to leave the room, certain I had done little to convince this woman of my suitability for the job. Not even my considerable charisma, I reasoned, could have shone through in the three words she allowed me between Clinton anecdotes.

But as we walked down the stairs back toward the lobby, Lionel turned to me and chuckled. "Well, it looks like you've got the job then," he said.

I stopped dead in my tracks and looked at him quizzically. "You can't be serious," I replied. "I barely got a word in edgewise. She didn't ask me a single question. All I did was sit there and nod." These were, I would learn later, two qualities that made me eminently qualified for the position.

It was early afternoon as I stepped out onto the street.

"So I'll be in touch to discuss particulars," Lionel chirruped as he waved me down the street.

"Right," I replied, doing my best to disguise the look of shock. "We'll be in touch." The shock then began to yield to a sense of rising panic. This wasn't part of the plan. It was just meant to be a day-trip jolly to Paris. A brief respite from the monotony of Sky News. A little jaunt to the Continent for a crepe and a carafe, and a random job interview squeezed in between.

With two hours to kill before my return train to London, I decided to walk back toward Gare du Nord, to clear my head and weigh the decision that I suddenly, unexpectedly had before me. The last of autumn's yellow leaves clung to the trees as I wandered past the Grand Palais. To my right, beyond the elegant arc of the Pont Alexandre III and framed by its ornate lamps, sat Les Invalides, its gilt-edged dome glinting in the afternoon sun. I thought of London—of the gray skies, the cold single mattress on the floor that constituted my bedroom in the tiny West London terrace house I shared with five other people— and wondered if my time there was up.

But to move to Paris? Where I knew no one, where my university-level French, last studied eight years ago, was certain to be wholly inadequate to the task of daily living, where I had neither lodgings nor family nor friends? To take a job I wasn't qualified for, much less interested in? It didn't make a whole lot of sense. But then again, this was Paris. The world's most beautiful city. The urban embodiment of all that is chic, stylish, and desirable. The most visited city in the world— rich in history, crammed with culture, and chock-full of possibilities for a single guy in need of a change of scene following the recent breakdown of a nine-year relationship.

Stepping out on the Place de la Concorde, I glanced to my left and took in the scene. Countless postcards, vacation photos, and picture books had rendered this scene familiar, yet its beauty still startled me. Elaborate twin fountains threw jets of water ostentatiously into the air, while the majestic Hôtel de Crillon kept silent watch.

It was madness, surely. What about my journalism career? What interest did I have in becoming a PR flack for an international business organization? But then how else was I ever going to have the opportunity to live and work in Paris? I had always fancied myself doing a stint in the City of Light, and here it was being offered on a platter. Sometimes, I told myself, life takes turns you cannot predict. Opportunities are presented that you could never imagine would come your way. I was twenty-eight years old with no girlfriend or wife, no children, and no mortgage to pay. I was as free as I was ever going to be in life. What's more, I had a broken heart in need of mending and was in a dead-end job in a city I had grown to resent. I might have only one opportunity in my life to live and work in Paris, and this was probably it.

The white gravel of the Jardin des Tuileries crunched underfoot. Kids dressed in immaculate woolen tunics pushed toy sailboats across a pond. Through the skeletal branches of carefully cropped plane trees, the baroque, honeycomb facade of the Louvre loomed large. The fast-sinking sun caught the top of the glass pyramid in the museum's courtyard. Reaching the courtyard, I took a seat and a very deep breath. I didn't know a soul in Paris. I would be moving to a city where I would be starting all over again. It was terrifying. I took my cell phone out of my pocket and dialed the ICC.

"May I speak with Lionel Walsh please?" I felt my heart pounding as I was put through. "Hi, it's Bryce. Bryce Corbett. When would you like me to start?"

Chapter 2

Goodbye to All That

W HERE TO THEN, GUV?" It was the taxi driver. His Ford Escort was idling outside the council flat in the down-at-heel south London suburb of Bermondsey where I had been staying with friends prior to my trip.

A month had passed since my phone call to Lionel. I had used the time to quit my job at Sky News, squeeze my belongings into a backpack and a suitcase, and bid farewell to my London friends. A pale morning sun battled valiantly to exude a modicum of warmth. The bare branches of trees cut an intricate black web into an otherwise nondescript, white-gray sky.

It had taken two years of living in London to come across a stereotypical London cabbie: soft-cloth cap pulled down over impish eyes, a beige cardigan reeking of smoke, and a bulbous nose sprouting like a mushroom from a face scored with lines. It seemed somehow fitting that this man was now taking me on my last drive through the streets of London.

"Waterloo Station, thanks," I replied. "Eurostar terminal."

"Right you are."

Row after row of council flats and terrace houses passed in a blur of gray and brown. London had its own charm, but I wouldn't be sorry to say goodbye. The cabbie didn't know it, but with each corner we turned, he was driving me farther away from a difficult period in my life.

I had arrived almost two years previously, the latest in a very long line of reverse colonials to try his hand at London town. Turning my back on a good job and a promising career as a Sydney gossip columnist, I had left Australia bent on European adventure—and determined to reinvigorate a flagging nine-year relationship.

My girlfriend of almost a decade—a high school sweetheart and my first great love—had made the journey to England, via India, some four months previously. The idea was that we would set up home together in a brand-new country, find ourselves whatever grotty bedsit our Australian pesos could afford, get a couple of jobs, and enjoy the freedom and anonymity of a city where no one knows your name. It was to be a fresh start. A new beginning. A leap of faith for the sake of a relationship that had accounted for—and defined—our entire adult lives. But this rearguard attempt to salvage the sinking ship that was our partnership was doomed even before my jet touched down in Heathrow.

Within weeks of my arrival, we decided to break up. To say that coming to terms with the end of a nine-year relationship, in the relative discomfort of a friend's council flat in a grim suburb in south London, far from family, without a job and in the dead of winter, was a difficult experience would be something of an understatement. As opening gambits for overseas adventures go, it wasn't the most promising.

The eighteen months that ensued were an excruciating exercise in postbreakup pain-prolongation. Sporadic contact, semiregular exposure to each other via a network of mutual friends, and a dogged sense of loyalty to the good years we had had together meant that neither of us had properly moved on.

I was ready for Paris. Ready for a change of scene and a shedding of some emotional baggage. I was well and truly finished with love. I'd given it nine years of my life, and watched it all come crashing down around me. I'd spent almost two years now wallowing in postbreakup self-pity. It was time for a bit of guilt-free, utterly indulgent, bachelor-inspired fun.

The taxi dropped me at the Eurostar terminal. Waterloo Station was typically manic. With a backpack and an oversize wheelie suitcase, I weaved my way through the Sunday-morning masses, struggled onto my train, and settled in. The train pulled out of the station and rocked gently toward Vauxhall and Clapham. Through gaps in buildings sep-arating the railroad from the Thames, I caught glimpses of Big Ben and the Houses of Parliament. As the city receded behind me, the weight of the moment took hold. So this was it, then. I was actually doing it. Leaving behind the comfort of the familiar for the adventure of the unknown. Turning my back on a life that—though certainly not perfect—was easy, filled with friends, and crucially, conducted in my mother tongue.

I thought ahead to Paris and how the sum total of my experience of the foreign metropolis in which I had chosen to live was two fleet-ing visits over a carefree summer spent backpacking across Europe as a student. I would be starting over. Beginning again. Turning my back on all that I knew and throwing my lot in with a country where I wasn't even sure I could speak the language. But then I reflected on how London and I had never really seen eye to eye. How, despite hav-ing enjoyed a brief, passionate fling, London and I were destined never to stay together.

Certainly London was vibrant, dynamic, and exciting. It was—and is—a hotbed of creativity, a global trendsetter, a world capital in the strictest sense of the term. But experience had taught me that if you weren't making buckets of pounds in London, only portions of that excitement were accessible. What's more, everything in London seemed so tepid compared to what I had been used to back home in Australia. Instead of bold colors and big skies, there had been shades of gray and perpetual cloud cover. Everything seemed washed out. The showers were pathetic dribbles out of the bathroom wall. The fresh produce in Safeway was pale, almost apologetic. Nothing in London had any robustness.

But more than that, London had been a bloody hard place to live. Every morning there felt like the start of a new campaign in an endless war of attrition. It was me against the city, in a daily test to see who would give in first. In London's armory were the Tube, the crowds, the weather, the food, and the prohibitive cost of living, the combined firepower of which I was powerless to resist. Every time I stepped out my front door, twenty pounds seemed to mysteriously disappear from my wallet. Just taking a breath seemed to cost me a fiver. At the end of some days out on the town, I would sit in my sparsely furnished bedroom, reflect upon the parlous state of my finances, and wonder if I wouldn't have made better use of my time simply by staying at home, making a little pile of cash on the floor, and setting it alight. At least that way I would have been momentarily warm and dry, neither of which I ever seemed to be when I stepped outside.

Moreover there are more than half a million Australians in the greater United Kingdom. For more than forty years Australians had been piling into London. From the Aussie enclave of Earls Court during London's swinging sixties to the modern-day proliferation of Walkabout bars, my countryfolk had worked hard to make their presence felt in London. To Aussies living in London, their new home was different from the homeland but not drastically so. The language was the same, the food was similar, and the cultural references were largely the same; it was all just a lot colder and wetter.

As one of the half-million, I had found that—thanks largely to our numbers and our tendencies to huddle together, assume good jobs, and excel at most international sports—an Australian in London had become, justifiably enough, little more than an annoyance. If I was going to be a foreigner in a foreign land, I wanted to be considered a novelty, not a nuisance. When encountering a local, instead of being made to feel I had nothing to offer beyond a reinforcement of already hardened stereotypes, I wanted to feel interesting, unusual—welcome.

That at least was the theory, as I rocketed across the plains of Picardy for the second time in as many months. Yet the Paris that loomed large on the near horizon was one big question mark. Did the city contain a host of potential new best friends just waiting for me to get off the train? Or was I headed for an endless series of lonely nights in front of television programs I didn't understand? Would I fall madly in love with a glamorous French mademoiselle, or was I destined to be spurned for my rudimentary command of *le français* and lack of continental sophistication? I strained to make sense of a conversation being held by the French couple to my left and realized, with rising panic, that my schoolboy language skills were going to need some serious work. By the time the train reached Gare du Nord, the panic had given way to a conviction that I was making a serious mistake.

The line for a taxi was long and seemed unusually charged with short-tempered Frenchies, all of them exhaling air dramatically, pushing rudely in front of me, and muttering under their breath. Once I was in the taxi and on my way to the hotel, scenes of Parisian life that on previous visits to the city had sent me into raptures now just looked foreign and threatening. What was I thinking? The absurdity of the enterprise I had undertaken—moving to Paris for a job I wasn't interested in and had applied for on a whim—was only now starting to sink in. Surely it could only end badly.

Turning a corner, we came upon Parc Monceau and a scene that calmed my nerves. Beyond the black iron grille of the fence, families strolled leisurely about the beautifully groomed garden, enjoying the sunshine on what had become a glorious Sunday afternoon. Under the boughs of leafless trees they walked in couples or in foursomes. The men pushed baby carriages while their wives walked elegantly alongside. The children, some even wearing berets, tottered along behind. Everyone was dressed immaculately. Long, dark woolen coats, stylish hats, and good shoes. It was picture-postcard Paris. It was shamelessly stereotypical. I drank it in like a tonic and told myself everything was going to be all right.

The adventure had begun—there was no turning back.

Chapter 3

The New Kid

T HE FIRST DAY of a new job is much like your first day at school. Your shirt is ironed, your pencil case is packed, your shoes are polished, and you show up on time. Filled with an anticipatory enthusiasm and an eagerness to please, you are unfailingly polite to everyone you encounter at your new workplace. The woman at reception is treated to your winningest smile, the maintenance man receives a warm handshake—even the guy filling the Coke machine finds himself the target of your charm campaign.

And just as in the school playground, you spend the first few days scoping the new territory—working out who the kingpins are, where the cool kids hang, how the office politics fall, where the pitfalls lie, and how best to avoid them. Most workplaces have enough people and are sufficiently multilayered that you need a good couple of weeks to get the lay of the land. At the ICC I had taken the measure of the place within an hour of arriving. Whether it was the gray walls, the all-pervading silence, or the generally sleepy ambience, I knew almost immediately upon entering the building that the ICC and I were not

going to be natural bedfellows. And that perception was only rein-
forced as the days passed.

A week into my new job I had been to three meetings that appeared to have nothing to do with me, had sat in on four briefings that
were definitely outside my sphere of responsibility, and had been
copied on at least a hundred e-mails that didn't concern me. Committees were being created to make decisions on important projects, then
subcommittees were formulated to review those decisions before they
were enacted. Though English was nominally the language in which
the majority of the work was conducted, people used words and expressions that were foreign to me.

"We'll need to drill down some of these key variables to make sure
we are all singing from the same hymn sheet," they would say, adding:
"And before we action any of this let's make sure we've given it some
blue sky thinking and put all our ducks in a row." Unsure what they
were talking about, I developed a habit of nodding sagely while scribbling in my notebook. I was getting a crash course in the strange world
of corporate office life.

Most disturbing, however, was the sudden drop in my pace of
workplace activity. All previous professional incarnations had seen me
working in the bustle of a newsroom. All the newspaper newsrooms in
which I had toiled as a hack, and certainly the twenty-four-hour TV
newsroom in which I had worked in London, had been notable for
daily scenes of barely constrained chaos. Even in the brief periods of
downtime, when a news story wasn't breaking or sixty reporters weren't
all frantically bashing their keyboards to meet deadline, a newsroom
always had an amazing energy. A buzz that invigorated everyone in the
workplace. The only buzz audible in this new working environment
was the sickly one emanating from the clock on the wall. Even the
timepieces at the ICC seemed apologetic, as if to tick too loudly might
jolt employees from their slumber.

And then there was the work itself. As the self-described "world
business organization," the ICC existed to create the rules by which
international commerce was practiced and to lobby bodies like the
United Nations and the World Trade Organization on behalf of the
private sector. For a former gossip columnist, more accustomed to red

carpets than red tape, it was a distinctly odd marriage. And it was a union that apparently had many of my new colleagues also scratching their heads. Barely two weeks into my tenure, a bet was running among my more savvy coworkers about how long I would last in the job. To their way of thinking, there was no way my particular species of fish would cope for long in the ICC's murky waters.

But if the institution was distinctly moribund, at least many of the people with whom I worked were young and dynamic. Like me, they had come to Paris from all corners of the world. English, Swedish, Swiss, Canadian, American, Togolese, Moroccan, Austrian, Russian, Brazilian, Finnish, Lebanese, Greek, Mexican, and Italian—there were even a handful of fellow Aussies and, of course, a healthy number of Frenchies. Like me, the younger members of staff had mostly come to the ICC for the chance it afforded to live and work in Paris. The work experience was definitely secondary to the life experience.

The fact that at least half of the staff were French—especially those at the administrative end of things—meant that my French would improve exponentially. It also meant I got to witness firsthand the impressive force of the powerhouse French work ethic. It wouldn't be long before I knew the French for "express delivery doesn't exist," "you must be joking if you think I can get it to you before the end of the week," and "that's not my department." If nothing else, I reasoned as I slowly got to know the place, this job was destined to be amusing.

During a session in my first week the human resources manager spelled out to me my benefits and entitlements as an employee under French law. I was contractually bound to work thirty-five hours a week—any more would be a contravention of French law. France's previous, Socialist-led government had legislated the drastically shortened work week in a failed effort to create jobs, and no attempt at compromise since had convinced the unions to relinquish it.

I was legally required to take a lunch break of at least one hour. Each day I was to be given one "ticket restaurant" in the value of eight euros. This state-funded lunch voucher system was designed to ensure that the entire nation had one good square meal a day. And I was entitled to six weeks of paid vacation each year, plus a week's worth of public holidays, which the French honor religiously.

This will be a laugh, I thought to myself. A seven-hour workday, public holidays every other week, a subsidized meal every day—talk about a free lunch!

Then the personnel manager turned to matters of superannuation and retirement.

"Once you have worked here for thirty years, you will have accrued quite a lot of superannuation and retirement benefits. You might want to start thinking about how you will want to invest it," she said.

It was all I could do to disguise my befuddlement. Thirty years? Was she serious? Did she really think I would still be here in thirty years? I was a twenty-eight-year-old Aussie drifter, on the run from London and in search of a good time in the City of Light. What possible need did I have for a retirement plan? I didn't know where I would be in the next six months, much less in the next thirty years. Certainly I had no greater ambition with this job than to give it a year, collect a salary, and live it up in this remarkable city.

And yet I left the personnel office feeling decidedly nauseous, wondering if in my enthusiasm to hop across the Channel, I had made a grave mistake. Was I trapped in this job and now destined to while away the best, most productive years of my professional life fighting with intractable mailroom staff and eating state-funded lunches?

I took myself to the Grand Corona café on the Place de l'Alma, sat alone on the terrace, and ordered a coffee. Paris bustled around me. Across the Place de l'Alma and on the other side of the Seine, the Eiffel Tower rose impressively toward the clouds. No, I reminded myself, I wasn't trapped. The vision was intact, and my motives for being here remained untainted. I had come to suck the marrow. If Paris truly was a movable feast, as Hemingway once famously asserted, then I was determined to take a place at the table, roll up my sleeves, and tuck in. If this job was a means to that particular end, then all the better. Besides, a position that offered international travel, a healthy salary, and (though it wasn't exactly my bag) exposure to the higher echelons of the corporate and intergovernmental worlds wasn't all bad.

If the ICC was prepared to put up with me for a year, then I reckoned I could just about try to put up with them. I was in Paris, after all.

Chapter 4

Le Marais

NOW THAT I HAD A JOB, it was time to find an apartment. Displaying a level of indifference to my new workplace that I would work carefully to maintain in the months to come, I spent the better part of the first month of my employment at the ICC out of the office, scouring the streets of Paris for somewhere suitable to live. As a refugee of fringe-dwelling, hand-to-mouth living in London, I had only one criterion for my Parisian abode: it had to be central. Living in Paris, I reasoned, was going to be a once-in-a-lifetime experience. If I was going to live here, I wanted to live in the dirty, sweaty, heaving heart of it.

The Marais was therefore earmarked as my neighborhood *du choix*. Otherwise known as the "trendy fourth arrondissement" or "le gai Marais," it is to Paris what Soho is to London, the Village is to New York, or Darlinghurst is to Sydney. Except that it was infinitely more charming than all of the above put together. Filled to overflowing with an eclectic mix of young urban professionals, a community of Orthodox Jews, practically every gay man in the city, and a bolt of old grannies (who had lived there for eons and refused to move, no matter how much public male-on-male action they were inadvertently exposed to), the quartier had all the elements I was looking for. It was as central as it was possible to be in Paris without actually being in the Seine, it had gay men and rabbis living cheek by jowl, it was picture-postcard perfect, and it was heavily populated with bars, cafés, and restaurants that were packed at all hours of the day and night. Having undergone a wholesale gentrification twenty years previously, the quartier had been transformed from a working-class ghetto to some of the most sought-after real estate in all of Paris.

Called Le Marais after the swamp that Louis XIV drained to build stately homes for his court, my new neighborhood had some of the most stunning old buildings in the city. The Place des Vosges, the Musée Picasso, Les Archives, and the Musée Carnavalet were just some of the beautiful former *hôtel particuliers* that populated Le Marais.

Turning a corner and finding yourself in the Marais was not unlike stumbling upon a wonderfully decorated film set. It was a labyrinth of narrow streets, lined on either side by tumbledown buildings, hole-in-the-wall bars and cafés, old streetlamps, and massive, ornate double wooden doors opening onto secret courtyards and honey-colored buildings. Every now and then, as if paid by the city's tourist officials to be there, an old woman would shuffle out of a *boulangerie* with a wizened old pooch on a leash and a baguette under her arm.

Coming as I did from a country where eighty-year-old inner-city row houses were as historic as buildings got, it didn't seem possible to me that people could actually live in what was surely just an elaborate facade for a very expensive period drama. When courtiers lived here back in the eighteenth century, just up the river from King Louis's modest pile the Palais du Louvre, the Marais had been a seething hotbed of drama and intrigue. Dangerous liaisons had gone on behind every door—heaving breasts, steamy boudoirs, tightly strung corsets, men in wigs, and sexually frustrated madames. Two hundred years later, not a whole lot had changed. But what had once been an eighteenth-century playground for kings was now a modern-day playground for queens.

Responding one morning to an ad in the real estate weekly *Parti-*

culiers de Particuliers, I found myself waiting outside the large brown wooden doors of 18 Rue Sainte Croix de la Bretonnerie. As well as being one of the longest street names in all of Paris, it also happened to be one of the best-known streets in all of the Marais. If the Marais had a thoroughfare, this was it. If the Marais was the pumping heart of gay Paris, Rue Sainte Croix was its major artery.

Entering the digicode numbers as instructed by the old woman proprietor to whom I had spoken earlier in the day, I stepped through the doors and into a pleasant courtyard. As I started to climb the stairs of Escalier B to the second-floor apartment, I was met halfway up by a long line of people, each of them clinging to their own copy of *Particuliers de Particuliers* and each of them wearing the same haunted look as me, the demented look of the temporarily homeless. Having been well advised by workmates to arrive with a complete dossier—including bank statements, references, salary slips, a large wad of cash, and a document authorizing the handover of my firstborn child, as and if required—I waited my turn with only a hint of smugness.

When I finally entered the apartment, I was met by a scene so shocking it was all I could do not to turn and run. The apartment was perfectly situated. It had a wall of floor-to-ceiling windows in a living room that was flooded with morning sunlight. The bedroom was large, the bathroom was serviceable, and it was fully furnished, meaning I would have to buy nothing. But the walls! The walls! They were like nothing I had ever seen before. As a child of the seventies, I think I can safely say that I have seen my fair share of orange home furnishings. But these padded, russet-orange-fabric-covered walls—with a swirling white floral and paisley pattern—were something else again. It wasn't so much that they dominated the room as they devoured it. Just standing in the middle of them felt like being trapped on some awful drug-induced trip from which there was no apparent escape. And when you looked closely, you realized there was none. By covering all access doors to the living room—be it to the kitchen, the bedroom, or the bathroom—with the same patterned orange fabric, the masterminds behind the decoration of this particular apartment had managed to achieve that highly sought-after interior design feel—the padded-cell effect.

And then there was the furniture. By virtue of having been purchased sometime around 1965, the bed looked like something straight off the set of an Austin Powers film. Its black-padded-vinyl headboard featured a set of built-in reading lights—or "bed headlights," as I came to call them. The porn-star bed was perfectly complemented by a pair of black and orange conical swivel chairs. The apartment looked nothing more than uninhabitable.

But I had been searching for a home for three weeks and was now being turfed out of the hotel for which the ICC had kindly been paying. Besides, orange walls aside, it was certainly no worse than other apartments I had seen. The week before I had almost put a deposit down on a place that would have required me to climb a ladder and crawl into a hole halfway up the wall each time I wanted to go to bed. The walls I could learn to live with. I just needed a roof over my head.

Faster than the old biddy proprietor could say "But you're an Australian blow-in with no rental record at all in France," I flashed my winning smile, blurted out the three French real estate phrases I knew, and threw a wad of cash on the table. The deal was done.

Two days later I transported my paltry collection of belongings from the hotel to my new apartment. I distinctly remember the first night in my new home. Having taken a whole ten minutes to unpack my bag, I sat on the bottle-green velour sofa in the living room and watched with a rising sense of claustrophobia as the orange walls closed in around me. So this was it. My Paris home. A naked lightbulb hanging from the ceiling cast a harsh yellow light over the room. The place seemed empty, cold, soulless. I put on my headphones and fired up my Walkman for distraction and comfort. But there was no escaping it. With the adrenaline of arrival fast ebbing and with the excitement of apartment-hunting over, it was now just me, in an empty orange room, in a job I wasn't sure about, in a city full of strangers.

Outside it was freezing cold. A dark, rainy winter's night in Paris. I could hear the hum of the metropolis outside, and standing at my window, I could see people walking in huddled pairs on the street below. I turned to look around my new apartment and suddenly felt very small, very alone, and very, very far from home.

Chapter 5

Rear Window

As INTERNATIONAL CAPITALS GO, Paris is about as small as they get. Though the greater metropolitan area contains some eleven million people, the twenty arrondissements inside the ring road, or *periphérique* as it is called, house only about two million. This, combined with the fact that the city is a national treasure, plus an admirable determination on the part of the city authorities to maintain a low-rise conurbation in the city's center, means that Paris is like one great big village.

You can walk pretty much anywhere in the city. The Métro, though stinky, is one of the most efficient public transportation systems in the world, and bike riding is encouraged by a comprehensive network of bike lanes all over the town. This big-city-with-a-village-atmosphere is only enhanced by the fact that under the leaden roofs and terracotta chimney pots that constitute the Paris skyline, people live on top of one another. The French call it *vis-à-vis* when the windows of your apartment look directly across the road or courtyard into the windows of your neighbor's apartment. What this creates is a fantastic, citywide version of the Hitchcock classic *Rear Window*. It surely also accounts for low TV-viewership figures in Paris. For who needs television when they have real-life dramas played out for them every night through their living-room windows?

Having an uninterrupted view into the living quarters of your neighbors creates the bizarre situation whereby despite the fact you don't know their names, you are acutely aware of the kind of underwear they sport, their sexual preference, the cereal they eat, how often they wash, and the state of their love life. From my living room I had the cross section of human experience on tap. And given that I was a new arrival in the city, without a network of friends to otherwise fill my extracurricular hours, I would often come home, whip up some dinner, stare out the window, and watch the drama unfurl before me.

Across the street and two floors up, behind the window boxes of carefully tended geraniums and beyond a set of red and white gingham curtains, lived the gay couple. They looked like a clone of each other and apparently had wardrobes consisting solely of white Calvin Klein underwear. Below them, and behind a set of comparatively grottier windows, lived the lesbian couple. They too had window boxes, but the plants were long dead, and the empty boxes now served only as receptacles for the butts of the cigarettes they seemed to be perpetually smoking as they hung nude from the window.

One floor down was the hetero couple. They didn't have any window boxes or plants. But they did have a lot of sex, which I guess they figured was a better use of their time. Next door to them lived the ironing man. He was, as far as I could tell, a young single guy with an unusual obsession with ironing. I am sure he had other interests, but none that I ever saw him indulge. Day and night, no matter what the hour, he could be seen shirtless at the ironing board, throwing his sunken hairless chest and skinny little arms into the de-creasing process of a seemingly endless pile of laundry.

After a month in my new apartment, I had seen all the characters in my window-framed drama in varying states of undress—as indeed, they had seen me. Given that we didn't know one another, and that if we bumped into each other in the street, we probably wouldn't have recognized each other out of context, it seemed perfectly fine that we had all been nude in front of one another. Besides, the occasional flash of a bare buttock was nothing compared to some of the stuff to which I eventually bore witness.

Though I had only recently begun tuning in to the nightly window drama, it had nevertheless been long enough to discern the sexual habits of the hetero couple—who were apparently the least concerned of all my neighbors about sharing the intimate details of their love life with the wider arrondissement. They had curtains on their bedroom windows but seemed incapable—or simply disinclined—to ever use them. It wasn't uncommon for me to glance up from my couch late at night and catch a glimpse of them doing their bit for French population growth, usually with admirable enthusiasm. As the weather began to warm and winter turned to spring, I would discover that not only was their curtain-drawing ability apparently impaired by the rising temperature, so too were their window-closing and scream-suppressing capacities. And people would marvel when they learned, after two months in Paris, that I still hadn't gotten around to connecting my cable TV.

Two months into my Paris sojourn, my sister Kirrily and her fiancé Damion came to visit from Melbourne. One night we went for dinner in the quartier and returned just in time to see the lights flick on in the hetero couple's apartment. Keen to share the fullness of my new Parisian life with my loved ones, I told them to kill the lights and gather round the window to take in the spectacle that I knew would inevitably ensue. Without for a moment considering how sad this made me look to my visitors (I could all but hear my sister thinking: *Not only does he watch strange people have sex, but he has an entire light-switching-off routine to do it*), I settled in and started up a commentary on the couple's lives, their other endearing daily habits, and the odd position of the girlfriend's birthmark. Suddenly, and with a twist of my head to get a better view of the two faces stuck to one another across the way, I stopped dead in my commentary tracks and took a sharp intake of breath.

"Hang on a minute. That's not his girlfriend."

I felt strangely affronted. It felt like he was cheating on me, refusing to stick to the script I had written and keep to the role I had assigned him in my rear-window soap opera. If he was going to cheat, I reasoned later, he could have at least closed the curtains out of deference to his better half.

As entertaining—and occasionally noisy—as my living-room-window characters were, they didn't hold a candle to the woman who lived in an apartment opposite my bedroom window. She was either possessed of a very punctual lover, or was a very big fan of a particular TV personality who came on the box every morning at nine. For how else to explain why her very loud orgasms were so regular that you could set your watch by them? I never had to fear missing my alarm or sleeping past nine o'clock as long as she was there. One Saturday morning her yelps were so sustained and so vocal that I found myself standing incredulous at the window, in admiration, envy, and concern. Across the street four of my neighbors, similarly roused by the ruckus, stood in their respective apartment windows seeking out the source of the clamor. We acknowledged one another with a sheepish wave, indulged in knowing grins, and retreated behind our curtains to let our quartier consoeur climax in peace.

And if it wasn't Miss Joy of Sex across the street keeping me from my slumber, it was the old couple who lived next door and downstairs. They were so old and had been in the neighborhood so long that the building had practically been constructed around them. They lived in the apartment next to mine, and also on the floor below, in an apartment directly underneath mine. This strange upstairs-downstairs arrangement was made all the more bizarre by the fact that no internal staircase connected the two living spaces, meaning they spent the better part of any given night on the communal staircase, opening and closing doors in a most unnecessarily noisy fashion.

She was a sprightly, mischievous-eyed eighty-something woman, rumored in neighborhood circles to be a white witch. She favored cardigans and tended to shuffle more than actually walk, always with her long blond hair pulled back in a loose ponytail. He was an amiable elf of a man, his bumper crop of dramatic gray hair swept back over his pate in that fashion so favored among older French men.

Dyed-in-the-wool communists—of the type you tend to find only in countries that have never really experienced communism—they had thrown rocks at police during the riots of May '68 and protested France's colonial war in Algeria in the late fifties, and, if the wizened face and hunched posture of Mrs. Commie was anything to go by, there was a pretty good chance they had even manned the barricades during the Revolution of 1789.

Every now and then I would pass them on the stairwell. I would be just home from my job in the service of rampant capitalism and heading out to a bar, restaurant, or shop to pay homage to the god of consumerism. They would be heading home, placards and banners in hand, after a hard day spent demonstrating against one of the myriad evils of the free market system. And given the regularity with which the French tended to strike and protest—plus the fact that a French person will join in a demo even if they have no idea what they are protesting—they usually had a pretty crowded dance card.

"*Bonjour*, Monsieur, Madame," I would say as I bounced down the stairs. "You've been out at a *manifestation* again? What was it today?"

"Oh well, you know, Monsieur Corbett," the old lady would reply seriously, in the perfectly enunciated French of the elderly. "Today we were protesting council plans to evict squatters from the building on the Rue Charlot."

"Oh—that wasn't yesterday's protest?" I would ask, confused.

"*Mais non!* Yesterday was a protest against the declining water quality of La Seine!" she would admonish me, incredulous that I was unaware of this most pressing social crisis.

At night, apparently not worn out by hours spent footslogging in a circle outside the mayor's office, they would shuffle endlessly from one of their apartments to the other. Up and down they climbed the stairs with the labored footsteps of the politically oppressed, pausing only to slam a door or shout at each other in heated, midstairwell philosophical debate. And if it wasn't a midnight tirade against the state that kept me awake, it was their habit of watching television at top volume at two in the morning. Whether because they suffered from industrial deafness, or because she was using the noise to cover the sound of virgin sacrifices, the TV was always switched on at top volume at two a.m. I never had to worry about listening to the news in the morning, as the TV news bulletins would reverberate up through my bedroom floor each night.

Noisy, exhibitionist, ideologically dogmatic, and distinctly claustrophobic, my new neighborhood had all the elements I required for an authentic Parisian experience. Certainly I was not destined to get much sleep. But with all this entertainment on tap—all of these lives being busily led, barely a curtain twitch away—I was destined to be endlessly amused. But as my sister quietly but firmly pointed out, living vicariously through the snatched glimpses of other people's domesticity was not much of a life.

"You should maybe get out more," she politely suggested.

I had to admit she had a point.

Chapter 6

Boys, Boys, Boys

A S ECLECTIC AS THE COMPOSITION of the Marais was, one particular social subset definitely shone the brightest: the gay community.

Parisian gays had long ago claimed the Marais as their own. Among the city's twenty arrondissements, the Marais seemed to please them the most. It was pretty, it was very well put together, and it featured plenty of bars that served a mean Cosmopolitan. Go figure.

What this meant for the Marais—as indeed it means for most other gay enclaves in major cities around the world—was that the quartier was full of funky shops, cutting-edge fashion outlets, groovy cafés, and more than its fair share of excellent restaurants. Living in the midst of it all was consequently pretty easy to take. Homosexuals, in my experience, tend to make excellent neighbors. They are house proud, meaning the place always looks good; their community boasts a disproportionate number of handsome members, relatively speaking; and they know how to have a good time. The boys with whom I shared the Marais were no exception.

If you were to break Parisian arrondissements down according to their respective soundscapes, the eighteenth, with Montmartre, Sacré Coeur, and the Place des Tertres, would be the evocative, mournful whine of that most French of instruments, the piano accordion. The sixteenth, with its bourgeois apartments and ladies-who-lunch, would be the elegant lilt of a symphonic movement. The fourth, with the Marais, where Kylie was queen and Lycra hotpants were de rigueur, would be the persistent throb of techno music.

Having now moved in and spent just over three months in my new apartment, it seemed to me that I was waking up and falling asleep to the rhythmic thud of techno music. And while for some, the prospect of sharing living space with the musical equivalent of a jack-hammer would be hell on earth, to me, it was all part of my new neighborhood's definite charm, aural proof that my new home was at the throbbing heart of a semisleepless international metropolis. What I found less easy to get used to was the nightly melodrama of love gone wrong, a recurring soap opera invariably played out, at volume, directly beneath my bedroom window. At around two each morning, as the bars were closing and the last of the boys spilled out onto the street, an invisible cue seemed to be given for many of them to strike up a forlorn, guttural chorus of *"Mais Jean-Pierre! Je t'aime!"* or something to that effect. Screamed at top volume by a spurned lover to the back of his hastily retreating paramour, the plaintive cry would bounce off the narrow walls of the buildings lining the Rue Aubriot and jolt me from my sleep. I never bothered to get out of bed to verify, but I could usually tell by the speed of the footsteps disappearing down the street that despite the declaration of undying love of which he had just been the subject, Jean-Pierre didn't quite feel the same way.

In honor of the countless hearts that were broken and the number of prematurely conceived visions of domestic bliss that were shattered outside my window each Parisian night, I christened the terracotta statue of the Virgin Mary, perched in an alcove above the corner of the Rue Sainte Croix and the Rue Aubriot, "Saint Jackie, the patron saint of melodrama." She got her name from a former colleague in the U.K. who was renowned for her propensity toward all things melodramatic.

Jackie stood watch over the Rue Sainte Croix, her head thrown back
to the heavens and her left arm thrust outward and upward in a sign
of genuflection. Her creators had no doubt fashioned her thus to con-
vey a sense of obeisance before the Almighty, but I preferred to think
of her in a perpetual state of exasperation.

And while Jackie bore silent witness to the high-camp, daily drama
played out on the Rue Sainte Croix, the numerous business establishments that lined its streets ensured that that drama, and the players
within it, were suitably well fed, well lubricated, and well turned out.
My personal favorite, among the gay-oriented small businesses in my
hood, was Le Gay Choc, which was ostensibly a bakery, though from
what I could gather, it was more highly valued in the neighborhood for
its cruising potential than for any of its actual breadstuffs. On Valen-
tine's Day you had to get in early if you wanted to nab one of the novelty loaves of bread baked in the shape of a penis—complete, rather
disturbingly, with poppyseed-speckled testicles. I was never sure exactly what was going on behind the flour sacks at the back of the shop,
but there was no question they baked the best baguette and most
mouthwatering *tarte au citron* in all of Paris.

Then there was the nearby Raidd bar. Beyond its smoked-glass
plate windows, boys would stand at the bar and sip beer while impressively muscular men bathed themselves in shower units built into the
wall. Around the corner, should you decide you needed a haircut, the
enigmatic barbershop of the Marais, Space Hair, was at your service.
So called because all of its stylists were perpetually spaced out, it was
more nightclub than hair-dressing salon. Clients were offered a gin
and tonic upon arrival, and haircuts were offered in any of three distinct styles: gay, very gay, or screaming queen.

Then there were the appropriately named Amnesia bar, the clothing store Boyz Bazaar, and the Sunday-night meat market otherwise
known as Café Cox, the name of which always struck me as a master-
stroke of marketing understatement. These establishments were all as
much a part of the neighborhood as the designer tea shop opposite my
apartment, the bakery owned by a cheery Moroccan family down the
street, and the unemployment office two doors up.

• • •

I SOON DISCOVERED that the sidewalk outside my door was highly valued preening real estate: impeccably groomed young men paraded up and down it at all hours of the day and night. Less good-looking and decidedly older men would occasionally drive slowly down the street, stopping at intervals and giving hopeful, yearning looks at their young, elusive quarry.

I had begun to cultivate a few friends at work and was slowly building a semirespectable social life. Male friends would drop in to visit me in the Marais and remark at how many men had propositioned them or commented upon their arse as they walked down the street. But for me there was nothing. Zippo. Nada. Not that I wanted to be hit on by another man—I just didn't want to be left out. I rationalized (as men are wont to do when it comes to questions of self-confidence) that as a local—a bona-fide, card-carrying member of the quartier—I had special status and had thus been earmarked by the boys to be left alone. It wasn't that they didn't *want* to make unseemly advances in my direction, but by restraining themselves they were respecting an unwritten neighborhood code.

As well groomed as my gay neighbors were, the beauty of my new quartier went much deeper than the multiple layers of fake tan on parade each night. Though the Marais was overtly gay in flavor, you didn't have to scratch too deep below the surface to discover that people from all walks of life also called the place home. Struggling artists mixed with well-known film actors and a smattering of media types. Young professionals had moved in and transformed pokey old apartments into architectural visions. Old-age pensioners, who had lived in the area since it was a tradesman's ghetto, still plied the streets, ensuring that nothing changed too fast and that the neighborhood retained its glorious old-world charm.

In their flashy way the gay community had made the most obvious contribution to the look and feel of the arrondissement, but they were closely followed in the neighborhood-influence stakes by the Jewish community, whose wholesale assumption of the Rue des Rosiers had created a mini-Zion in the heart of the French capital. This wonderfully colorful cultural influence in my newly adopted patch of Paris included the amusing spectacle each Sunday of what appeared to be every Jewish teenager in the greater Paris metropolitan area "hanging" on the Rue des Rosiers. Girls on one side of the street, boys on the other. They never appeared to do anything other than jostle and point and text and pout at one another—in that way teenagers do. The boys were especially entertaining. Dressed to a person in tight white long-sleeved tops, white Diesel shoes, and distressed Energie denim, the very sight of them would have warmed the hearts of hair-product manufacturers everywhere. It was a veritable Festival of Hair Gel. I worried that should a naked flame get too close to any of the boys' carefully coiffed crowns, the entire street would go up in a spectacular fireball.

Having Jewish neighbors also meant enjoying a ready supply of delicious Middle Eastern cuisine. Indeed, if it hadn't been for the falafel roll with pan-fried eggplant from L'As du Falafel, it is doubtful that I would have regularly encountered at least three of the five basic food groups during my first few months in Paris.

Not being of the home-cooking persuasion, I started to rely heavily on the fast-food wares of my friendly neighborhood small businesses. When it got to the point that I could walk into the extremely down-at-heel yet always delicious Minh Chau Vietnamese restaurant on the Rue de la Verrerie, to be greeted warmly by the old grandma owner and asked, "Would you like your usual?" I knew I was being accepted as a local.

Also helping me to make the transformation from blow-in to local was a trio of café-bars at the end of my street, whose mortgages I would help to pay off with my faithful custom in the years to come. All owned by the enigmatic Xavier—the Marais café scene's very own version of the Godfather—and packed to their heaving rafters with a cool collection of beautiful people, L'Etoile Manquante, Les Philosophes, and Au Petit Fer à Cheval sat side by side on the Rue Vieille du Temple. Working on the Monopoly-board theory of buy-up-a-block-and-stack-it-with-small-businesses, Xavier had become the Don of Coffee in Paris's hippest arrondissement. By designing each of his café-bars in a style that played on the Marais's rich tradition yet still appealed to the city's style set—and by employing only dark-haired young men and insisting that they dress in the traditional French waiter garb of black apron over white shirt—Xavier had created a one-man French café empire.

As I sat one evening sipping a beer alone on the tiny terrace of the Petit Fer à Cheval, watching the nightly parade of boys, Jews, and beautiful people, it occurred to me that the experience would be all the more enjoyable if I had someone to share it with. Paris was doubtless an exciting city. I had rather fortunately landed in the heaving heart of it. But without friends to share it with, the novelty and excitement of being a stranger in a new city were destined to prove short-lived.

It was time, I decided, to launch Operation Find Some Friends.

Chapter 7

The Paris Posse

I'S A FUNNY THING moving to a city where you don't know a soul. It's simultaneously liberating and terrifying. Liberating, because you are completely free. You have no family commitments to honor, no sprawling networks of disparate friends to maintain. And because no one knows you, there are no widely held expectations, built up over years of familiarity, of who you are and what you do. Terrifying because you are essentially alone. Sure, you have countless friends and family at the end of a phone line, but at the end of the day, when the lights go out and you pull up the bedcovers, you are all by yourself.

Almost four months had passed since I had arrived in Paris. I had a job that looked like it was going to be a breeze, and an apartment that was slowly becoming a home. Now all I needed was a troupe of cohorts with whom to infiltrate the city's seedy underbelly.

With the same misguided optimism I would see reflected in countless other fresh-faced expats after me, I reasoned that the best way to develop a circle of friends and get under the skin of the City of Light was to ingratiate myself with the Frenchies. Through contacts at work and a relatively well-established expatriate network, a variety of social opportunities began to present themselves, and Project Assimilate was officially launched.

As a result, on any given night of the week, and especially on precious Friday and Saturday nights, I would find myself standing in a room half full of Frenchies and half full of expats. The expat department usually contained a smattering of American princesses on Daddy-funded six-month study tours, Swiss banking nerds who had been transferred to their private bank's Paris office, and German government-employed energy experts "on mission" at the Paris-based Organization for Economic Cooperation and Development, or OECD as it was known in the local lingo. Dismissing out of hand the conversational potential of this most rich sample space of fellow expats, I would invariably concentrate on getting to know the Frenchies—determined to improve my grasp of the language, develop some friendships with the locals and deepen my appreciation of this remarkable culture I had come to live in.

As someone who loves to talk, I quickly learned to appreciate the awful frustration of being party to a group conversation and having something intelligent or witty to contribute to it but possessing neither the vocab nor the requisite facility with the language to express it. In pretty much every situation, the scene would play out as follows: I would keep up with a group conversation delivered in rapid-fire French, nod enthusiastically, and think of something erudite or funny to contribute, and by the time I conjugated the verb, decided whether the subject was masculine or feminine, and worked out whether to use the familiar *tu* or the more formal *vous,* the conversation had moved on.

Where in my own language I was the life and soul of a party, in French I became a conversational wallflower. Eventually someone would take pity on me, notice my pathetic earnestness, and throw a question in my direction. It was invariably a mercy query, motivated more by a desire to draw me into the proceedings and put me out of my misery than by any actual interest in the answer. But as it turned out, being obliged to repeat their inquiry three times before I actually understood it, or worse, receiving an answer that had nothing to do with the question they had posed, did little to encourage them to further extend the tentative hand of new friendship.

And it wasn't as if I could take refuge in the bottle. French parties, I soon learned, were among the driest affairs on the planet. Everyone brought a bottle, and everyone placed their bottle on a large table in the corner that was straining under the weight of painstakingly prepared finger food, but no one, it seemed, was allowed to actually open those bottles. Convinced that fluency in French lay only four swift drinks away, I used to shift nervously from foot to foot, eyeing the alcohol and willing someone, anyone to open it up and offer it around. But French social etiquette stipulates that under no circumstances do you ever pour yourself a drink. Rather, you wait patiently until someone notices your empty glass and offers to refill it. However, as my party pariah status was growing with every passing minute, there was no way I was prepared to stand on ceremony. Trample all over it, more like.

And so it was that I would eventually risk social death and march over to the drinks table and help myself. Ignoring the sharp intake of collective breath from shocked fellow revelers, I would then proceed to get as drunk as possible as quickly as possible.

Once suitably steeled by the numbing effect of two glasses of Bordeaux in quick succession, I was just about able to cope with another half-hour discussion of the volatility of oil markets with the German energy geek, before making my excuses and leaving. To say that I prematurely abandoned Project Assimilate would be an understatement. Perhaps with persistence I would have found a group of slow-talking, alcoholic French friends, but it was patently going to take a lot of fruitless air-kissing and tedious conversation before I found my social saviors. This French social lark was all well and good, I finally decided, but if it meant standing around a silent room (would it have killed them to put some music on?) and boring one another to death, then it probably wasn't for me. Besides, my Australian upbringing had taught me to be naturally suspicious of any party at which there was more food than alcohol.

So it was that I dug out the one Parisian telephone number with which I had arrived. I had been keeping it to one side, vowing only to use it in an emergency. It was the number of an English girl named Fiona who had recently moved to Paris. She had once taken a salsa class with one of the TV reporters with whom I'd worked in London. As contacts went, it was about as tenuous as you could possibly get. But the nights weren't getting any less lonely, and I was damned if I was going to spend another evening listening to the relative merits of the Swiss private banking code.

I picked up the phone, dialed the number, and made a date to meet up the next night. The Paris Posse was officially conceived.

Now, as a general rule, I'm not a great believer in fate. I believe most things can be explained as a result of circumstance, planning, or good old-fashioned coincidence. But meeting Fiona set in motion a random chain of events and chance encounters that would irrevocably change my Parisian life and lead me to consider if perhaps there wasn't some heavenly ordination at work.

The event itself was ordinary enough. Two relative strangers meet in the 7 Lézards jazz bar on the Rue des Rosiers, share a few drinks, establish a rapport, and silently—separately—decide that this is a friendship with definite potential. Fiona was a lawyer, transferred to Paris by her large London-based corporate law firm. Petite, vivacious, and possessed of a set of dazzling baby-blue eyes, she made a very good first impression. Law, as is often the case with lawyers, was not her thing. Like thousands before her and thousands to come after her, she had simply got the grades to study law and figured she was therefore obliged to do it. Her real passion was photography. And dancing. And rather fortunately for me and our budding friendship, drinking and smoking. Within half an hour of our sitting down and engaging in effortless conversation, she ordered a second carafe of Sauvignon Blanc with nary a bat of an eyelid. I knew we were destined to get on like a house on fire.

Fiona had been in Paris for only four months. By virtue of the fact that she had lived in France as a child, she had pitch-perfect French and a budding network of French friends. But she too had stood sober at enough French soirées to know that if she was going to survive—and indeed enjoy—her time in Paris, she needed to develop a reserve of like-minded expats. In her wanderings Fiona had crossed paths with another lawyer, Sylvie, who was also from England and had been relocated to Paris by her mega–law firm. Among her myriad other talents, Sylvie was somewhat of a prodigy in the specialized field of international arbitration law. She was also of Spanish-Iranian extraction, a combination that gave her striking beauty and, as I would later discover, the ability to salsa dance with the best of them. By day she worked with governments and industry chiefs prosecuting cases in international courts of arbitration; by night she liked nothing more than to down a few glasses of white wine, take to the dance floor, and work up a sweat. I decided I could get to like her too.

Sylvie knew of another young English corporate lawyer, Gavin, who was doing a six-month stint in the City of Light. Lawyerly transfers to Paris from firms in London, I quickly learned, were not only common but highly sought after for the opportunity they provided the next generation of legal eagles to let down their hair before being sucked into the great gray vortex of corporate law.

Gavin was dashingly good-looking in a kind of James Bond, terribly proper English fashion. He was debonair in a way that seemed almost to belong to a bygone, more elegant era, as if he had been plucked straight from a P.G. Wodehouse novel and plonked down in modern-day Paris. A raconteur par excellence with a razor-sharp wit, Gavin could enthrall a dinner table with an endless supply of anecdotes and comedy routines.

During one sunny spring Sunday afternoon of Bloody Mary–quaffing on the Left Bank, Sylvie, Gavin, and Fiona had been distracted from their boozing by the sight of a Vespa spontaneously combusting on the sidewalk opposite their Saint Germain outdoor café. Not an event, it should probably be pointed out, that was all that common. Sitting two tables away at the same café was a similarly gobsmacked expat, Eric the Canadian, who had just arrived in Paris on assignment from the Zurich-based Swiss bank for which he worked.

As the Vespa burned, jokes were swapped and numbers duly exchanged.

Eric was a fresh-faced twenty-three-year-old from Toronto, three years out of university and hell-bent on having a no-holds-barred Paris experience. Like many of his countryfolk, he was partial to the odd bit of polar fleece clothing. Like every one of his countryfolk I have ever met, he was also warm, genuine, and funny. His enthusiasm for life and thirst for experience were infectious, and his habit of staring wide-eyed while you spoke was endearing—though whether it was because he was genuinely amazed at what you were saying or simply because he couldn't decipher your accent, it was never easy to say.

Some weeks prior to the burning-Vespa incident, Sylvie had crossed Parisian paths with an English girl called Charlotte. Charlotte was an English rose with a personality that seemed either reluctant or simply incapable of being contained within her tiny frame. She had an effervesence and enthusiasm for life that were contagious—two qualities that made her extremely good at her job as an advertising sales executive in *The Wall Street Journal*'s Paris bureau. Her colleague Claudio, from Italy, was also a new arrival in Paris and on the lookout for like-minded expatriate distraction. For though Claudio shared Latin roots with his French cousins, he felt much more at home in the company of similarly exuberant Anglo-Saxons than with their more staid French counterparts. Claudio was a born performer, a class clown with a richly sentimental side that was typically, effusively, adorably Italian. A set of big brown eyes and a Dolce & Gabbana wardrobe also made him a hit with the ladies.

Not long thereafter, on a random night out in the Marais, I came across an amiable English lad from Yorkshire. James had just arrived in Paris to assume the hilarious job title of "Energy Analyst—Emergency Planning and Preparations Division of the Directorate for Oil Industry, Markets and Emergency Preparedness" at the International Energy Agency. Hailing from Sheffield, in England's working-class industrial north, James's smarts had transported him to bourgeois Paris, where he was now busily absorbing and processing his new foreign surroundings. You could tell that a chameleonlike ability to blend with his surroundings, no matter what the social milieu, had served him well in life. A cheeky grin, brooding good looks, and more than his fair share of charm hadn't hurt either.

Meanwhile, through a friend with whom he had briefly been at university in Aix-en-Provence, Gavin had made contact with a young French lawyer named Julien, who (undoubtedly to his undying regret) found himself drawn into the fast-evolving expatriate circle. Julien had grown up in Macon, at the edge of the Burgundy region, southeast of Paris. He appeared to take his role as token French friend seriously, ensuring that his newfound band of foreign acquaintances were daily exposed to the best his country had to offer—whether it was cheese, wine, a hidden gem of a restaurant, or the perfect spot for a midsummer Seine-side picnic.

Completing the troupe of new buddies was Will, another English lawyer with whom Sylvie had studied at Cambridge University. Tall, handsome, and with a chiseled physique from his days of playing university rugby, Will had arrived in Paris to work in the noble pursuit of international human rights law. When he added his hat to the ever-growing pile, the Paris Posse was born.

ALONE, EACH OF the random connections that had brought us into one another's orbit was relatively inconsequential, but put together, they would turn out to be among the most significant coincidences in the Paris years that lay ahead of us. Thanks to a salsa class in London and a burning moped in Saint Germain, a core network of friends had been accidentally formed which would go on to have a massive influence not just on me but on all who were part of it. Over time the Posse's numbers would swell and ebb as each of us moved on, took a partner, dumped a partner, or otherwise introduced new recruits to the circle.

We all came from different countries and different backgrounds. We each had a different level of proficiency with the French language and culture. On the face of it, we had little in common except a coincidence of geography. Our reasons for being in Paris were as diverse as our nationalities, yet common to all of us was a passion for France, a love of the French, and a fascination for their language and culture. With the exception of local lad Julien, we were all of us chancers, in that we had willingly left comfortable existences at home to travel to France, where none of us knew a soul, just to sample the fabled delights of *la vie parisienne.* We became very close to one another in what seemed a ridiculously short amount of time.

Far from family and friends, and dealing daily with a set of linguistic and cultural challenges that were invariably either highly amusing or utterly exasperating, we each of us needed a ready series of empathetic shoulders on which to lean. That all of us had passed through the same social filter to find ourselves in Paris (adventurous, passionate about all things French, and willing or stupid enough to throw ourselves into a new country where we had no friends) meant that we formed a network whose members immediately had plenty in common. Enough, certainly, to be the natural, easy-to-reach substitute for family members or friends who were either one too many time zones away or too far removed from the day-to-day challenges of Paris life to properly understand what we were experiencing.

In an age characterized by the sitcom *Friends*—where networks of independent, geographically mobile, unmarried late-twenty-somethings roamed cityscapes the world over—we had formed our very own urban tribe. Unbeknown to us then, this tribe would remain close for years to come: traveling together to exotic destinations all over the world, exulting together in times of happiness, and drawing together in a protective ring in times of distress, hardship, or sadness. It wouldn't matter that time would eventually see some of us depart for our respective homelands or witness others move on to new horizons—the bond that was forged in these first six months of our Parisian existences was such that neither time nor distance would erode it.

But that was all years ahead of us. For now, all we knew was that Paris was our new, largely unexplored terrain and that in the Posse we had found the perfect unit in which to explore it. We were loud, we were brash, and we were all very fortunately in possession of handsomely paying jobs that required little more than our physical presence each day.

You could almost hear the city quivering in nervous anticipation.

Chapter 8

Summer of Love

IT HAD BEEN FIVE MONTHS since I had arrived in France. Summer was now in full swing, and in that way typical of countries that actually experience four distinct seasons (unlike my own, where there are only two: hot and cold), the city of Paris was coming out of its shell. Off came the scarves and overcoats beloved of all Parisians whenever the mercury dipped below 68 degrees Fahrenheit. Down went the guard they had spent all winter honing. And out the door flew that particular brand of Gallic indifference so often confused with arrogance.

For us new arrivals, it was a magical time to be in Paris. It was a summer of love, and no corner of the city was safe from our rapacious appetite for discovery. It was a time where no connection to the host of a house party was too tenuous. No bar, club, or restaurant was in a corner of the city too far-flung for us to sample. And no French person sitting in a bar was safe from our enforced (and usually drunken) company. We were strangers in a new city and high on the feeling of liberation that our anonymity afforded. We were alive with a sense of the possible and infused with the enthusiasm of the truly uninhibited.

We would routinely leave a bar with our cell phones full of new telephone numbers, having foisted ourselves upon anyone foolish enough to sit still for more than a minute. Each new acquaintance was at best a possible close friend and at worst a possible new entrée into *la vie parisienne*. No invitation, no matter how sketchy, was rebuffed. Every soirée was attended, and every avenue was explored in our attempts—whether joint or individual—to get under the city's skin. We had all seen the postcards and, on previous trips, had checked off all the boxes on the Paris tourist to-do list. We were none of us in the City of Light to spend hours in front of Monet's water lilies. What we wanted was a front-row seat at the seedy sideshow of underground Paris, and we found no shortage of willing local guides to aid us in our quest. Mild-mannered business executives by day, we would shed our corporate skin at night and follow our newfound friends to warehouse parties in outer suburbs of Paris where even taxi drivers refused to go.

After a few months of concerted bar-hopping and handing out our phone numbers to anyone who would take them, we found we had been unwittingly added to the e-mail list of a too-cool-for-school events company responsible for organizing legendary underground parties in a series of mystery Paris locations. Calling themselves Les Templiers, in a nod to the Knights Templar (the Christian military order made famous in *The Da Vinci Code* and that, legend has it, still operates secretly within French society), the events company had forged a reputation for hosting enormous, invitation-only, fancy-dress bashes all over the city. You would never know the location of the party until the last minute—you'd receive a furtive e-mail hours before it was due to begin. Each fiesta had a different theme. Each was packed to its heaving rafters with young, bright-eyed Frenchies, and each was sustained by a steady flow of free alcohol provided by one drinks company or another keen to hawk its wares to what it believed was a trendsetting demographic.

One Soirée Templiers had a futuristic theme, requiring us to dress all in white and assemble at a recently decommissioned electrical power station on the outskirts of Paris. Inside the cavernous power station, a roster of well-known international DJs whipped the crowd into a dancing frenzy, while trampolinists bounced in one corner and trapeze artists swung overhead. A bar made entirely of carved ice dispensed industrial quantities of a new designer beer, while across the way, in what once had served as the power station control room, an experimental electronica band turned the tiny space into a seething mosh pit.

At another Templier shindig James, Fiona, and I were summoned to a disused lime quarry thirty miles north of the city. The theme was graveyard chic, requiring everyone to dress as the living dead. We knew we were getting close to our destination as, with each turn off the highway, the concentration of cars packed with Morticias became more noticeable. Arriving at the quarry, we parked the car and, in full costume, joined the black-clad throng disappearing into the side of a hill to lose themselves in the labyrinth of subterranean dance floors, bars, and makeshift boudoirs. Turn a corner in one dimly lit tunnel, and you stumbled upon a space filled with beds, chaises longues, and appropriately reclining people. Take another passageway deeper into the maze, and you stepped into a vast cavern, crammed with masked, fancy-dressed French people dancing before a DJ with uncharacteristic abandon.

It was all good clean fun and only further aided our infiltration into the ranks of Paris's so-called bobos—the term coined for the city's army of part-time, halfhearted counterculturalists, the bohemian-bourgeoisie. It also made a mockery of the reputation the French have for being cold, aloof, and arrogant. Every local we met seemed genuinely excited at the prospect of showing off their city and sharing their culture with a ragtag bunch of foreigners.

But Parisian life wasn't all louche underground parties and post-midnight debauchery. Flush with the excitement of actually living in Paris and inclined to pinch ourselves each time we crossed the Pont des Arts, caught a glimpse of the Eiffel Tower, or rounded a corner to fall upon yet another spectacular Parisian vista, we wasted no time milking every moment of daylight too. Lazy Sundays were spent lying in the Parc Floral in the Bois de Vincennes, listening to free jazz concerts and sleeping off hangovers. The long stretch of lawn running from Les

Invalides to Pont Alexandre III became the venue for regular Saturday afternoons of amateur soccer, followed by beers in a nearby sunny outdoor café. The tennis courts at the Jardin du Luxembourg bore regular witness to our spectacular collective lack of sporting prowess. But what we lacked in style, we more than made up for in enthusiasm.

During the week we spent most of our hours at work on e-mail, dissecting the night before and making plans for the evening ahead. If we were feeling particularly energetic and the evening was especially balmy, we would rendezvous on Rollerblades and tear through the city's largely deserted streets. Spectacular sunsets would cast a pink hue over the entire city, giving the limestone facades of Haussmann's architectural handiwork a soft-focus, ethereal quality as we skated through the streets below.

Rollerblading down the middle of the Rue de Rivoli at midnight, toward the Place de la Concorde and around the huge, brightly lit Ferris wheel installed there for the Millennium celebrations would always involve making a brief stop on the Pont de la Concorde, to stare up the Seine toward the Eiffel Tower. Blading homeward through the empty, softly lit courtyard of the Louvre and around the base of the glass pyramid—which, lit from below, was a scintillating shard of glass and light—we would sit for a while in silence and breathe it all in. Staring intently at the scene before us, we would attempt to commit to memory every shadow, every play of light, every subtly illuminated feature of the Louvre's baroque exterior. If, heaven forbid, we were sent from the city to never spend another hour in Paris in our lives, we wanted to make sure these moments were locked in the memory bank, to stay with us forever.

On some nights after work we would assemble in the Jardin des Tuileries for evenings of rosé-sipping or make our way up to the Parc de la Villette where, on a vast stretch of grass (reclaimed parkland from what was once a large industrial site), we would put out blankets, lie back, and enjoy an evening of open-air cinema. It was a summer marked by twilight picnics on the Pont des Arts, eating cheese, drinking red wine, and watching the sun set behind the Grand Palais to the sound of bongo drums and amateur strummed guitar. It was a summer, moreover, during which the human capacity for sleep deprivation was severely tested.

Most weeknights would end with James, Eric, and me retreating to Eric's eighth-floor apartment on the Rue Saint Martin, just next to the Pompidou Center. Not content to simply take in the spectacular view from his living room—across the rooftops of Paris to the Eiffel Tower and beyond—we would arm ourselves with a bottle of whiskey, climb through the manhole in his hallway ceiling, clamber over a greasy elevator shaft, and emerge onto the roof, so that only the stars were above us. With the cold gray lead of a Paris rooftop under our bums, we would sit and stare out over the city, smoke whatever we had managed to score on the Pont des Arts, sip our whiskeys, and put the world to rights.

Weekends were different only inasmuch as the venues we patronized were busier and the sleep-ins the next morning more sustained. An average Saturday night might begin with a quick meal in the tiny brasserie behind our favorite bar, Au Petit Fer à Cheval, followed by a series of beers in quick succession at nearby Chez Richard. Then it was on to Favela Chic, a heaving little sweatbox of a nightclub near the Place de la République. Brazilian-themed, and keeping its eclectic clientele very well lubricated with the most potent caipirinha in all of Paris, Favela nightly transformed from a noisy restaurant to a salsa-dancing sauna.

Thanks to a door policy that allowed at least twice as many people into the establishment as were legally permitted, the dance floor was invariably so packed you often found yourself grinding pelvises with a complete stranger. Thanks to low ceilings and completely inadequate ventilation systems, shirts became a sweaty second skin and hair was plastered to foreheads within minutes of hitting the dance floor. It was so steamy, the bar staff would regularly spray the writhing dance floor masses with a shower of ice water. The combination of highly potent rum cocktails, tightly pressed bodies, and lack of oxygen made for an intoxicating couple of hours—literally and figuratively.

Stumbling out onto the street at two a.m., the still summer air caressing our sweat-soaked limbs, we would troop en masse back to the

Marais and install ourselves at the Low Rider Café on the Rue de Rivoli. This twenty-four-hour eatery, which mercifully served *croque-monsieurs* and *frites* until six a.m., was a mustering point for the flotsam and jetsam of the Paris night. Drag queens from nearby Marais gay bars shared the early-morning space with insomniac poets, artists, and actors who had emerged from surrounding garrets. Dodgy-looking characters stood alone at the bar, shirt collars turned up over artfully unshaven jowls. "I was riding low last night" was a phrase that entered the Posse vernacular, referencing our late-night eatery of choice, and it became the standard response to any inquiry the following day as to why we were looking so rough.

All of this activity was only repeated, and with greater intensity, when visitors were in town—which had started to become pretty much constantly. Feeling obliged to show them a good time, and determined to ensure they left thinking I had the swingiest lifestyle since the Great Gatsby and that my apartment, now dubbed the Love Pad, was the Parisian incarnation of Studio 54, I would take them out on marathon evenings of eating, drinking, and rabble-rousing.

THE ONLY TWO THINGS more remarkable than my stamina to endure these back-to-back all-night sessions—which stretched long beyond the first summer and easily into the ensuing autumn, winter, and spring—was the apparent resilience of my liver to withstand them and the sustained patience of my employer to put up with them.

"Been out Corbetting again, have we?" would be the daily inquiry of me from one superior or another as I dragged my sorry arse into the office each morning. The fact that my surname had become a verb to describe drunken behavior of a most unbecoming sort should probably have given me cause for concern, but I was too busy dealing with a perma-hangover and marveling that instead of discouraging my behavior, my immediate superiors seemed to find it amusing—refreshing even. To them I was just a young man in Paris having a whale of a time. Variously married, most with adult children, they seemed to not only indulge my behavior but actively to encourage it, as if to live it vicariously (and olfactorily, given what must have been a permanent reek of alcohol) conferred a kind of vitality.

I spent most mornings in my office nursing a tepid espresso from the coffee machine and watching imported Berocca tablets dissolve in plastic cups of water from the communal drinking fountain. On the odd occasion that I was called in to a meeting or expected to make a presentation, I would do so channeling all the sobriety I could muster, before retreating once more to my office to pass out.

After a while I came to recognize that the midafternoon pledge I would regularly make to myself to "never get that drunk again" was essentially hollow. Besides, it wasn't my fault that my life had morphed into an ambling series of hedonistic escapades. It was the fault of that old temptress Paris, the lurid corruptor of many a good man before me. And what had I come to Paris for anyway other than to lose myself momentarily in its famed bohemian nether regions?

Living a bachelor's life, and as the master of my own orange-walled domain, I had no one to answer to and no one to disapprove of my gleeful skip down the path to certain rack and ruin.

Chapter 9

Lesson in French Love 1:
Run for Your Life

SIX MONTHS into my Paris experience, I felt I had done a reasonably good job of assimilating. In my neighborhood I had been accepted as a local to the extent that the baker had stopped routinely giving me the most stale baguette in the shop. At my local drinking hole, Au Petit Fer à Cheval, I was greeted upon entry with a chorus of *"Le kangarou!"* Even the transvestite who ran the leather goods and piercing emporium under my apartment had begun to acknowledge me in the street.

And so I was beginning to carve my own niche in Paris. Six months of immersion in the culture meant that I was starting to get a handle on the French and their idiosyncratic ways. What's more, my French language skills were improving with every passing day—on a scale of *crap* to *excellent,* I was hovering somewhere near *not too bad at all.* And yet I still felt my cultural education was advancing at a snail's pace and that I needed some intense immersion therapy to really get under the skin of my adopted country.

There was nothing else for it: the time had come to take a French lover. Until now I had actively avoided becoming involved with a French girl. Quite apart from the fact that a steady stream of young English and American ladies were always passing through Paris, keen for a holiday romance, the French woman was a species that scared the living crap out of me. God knows they looked fantastic, all pouting lips, elegant poise, and demure posturing. Take a stroll down a Paris rue on any given day, and you cannot help but be struck by the number and variety of attractive women. Their hair is always beautifully coiffed, their clothes are stylish without being fashionable, and they carry themselves with an incredibly sexy air of haughtiness. They give off the impression of being untouchable—and it made me want to touch them all the more.

I spent the longest time thinking that Paris had more than its fair share of naturally beautiful women. But upon closer inspection, I discovered the secret to their stranglehold on beauty: French women go to an awful lot of trouble to look as if they haven't made an effort. They spend hours in front of the mirror to make themselves look natural. And like family recipes for cassoulet, the art form is passed down through the generations from mother to daughter. The average French woman spends thousands of euros each year on a raft of beauty products and anti-aging cosmetics that are as outlandish as they are plentiful. From creams that promise to "drain" recalcitrant thighs of liquid (who knew thighs were full of liquid?) to balms that magically erase wrinkles and tonics that prevent cellulite, the average Paris *pharmacie* is so chock-full of snake-oil beauty products, it's impossible to find anything of any medicinal value on its shelves.

As a newcomer to the country, I was in awe of *la femme française*. They had a practiced aloofness that was at once repulsive and irresistible. They could disintegrate you with a single withering look. Their manner of sucking on a cigarette, throwing you a disdainful look, and exhaling with contempt could reduce a grown man to a blubbering wreck. French men were used to this complex mating ritual. For them, a cutting putdown from a clearly uninterested woman was tantamount to a marriage proposal. They relished the cuts, seemed titillated by the flesh wounds, and threw themselves gleefully into the path of a full-scale French female dressing-down. It was a kind of public S&M, played out nightly in bars and clubs all over the country.

But for me, a simple lad from the suburbs of Sydney, such blatant rejection in the face of what were, admittedly, some fairly clumsy attempts at pickup lines, represented little more than humiliating failure in my attempts to seduce a French woman. Many had been the night I had leaped hopefully into the abyss that is a French woman's psyche and made valiant attempts to engage her in simple conversation, only to plummet onto the jagged rocks of her disdain. My French was functional, albeit heavily accented. As *un étranger,* I was relatively exotic. I may not have been Brad Pitt, but neither was I hideously disfigured. And unlike my French male counterparts, I had neither appalling fashion sense nor acute halitosis. Why then was I failing at every turn? On nights out with the boys, we would take turns approaching French women. It became a kind of sport, with the winner being whoever attracted the most withering look or spirited putdown.

And so I relegated French women largely to the "too hard" basket. And then I met Josephine. At first glance she seemed like a nice enough girl. Pretty in the insouciant way of all Parisian women, intelligent, and seemingly available, she satisfied the three criteria I had set as a benchmark for any cross-cultural relations of an intimate kind. Josephine was a journalist. She worked by day for a news agency, reporting on stock movements and financial markets. By night she studied Hebrew, in preparation for her planned journey to Israel, where she meant to one day live, work, and join the struggle for an uncontested homeland. Josephine was, she told me, a late convert to the Jewish religion. Having spent the better part of her twenty-eight years living in a blissful state of atheism, Josephine had delved into her mother's Jewish heritage and discovered a late-life passion for all things kosher. All of which was fine with me. As long as she spoke French, smelled good, and made for a stimulating dinner and drinks companion, I was happy to weather the occasional lecture about Ben-Gurion.

After the requisite two dates, and no doubt won over by my preternatural charm, the winsome young damsel was lured back to the Love Pad. The fact that once in the apartment, she insisted I call her

Judith—which, she informed me, was her chosen Hebrew name—failed to ring any alarm bells.

"Sure," I replied, not wanting to scare her off. "Whatever floats your boat."

The fact that upon returning home from work the next evening to find she had left a note under my door, written in Hebrew, also failed to set off alarm bells was perhaps, in retrospect, a little naïve on my part. So she was passionate about her new faith—good for her. It was only after we had spent our second night together and I received a call at work the following day that I began to realize just how deep I had inadvertently gotten myself.

"Salut, c'est moi," she announced.

"Hey!" I replied, mustering all the nonchalance I could—desperate to appear postconquest cool. "What's up? Did you manage to let yourself out of the apartment okay this morning?"

"Oui, no problem. I left the keys in the mailbox like you told me."

"Oh great, thanks." Awkward silence. "So. We should meet for a drink or dinner over the weekend, if you aren't busy."

"Sure, that would be nice." Long pause. "Umm. About the keys," she said.

"Yes," I replied, suddenly aware of a sinking feeling in my gut.

"Well, the thing is, I kind of noticed a spare set of keys on the dining room table and put them in my handbag as I left the apartment."

It was my turn for a long pause. "Ummmm. Why?"

"I don't know. I just saw them there, and before I knew it, I was putting them in my handbag."

Now I was starting to feel spooked. "Right," I stammered. "Um. Well. The thing is, I kind of need them back. You know, for guests who come to stay and stuff."

It was lame, but on the spur of the moment, and with red alert sirens blaring in my head and great neon signs flashing in my mind's eye—"Stalker! Bunny boiler! Call a locksmith immediately!"—it was the best I could come up with.

We arranged to meet that evening at a café for the handover of keys. I purposefully chose somewhere outdoors and very public, reasoning that if we were surrounded by people, she was less likely to come at me with a meat cleaver or otherwise make a scene.

As I arrived at the café, she was already *in situ,* enjoying the last rays of sunshine on a perfect late summer's evening. We shared a drink, indulged in chitchat, and generally skirted around the topic. I wanted the keys, and then I wanted out. Quickly.

"Look, I'm really sorry about the key thing," she offered finally, as she dug into her bag and fished out my house keys. "I don't know what came over me. My therapist would be horrified if she found out."

Therapist? It was all I could do not to spit a mouthful of beer across the table. With keys safely in my pocket, I made to leave. Yes, we would definitely keep in touch when she went to Israel. Of course I would look into coming to visit. No question that we would see each other again before she left in a couple of weeks' time.

I pecked her on the cheek, turned on my heel, and walked away. Briskly.

Chapter 10

Dial H for Help Me!

B Y THE TIME my first full winter in the City of Light swung around, I had welcomed so many guests to the Love Pad, I began to wonder if my apartment was being advertised without my knowledge in the Air France in-flight magazine. Though records are shaky, I conservatively estimate that during my first eight months in Paris my humble Marais abode played host to some sixty-four guests. Many of them were friends or family. Most were Australian. Some were even people I vaguely knew. Some stayed a night, others stayed a week. All enjoyed the dubious comfort of the world's worst sofabed (which I refused to replace, working on the theory that if I couldn't get rid of a guest, eventually the sofabed would do it for me). And each one of these guests helped to ensure that I continued to pour my salary into the mortgage payments of the five or six bars within crawling distance of my apartment.

Mostly I liked having guests—it was a welcome opportunity for me to show off my new Parisian life. Nothing was sweeter than stepping out my front door with them, onto the bustle of the film set that was the rue Sainte Croix, and watching their faces twist with awe and envy. It was also a welcome reminder to me of how lucky I was to be living that life.

When the first wave of guests descended during that first summer, I made the mistake of feeling obliged to personally escort each one on a guided tour of the city. Perhaps not realizing that they were really in Paris for the city and not expressly for my company, I would drag them along what became a very well-trodden track. Setting out from my apartment, we would walk past the Hôtel de Ville, in front of Notre Dame, down the quai past the booksellers to the Pont des Arts, across the bridge, into the courtyard of the Louvre, through the Tuileries, and on to the Ferris wheel at the Place de la Concorde. From the vantage point afforded by the Ferris wheel, we would take in the remainder of the city's iconic monuments—the Grand and Petit Palais, the glorious gold-domed Invalides, the marshmallow Sacré Coeur atop the Butte de Montmartre, the Champs Elysées, the Arc de Triomphe, and of course the Eiffel Tower. Striking her impressive pose upriver, Gustave Eiffel's iconic steel tower never failed to excite my charges. Cameras clicked furiously as a kind of deferential silence settled over us. Here finally, and undeniably, was proof they were in Paris.

Every now and then, motivated either by pure boredom or by horror at the prospect of having to do the circuit one more time, I would push out the tour guide boat and come up with a truly original Paris sightseeing idea. Like the time I suggested visiting the Paris sewers to my visiting Australian friends Madeleine and Alister.

"No, really," I quickly sought to explain. "The Paris sewers are supposed to be amazing. They were used as an underground network by the Résistance during the Second World War and also by revolutionaries during the French Revolution. There's a museum and everything. And hardly anyone goes there—it's completely off the tourist beat. We'll have the place to ourselves."

As indeed we did.

ARRIVING AT THE ENTRANCE to the *égouts de Paris* near the Pont de l'Alma on the Seine, we watched smugly as busloads of tourists careened past us to make their appointment with the three hundred other busloads of tourists at the Eiffel Tower. By stark comparison, the entrance to the sewers was distinctly void of other tourists.

Having paid our fifty francs to get in, we took a spiral steel staircase from the street down into the bowels of the city. And when I say bowels of the city, I mean it literally, not figuratively. Instead of an edifying and moving historical account of the vital role the Paris sewers played in the establishment and maintenance of the modern French state, we were treated to a half-hour tour dedicated to the technical logistics of how a modern metropolis moved its effluent.

The only thing more disturbing than the fact that such a museum even existed was the amount of effort that had obviously gone into creating it. Elaborate, interactive dioramas allowed you to follow a movement from its first flush to final treatment. Mannequins wearing thigh-high waders and rain hats accompanied a recorded tape explaining in three languages how Paris *merde* was processed. The curators had even thought to place the occasional stuffed rat atop evocatively seeping pipelines at occasional intervals. And as if to enhance the authenticity of the entire experience, the entire museum was laid out above a working drain. A metal-grille boardwalk, constructed expressly for the purpose of transporting museum attendees from one end of the oversize drainpipe to the other, hovered precariously above a fast-flowing stream of muddy brown water of distinctly dubious origin. It was, we decided afterward, one of those unorthodox tourist attractions that, once visited, need never be talked about, much less revisited.

Scarred by my failed attempt to inject a bit of originality into my personalized tourist trail, and tired of beating the same path each weekend and hearing myself narrate the same boring tourist fact for the umpteenth time, I finally took to sending my guests out on their own.

"Here's a set of keys, here's a map of the city. Knock yourselves out," I would say, before shuffling them out the door and getting on with my life. Most guests probably breathed a sigh of relief, finally left alone to enjoy the city without the noise pollution of my incessant gibber.

• • • •

WHEN OPENING my apartment to guests, I always tried to operate along the lines of *mi casa es su casa*. I enjoyed welcoming friends to my new city, and more than anything else, I wanted them to feel relaxed, to treat my apartment as they would their own home. It usually worked just fine, since most guests understood that this principle had its limits. They would drop their towels on the bathroom floor, for example, but would never clip their toenails on the sofa. They might venture a cheeky cigarette in the living room or help themselves to the coffee machine, but they would never walk around the kitchen naked.

For the most part, my guests were acutely aware of the imposition they caused by showing up on my doorstep, and they would go out of their way to express their gratitude, minimize their impact on my daily life, or shower me with gifts when they left. All of which was greatly appreciated. And most guests, it has to be said, behaved impeccably when it came to not abusing the hospitality.

But every now and then a guest would become a little too comfortable in their surroundings.

Sophie (which, for what will become obvious reasons, is not her real name) was one such friend. Ours was a friendship that stretched back years, and during the three and a half years I had been in London and Paris, she had visited once or twice from Australia and had always stayed with me for a week or so. Partners in debauched crime, we would usually crawl the bars of wherever I happened to be living until the wee-small hours, reminiscing about the old days and making mischief with the locals.

Alighting in the Love Pad on her first visit to Paris since I had arrived, Sophie dumped her bags and sped out the door, explaining as she went that she had a date with a Frenchman she had met the week before at a thirtieth birthday party in Marseille. I bade her goodnight and good luck, threw her the keys, and told her to let herself in when she returned.

"I'm having a quiet one tonight," I yelled down the stairs after her.

Around midnight, as I was preparing to go to bed, I heard keys in the door and got up to greet her and grill her about her hot date. Walking toward the front door in naught but my boxer shorts, I heard the unmistakable grunt of a male voice. In a panic, I rushed back into my room and closed the door. Sophie, already drunk, sailed into the apartment, settled onto the lounge, and invited her new friend to join her. I could only assume she thought I was out for the evening, or fast asleep. As the only way out of the apartment was through the living room, I was trapped. I decided to bide my time, lie on my bed in the dark, and wait out the nightcap scenario that was unfurling on the other side of my paper-thin bedroom door.

Just as I was drifting off to sleep, lulled by the low murmur of their voices, I became suddenly aware that the living room conversation had abruptly stopped, and in its place was a lot of heavy breathing. The breathing sooned turned to panting, the panting turned to grunting, and the grunting began climbing to such a fever pitch that I began to worry about the ability of my poor sofa to withstand such a concerted pummeling. Surely she had to be aware I was in the next room? Certainly she couldn't be copulating loudly on my sofa in the knowledge that I was trying to sleep not ten feet away?

For the sake of what was left of her dignity, I had to let Sophie know I was next door. But how? Walking into the living room would have exposed me to a scene too horrible to contemplate. I had an idea. My cell phone was on the living room floor next to the sofa. I would simply call my cell from the landline next to my bed, Sophie would answer, and I would quietly inform her that her intimate twosome had inadvertently become a threesome.

The phone rang once. The phone rang twice. Then in midcoitus— and in a maneuver that I can only imagine required no small amount of flexibility—my raunchy houseguest reached across the sofa, switched off the phone, and continued rutting. Loudly. I covered my ears with my pillow, desperate not to bear silent witness to the climax. When I resurfaced, it was to smell the first whiff of a postcoital cigarette and hear the first strains of some of the most bizarre pillow talk ever conceived.

"So I'm interested to know a little bit more about the separation of church and state in France," I heard Sophie inquire of her paramour. Which instead of turning him off, as it would most men, seemed only to further excite his ardor. Before you could say "is that a *saucisson* in your pocket or are you just a horny French man," they were at it again. This time in the kitchen—and by the sound of the crashing plates, not far from the sink, if not in it.

Desperate now, I realized the landline was my only hope. I had to get it to ring, to compel her to answer it. But I couldn't call myself. I had to call a friend, explain the situation to them, and get them to call the house. The fact that it was past one a.m. immediately ruled out the Paris Posse. I did a mental checklist of time zones around the world and cross-referenced it with the telephone numbers of friends I knew by heart.

When Claire, a mutual friend of both Sophie's and mine working at a newspaper in New York, returned to her desk after a meeting with her editor, it was to receive a hurried, whispered voice-mail message from her friend Bryce in Paris:

"Hi, it's me. Listen, I know this is going to sound really weird, but I just need you to call my home number as soon as possible. Sophie will answer the phone. I just want you to tell her that I am in the bedroom next door and that she needs to stop having sex with that French man."

But before Claire had time to hear her messages and return the call, the French man was sated, zipped up, and out the door. And judging by the brief amount of time between her paramour splaying her over the gas range and hightailing it, I guessed Sophie would have been lucky to get a peck on the cheek, much less her requested explanation of the comparative advantages of secularism in France.

Apparently not content to fall onto the sofa in a state of euphoric exhaustion, Sophie then picked up the phone and dialed her grandmother in Australia.

"Hi, Nan, it's me, Sophie," she said, as I lay incredulous in the next room. Not only had she had noisy sex in my living room with a relative stranger, she was now using this apparently unexpected hole in her

Friday-night social schedule to use my phone to call her grandmother. Long distance.

"I just had a date with a lovely French man," she said. "It's so nice to be in Paris and go on a date with a French man. They are such gentlemen. Much better than the men at home."

It was more than I could stand. To be prevented from sleeping by a noisily shagging friend was one thing, but to have the gallant credentials of my Australian brothers impugned by someone who seemed to think a complete disregard for foreplay, a gruff bedside manner, and a thick French accent were the height of chivalry was more than I was prepared to put up with. I picked up the telephone on my bedside table and intoned into the receiver: "Soph, it's me. I'm in the room next door. Can we talk when you get a minute?"

She hurriedly wound up the conversation with her grandmother and came bounding into the bedroom, hand slapped over her mouth in a look of total horror.

"Oh my god! I thought you were out. I thought you had gone to a bar or something. How long have you been there? What did you hear? This is so embarrassing."

"Never mind that," I replied. "How dare you suggest Australian men are not gentlemen after that little performance! As God is my witness, if I ever hear you say a bad word about Australian men again, I'll tell the world about the French lesson you just had in my kitchen."

And though in years to come Sophie would continue her love affair with all things Gallic, she never again voiced a bad opinion about Aussie men in my presence. Sure, the Frenchie may have had his way with Sophie, repeatedly in my living room and kitchen, but in my own quiet way I had struck a blow for non-French men everywhere.

As I lay in bed, drifting off to sleep, I puzzled over the international reputation the French have for being good in the sack. While you can certainly never generalize about an entire nation and its lovemaking prowess, from all the accounts of female friends who had had relations with French men, the male Gallic lover was a species especially averse to foreplay, wholly uninterested in pleasuring his partner, and on the whole particularly perfunctory when it came to the making of love. Sophie's little interlude with Monsieur Church and State may have deprived me of a few hours' sleep, but the experience hadn't been a complete waste of time. Now I knew with a greater degree of certainty that the French man's reputation for being a gifted lover was a fallacy. The cultural education continued.

Chapter 11

All Roads Lead to the Connétable

PARIS HAS LONG BEEN a magnet for poets, writers, and musicians. *La vie bohème* had its origins in the narrow, cobbled streets of Saint Germain and the licentious laneways of La Butte de Montmartre. Celebrated writers including Hemingway, Joyce, Beckett, and Pound have all called Paris home at one stage or another, drawn by the city's healthy respect for all things intellectual.

The literary heritage of Paris is so rich, it has spawned a cottage industry. Establishments all over modern-day Paris shamelessly trade on whatever tenuous link to an influential philosopher, musician, or writer they can muster. The result is a city crammed with plaques announcing that a writer once scribbled a few paragraphs in an attic here or a painter died of consumption in a garret there. Iconic places like the Café de Flore, where Jean-Paul Sartre and his missus, Simone de Beauvoir, used to smoke and think themselves to death, are able to charge seven euros for a coffee off the backs of a couple of long-dead philosophers. And the tourist hordes just cannot get enough.

And while it has a lot of competition, the grand pooh-bah of

Paris's Great Literary Heritage Cash-In is Shakespeare and Co., a tumbledown bookstore on the bank of the Seine opposite Notre Dame. Trading on a tenuous historical connection to Hemingway's publisher, Sylvia Beach, the shop is a river-hugging, oversize dust collector in which it is nearly impossible to actually find a book, much less purchase one. So dilapidated is the interior, it probably would have been condemned years ago were it not for the legions of impressionable American teens who continue to flock there on their "big European trip" to spend a few nights sleeping for free on foam mattresses in the attic in exchange for helping out around the shop.

On the ground floor a maze of precariously piled books are arranged in a system that seems to defy all logic. The one good thing about the store, as far as I could see, is that it serves to keep the legions of tortured artists and barely postpubescent Beat poets concentrated in one tiny pocket of Paris, away from the rest of us.

I discovered that were you to stroll along the stretch of the Seine in front of the bookstore on any given Friday night during summer, you were guaranteed to be confronted by a phalanx of aspiring poets and philosophers, emoting all over the riverbank. Filling the night air with their artlessly rendered poetry and polluting the otherwise stunning scene with their bad complexions, they regularly stage riverside poetry readings, always involving bottles of cheap red wine, lots of candles, and at least one guitar for a tuneless rendition later in the evening of "No Woman, No Cry." I learned from bitter experience that the only thing worse than listening to a preppy nineteen-year-old from Connecticut singing Bob Marley songs is listening to a preppy nineteen-year-old from Connecticut reciting his angst-ridden poetry. And it was an ordeal made all the more nauseating by the distinct impression you got from their designer bohemian wardrobes that the only real angst they had experienced in their short lives was that caused by the late arrival of Daddy's weekly check.

Shakespeare and Co. had become more of a memorial to Paris's famed *la vie bohème* than any living embodiment of it. Whatever artistic or literary credibility it might once have enjoyed had long since been replaced by the distinct aroma of upper-middle-class America—

a mixture of Snapple Ice Tea, sweaty Teva sandals, and Tommy Hilfiger cologne. Indeed, the entire Left Bank long ago lost its bohemian credentials. Except for a few pockets around the Sorbonne, it has been years since anyone even resembling a bohemian has been able to afford the astronomical rents of the fifth and sixth arrondissements. *La vie bohème* long ago packed its tatty cardboard suitcase and moved across the river. Its new home, as I was about to happily discover, was a place called Le Connétable.

Perched as it unobtrusively was on a nondescript corner behind the Archive National in the Marais, you could easily walk past the Connétable without guessing that its front door was in fact the secret portal to the seedy underbelly of modern-day Paris. From the outside there was nothing particularly remarkable about the bar-restaurant at all. The paint was peeling, the menu in the window was faded yellow and curling at the edges, and the sign above the door was missing the C, announcing the establishment to the world as the ONNÉTABLE.

Food was served in a second-floor restaurant area. The low-slung roof featured dark rows of seriously bowed rafters, and the walls were hung with faded tapestries. The basement had been cleared out and fashioned into a performance space of sorts. Musty black curtains hung over dank stone walls. A few battered stage lights were trained on a wilting microphone stand. The ground floor played host to the main bar area, a poky space crammed with odd bits of furniture, including an upright piano and a tattered sofa. The bar, which was squashed into one corner of the tiny room, seemed to be permanently propped up by a bedraggled cast of aging regulars.

The most unspectacular of bars, the place was so unobtrusive as to be instantly forgettable. But unobtrusive was exactly what its regular patrons wanted Le Connétable to be. To them, it was a haven. They were themselves refugees from a more idealistic time, when the ubiquitous French battle cry of *Liberté, egalité, fraternité* actually meant something. A ragtag bunch of sixty-something artistes, they considered Le Connétable their last refuge. A welcome, reliable respite from a Paris they found too busy, too materialistic, and far too full of loud, disrespectful foreigners for their liking.

So it was much to their collective chagrin that James and I stumbled across Le Connétable. We were introduced to the place by a mutual Dutch friend, Roebyem, who, by virtue of the fact she lived above it, had come to use the restaurant as something of a canteen. James, while out on a random midweek bender with Roebyem, or "the Dutchie," as we affectionately called her, had summoned me to Le Connétable, where they were busy polishing off a bottle of wine. I joined them, and over a few more bottles of wine, our love affair with the place was born.

The bar had been bought some ten years previously by a small blond French woman called Françoise. Now in her late fifties, Françoise had once been quite the woman about Paris, a celebrated beauty and the love interest of the late French folksinger Maurice Fanon. Fanon had been a child of the sixties, a social-protest folksinger. After hurling paving stones during the French student riots of May '68, he had gone on to forge a mildly successful career as a singer-songwriter. At the height of his popularity Fanon was a poor man's Serge Gainsbourg. Bob Dylan without the album sales.

Françoise had turned Le Connétable into a shrine to her late paramour. Posters of the brooding artist, his face barely discernible through the curl of smoke from an artfully poised Gitane, hung in the bar, and each night toward midnight his music would be played as a homage. Helping her run the good ship Connétable and responsible for waiting tables and tending bar were the oddest couple ever to wield a beer tap. Daniel, a hulking mass of brackishness, had jowls you could swing off, doubtless the product of too many years spent with his face in that default French hangdog expression that personifies disdain. His shoulders seemed to be constantly slouched, and his face was contorted into a perma-scowl. He seemed to detest every moment he was forced to serve at Le Connétable, resenting every customer for the inconvenience they caused him of actually having to work. His partner in service-industry crime was Marie. Preternaturally disinclined to prepare or serve drinks, Marie spent the better part of most nights leaning against the bar, smoking with an air of carefully cultivated indifference, and pointedly ignoring any requests for service. We called her Marlene, after Marlene Dietrich, because she had all of the Blue Angel's haughty attitude but none of her warmth.

There was talk that they were a married couple, but it was scuttle-butt that owed itself to nothing more than the fact that they treated each other with barely disguised contempt. Chief among Marie and Daniel's myriad talents was their ability to make up drink prices as they went along. The pricing structure never had any consistency, swinging from extremely reasonable to vastly overpriced according to the amount of alcohol Daniel himself had imbibed. A demi of beer that cost two euros fifty at eleven p.m. might mysteriously cost five euros eighty at three a.m. A bottle of bad red wine, whose only reliable quality was its surefire ability to cause a stinking hangover the next day, might cost fifteen euros at midnight and twenty-eight euros at five a.m.

The Posse became so enamored of Le Connétable that we adopted it as a second home, its wildly fluctuating pricing structure notwith-standing. Before long, it became the default venue where every night on the town would end. Our infiltration of the place was gradual. It was also met with a complete lack of enthusiasm by the regular patrons who had been coming to the bar for so long the barstools featured dents that perfectly matched their buttocks. Marie and Daniel—who, behind their gruff exteriors, had been revealed to be a pair of big old softies—were far more pleased to have us there. But whether that was because we brought in waves of young urban professionals who livened up the proceedings, or because each of those young urban pro-fessionals had a fat wallet whose contents they became less attached to as the night wore on, was hard to say.

Joining us most nights on this magical mystery tour to the depths of depravity was an ever-changing cast of actors, poets, singers, and musicians. The musical heritage of Le Connétable, plus the fact that in its basement it regularly hosted concerts of obscure traveling min-strels, ensured that the establishment was deeply credible among the younger Parisian thespian set.

On weekends, when the clock struck two a.m. and its license to serve alcohol technically expired, the Connétable would go into lockdown mode, drawing the curtains and lowering the shutters so as to appear closed to the outside world. It was only then, and with the bar packed to its low-slung rafters, that the real action would begin. Guitars would be pulled from cavities in the wall, violins would mysteriously appear, and the piano stool would be dragged out, signaling that the festivities were about to commence. While Daniel and Marie made little or no attempt to keep up with the steady demand for drinks, songs were sung, impromptu bouts of Beat poetry were performed, and the piano's ivories were furiously tinkled. Smoke hung heavy in the air as mournful odes to love lost and rambunctious jigs bounced off the claustrophobic walls. Strangers made drunken eye contact before falling onto the sofa in a mad snogging frenzy. A night at the Connétable was always louche and always late.

After six months of faithful patronage, we became grudgingly accepted as locals. It became our bar of choice when all others had closed. As a mark of our respect for the place, Will finished one drunken evening at the eclectically decorated Favela Chic bar-restaurant by stealing a stuffed toy camel and offering it up to Daniel as Le Connétable mascot. Daniel immediately called it *"mon chien"* and gave it pride of place atop the sofa. Taking a cue from the French film *Amélie,* we took to kidnapping the camel whenever we went on an overseas work trip. We would then photograph it in far-flung international locations, either in front of a recognizable landmark or somewhere otherwise expanding its cultural experience. The photos were mailed back to Daniel, whereupon he would stick them on a bulletin board titled "Les Voyages de Mon Chien."

For years afterward the wall behind the bar in Le Connétable was decorated with photos of a toy camel atop the Empire State Building, on horseback at a Denver rodeo, on a beach towel in Biarritz, dancing tango in Buenos Aires, and surfing in Bali.

But the fact that we were slotting our Connétable all-nighters in between international jaunts did little to enhance our already shaky credibility as bona-fide bohemians. We came to be known as *faux bos,* slumming it as bohemians into the wee small hours of a seedy Parisian night, but only insofar as it didn't interfere with our conference call the next morning.

In subsequent years Le Connétable would find its way into the *Time Out* guide, and, disastrously, not long thereafter, into *Eurostar* magazine. Almost overnight it would be transformed from a hidden gem into an oversubscribed tourist trap.

But for the time being the Posse had found its unofficial clubhouse. And as long as the variously priced beer flowed and the bar stayed open until six a.m., our custom was assured.

Chapter 12

Turquoise Spandex, Anyone?

LIKE MOST NATIONS, the French take their sports very seriously. The French rugby team is one of the best in the world, the French soccer team has been a World Cup winner, and French tennis players regularly jockey for top-ten positions in world rankings. But if you take a mega–sporting event like the Olympics and peruse the statistics, it becomes clear that when it comes to winning the big medals, the French are disproportionately underrepresented. Sure they sweep the field in such obscure Olympic sports as fencing and judo, and they perform well in events like equestrian and shooting, but for any sport actually requiring a modicum of aerobic exertion (except perhaps cycling, thanks to a national obsession with the Tour de France), they are pretty much nonstarters.

You only have to look around you in Paris to discover why. Life there entails a lot of sitting around. Be it in cafés, restaurants, or bars, sitting, eating, smoking, drinking, and talking, are about the only activities your average Parisian will undertake on a daily basis. Occasionally they might multitask by combining rugby- or soccer-watching with their smoking and drinking, but a brief moment of tension in front of the TV during a World Cup penalty shootout is the closest most Parisians ever come to breaking into a sweat.

Make no mistake, Parisians love their sports, but not so much that they ever feel compelled to actually play them. You might see the odd jogger and the occasional Rollerblader on the streets of Paris, but generally speaking, the French are a relatively sedentary bunch.

Largely due to a complete lack of space for sporting activities (a city crammed with Louvres, d'Orsays, Jardins du Luxembourg, and Notre Dames has little space for soccer fields), and compounded by the fact that what little grass there is in Paris is patrolled and protected by a particularly heinous breed of Paris Park Police (or grass nazis, as I liked to call them), the outlets for sporting expression in Paris are few and far between.

As a direct result, Parisian kids are remarkably uncoordinated. Coming as I do from a nation where children learn to tackle before they learn to walk, I was shocked to discover upon arriving in Paris that France is raising entire generations of children with no hand-eye coordination. What little time Paris kids are allowed to dedicate to sports each day is usually played out on a patch of gravel, sandwiched between two apartment buildings. These pasty, sallow, sunken-chested little mites kick-and-miss their little hearts out on ten square yards of dust. Sure, they might be able to tell you the entire history of the Impressionist movement, but they can't kick a ball to save their sheltered lives.

As a self-confessed member of that rare breed, the Australian male who is largely uninterested in sports (yes, I've been through counseling, but it doesn't seem to work), I felt at first that in sports-averse Paris I had found my spiritual home. But it wasn't long before I began to crave exercise. A year of drunken debauchery had taken its toll on my waistline, and something had to be done. Determined not to crawl toward middle age without once seeing proof that I possessed biceps, I decided to join the only chain of gyms that Paris boasted. Called Le Gymnase Club, the chain featured some ten locations around the greater Paris metropolitan area. Each one was as smelly as the other, and each had been painted by an interior decorator who obviously had a glut of unused orange. Together with poor ventilation and severe fluorescent lighting, it was about as convivial an atmosphere for exercise as the surface of Mars. A bunch of green-uniformed, mop-wielding cleaners would move in a desultory fashion from one room to the next on a never-ending circuit, and yet the place felt perpetually dirty. Every time I entered, I would ponder the viability of performing my exercises in a full-body prophylactic. God knows if my mother had seen the place, she would have whipped out her yellow gloves, pushed aside the cleaning androids, and given the place a good bleaching. But as it was, there was no gym alternative in the entire city of twelve million people. It was the stinky Gymnase Club or nothing.

Because the exercise fad had come relatively late to France, the nation was at least twenty years behind the rest of the world when it came to fitness fashion. A French man in shorts looks uncomfortable at the best of times. Put him in a pair of high-cut nylon running shorts—of the sort favored by long-distance runners—and finish the look with tucked-in tank top and a pair of black socks with white sneakers, and you've got your average French gym junkie, looking for all the world like a refugee from Olivia Newton-John's *Let's Get Physical* video. The more daring French gym junkies had a penchant for sweatbands and spandex Lycra—of every hue. I learned by observation that, generally speaking, turquoise spandex and men's pasty white thighs do not a happy marriage make.

Like gyms the world over, the Gymnase Club had stumbled upon the happy realization that you can take a large sum of money from people at the start of any given year for services that, in the throes of a New Year's resolve, they fully intend to use but never actually do. As I signed my check for membership, I did so smug in the knowledge that I would not become one of those statistics. I had been raised by a mother who made her children bring home the Glad Wrap from their sandwiches so she could wash it and reuse it. There was no way I was not going to get value out of the money I spent on my gym membership.

What this meant initially was that I experimented with the different classes the Gymnase Club had on offer, to see which best suited my needs. After discovering I didn't have the coordination required for step class, and after spending the majority of the low-impact aerobics class in a heap of sweating, jellied flesh on the floor, I stumbled upon Body Pump. Body Pump was part aerobics, part weights, requiring participants to lift dumbbells and barbells to the beat of a medley of pop songs. Emboldened by this happy marriage of my stated aim (to get into shape) and my guilty pleasure (cheesy pop songs), I soon became a regular Body Pumper and found myself inadvertently part of a bizarre community of fellow pumpees.

Foremost among my pumping pals was Nathan, an expat from America who was similarly bamboozled by the strange French gym world into which he had stumbled. Together we would take up position at the back of the class and gleefully assume the role of sniggering troublemakers, performing our assigned tasks badly while concentrating on the serious business of making fun of our classmates.

There was Boney Maroney (not, I suspect, her real name), who was in her early twenties, had a shock of fuzzy brown hair, and was surely the skinniest human being alive. The sight of her spindly legs quivering as she lifted a barbell above her head defied all laws of physics. I used to worry that one day she would put one weight too many on her barbell and snap clean in half, only to be swept up by the cleaning robots, never to be seen or heard from again.

Then there was the Brick (full name: Brick Shithouse), so called because of his thickset muscular torso. The Brick would always take up position at the front of the class, just next to the instructor, with an unobstructed view of himself in the mirror. As far as we could tell, he spent almost as much time preening as he did actually performing the exercises.

Farther back in the class, but always in a position to have at least half of the class directly behind her, was the Freak. We were never entirely sure of her gender, blessed as she was with one of those harsh female faces that suggests a former life as a man. What we were sure of, however, was the color, texture, and mood of each of her buttocks, revealed as they constantly were in a series of barely there g-string leotards. The leotards were emblazoned with such sequin-encrusted slogans as "Sexy" and "Gorgeous." Stretched over a pair of red fishnet stockings, and possessed of a tendency to disappear up her crack each time she bent over, the g-string leotards ensured that little about the Freak was left to the imagination.

But our favorite among all the gym regulars was definitely the Energizer Granny. She must have been seventy yet seemed to have more energy than most teenagers. She would bounce straight from a step class to the Body Pump room, never breaking a sweat and performing all of her exercises with an undue amount of enthusiasm and a crazed, almost delirious grin pasted to her face. I concluded that she was quite obviously on drugs.

While iron was pumped and cardio-funk was performed in the gym proper, all the real action appeared to go on in the locker rooms. I could have been wrong, but it seemed to me that there was a large number of people who had taken out gym membership for the sole purpose of indulging in a regular series of very long, very public showers. Now, I'm no prude when it comes to getting my gear off. I've performed the occasional midnight streak and skinny-dipped with the best of them. But there is gratuitous nudity, and then there is gratuitous nudity. And in my book it is not strictly necessary to weigh oneself on the communal scales, blow-dry one's hair in front of floor-to-ceiling mirrors, or rigorously apply moisturizing lotion to one's inner thigh while in a state of undress. I couldn't help but notice that some boys would be loitering naked in the locker rooms when I arrived for my gym session, only to be still loitering—apparently unable to find their clothes—over an hour later when I would leave.

For his part, Nathan had long since abandoned the practice of showering at the gym after a confronting experience with his sometime personal trainer, the ever-affable Loic. Quietly minding his own business in the communal shower one evening, he was horrified when Loic bounded in naked and struck up a conversation.

"So, let's see how you are coming along then," Loic said, motioning for him to turn around.

"Umm. Sorry?" asked a confused Nathan, glancing nervously over his shoulder.

"Come on! Don't be shy! Turn around and show me those pecs of yours! Let's see if all of this personal training is paying off!" replied Loic, apparently unfazed at the prospect of comparing muscle tone with a relative stranger, in the buff, surrounded by a troupe of similarly naked men taking suspiciously long showers. Whether he was simply a health professional who took his work way too seriously, or a seasoned shower stalker with more on his mind than burgeoning pecs, Nathan could not be sure. Either way, he never risked the Gymnase Club showers again.

For me, the gym became a semiregular weekly habit. Whether it was to clear out the cobwebs, to escape from the office, or simply to get an endorphin fix, I became a part-time gym junkie, visiting up to three times a week. Imagine then my delight at receiving in the mail one day what I can only describe as a "fat bastard letter" from the gym management. It came in the guise of a Satisfaction Questionnaire but was really just a postman-delivered cheap shot at my supposed lack of commitment to the fitness cause.

Dear Client, it began. *We're so glad you chose Gymnase Club to help you keep fit, but disappointed not to see you here more often. What a shame you don't make better use of your membership. Perhaps you would like to fill out the following questionnaire to help us better understand why you never come to the gym.*

Quite apart from the fact that it was untrue, it beggared belief that a service provider, to whom I had given a not inconsiderable amount of money at the start of the year to furnish me with gym facilities, was now taking potshots at my level of dedication to the fitness cause.

Are you lazy? the questionnaire went on to inquire. *Do you have too many other work or family commitments? Or do you simply not like gyms?*

Now, in some countries, a customer questionnaire might seek to discover if the service provider could in some way improve the service it was offering clients. Before accusing customers of slackness, apathy, and abject laziness, a gym might, for example, inquire whether its equipment is sufficiently state-of-the-art or whether the hours are convenient or the facilities generally clean. But this was France, I had to remind myself, a country where the customer is never very important, much less right.

I considered my options. It was too huge a slight for me to let slide. I had to confront it. But how best to do it? I started scribbling an outraged note in the "additional comments" section of the questionnaire, explaining that I did indeed use their facilities often, despite the fact they were out of date and constantly filthy. I thought of pointing out that were it not for the fact that they had a gym monopoly in Paris, they would have gone out of business long ago. I even contemplated telling them that orange walls and fluorescent-lit gym interiors went out of fashion with leg-warmers.

But then the futility of it all overwhelmed me. I knew the questionnaire would only be opened by some wholly uninterested work-experience kid who would throw it directly in the trash. So instead I went onto the Internet and printed out the respective medal tallies for Australia and France from the Sydney Olympics and scribbled across the top: *Australia: population 20 million, fourth place. France, population 60 million, sixth place. Where do you get off telling me I'm lazy?*

I slipped it inside the postage-paid return envelope and dropped it into the mailbox outside my front door. It was petty and would doubtless be ignored, but it made me feel so much better.

Chapter 13

Patron Saint
of Prescription Drugs

WHEN IT CAME to communicating with the natives, I soon discovered that in certain situations it was good to persist in French, and in others it made infinitely more sense to communicate in my mother tongue.

Talking to the woman on the phone to get the gas connected was, for example, a conversation I was willing to have in French. So were dealing with the plumber, chatting to my friendly neighborhood *boulanger,* and explaining the intricacies of my oh-so-complicated visa situation to the immigration authorities at the *préfecture de police.* Each one of these daily scenarios was important in its own way, but not drastically so. If I got something wrong, misunderstood a verb, or left the conversation with no idea what had just been said, it wasn't going to be life threatening. But when it came to my health, I discovered pretty quickly, conversations were best managed entirely in English.

During my first year in Paris it took two visits to a French doctor before I resolved to find an English-speaking one. My first foray into the mystical world of French medicine saw me sitting in a doctor's office in a state of high confusion while a meek excuse for a medical practitioner timidly examined my elbow despite the fact that I thought I had carefully explained to her that I had a sore throat. My second visit to a French doctor saw me walk away with a prescription as detailed and packed full of recommended drugs as the average French lunch is long. Perhaps because they are all in the employ of drug companies, or perhaps because they figure all medicines are practically free under the universal health care system, doctors in France will prescribe you at least twice as much medicine as you require. And suppositories are a particular favorite among the French, who don't really feel they have been properly treated unless they come away with an awkward gait and an uncomfortable feeling in the posterior.

Which brings us rather neatly to Dr. J (not his real name), or the Dick Doctor, as he became affectionately known. Dr. J was an English-speaking doctor in a nearby arrondissement. He ran a ridiculously successful practice not far from my apartment. Situated as he was on the outskirts of the Marais, Paris's heaving gay district, a great deal of the good doctor's practice was given over to treating the myriad venereal diseases that passed through his waiting room. Dr. J was also known for his brusque bedside manner, especially if you were female or heterosexual. But that was nothing compared to his apparent determination to diagnose every single ailment known to man as some variant of a sexually transmitted disease.

You could go in to see Dr. J with a slight cough and a runny nose, and immediately he would ask when you last had an AIDS test. Make the mistake of wandering into his surgery with what you were certain was a case of the flu, and he would find some way of ascribing your illness to a venereal disease. Syphilis and gonorrhea were perennial favorites, though crabs, genital warts, and AIDS also got a run for their money with Dr. J.

While seeing Dr. J meant I could conduct all health care matters in English, it also meant owning up to myriad sexual habits that I simply didn't enjoy.

"It's about my throat," I would say to him during a winter bout of tonsillitis. "It does this every year. My body gets run down, I push myself too hard, and my throat is always the first to go. It usually just needs a hit of antibiotics, and it's fine."

He would look at me as if I were delusional. As if he and I both knew that my throat wasn't really the problem and that my real affliction—the one I had come here for him to treat but had not had the gumption to talk about—was really much more sinister and embarrassing.

"Have you been practicing safe sex?" he would ask.

"Um, I guess so," I would reply, baffled.

"Because you know there is a lot of syphilis going around, and all it takes is one careless incident."

It was a world of medical euphemisms, a medical examination so loaded with high-camp innuendo, you sometimes felt you were an extra in a *Carry On* film and that a giggling Barbara Windsor would appear at any moment with her boobs spilling out of a nurse's uniform.

Experience soon taught me that if I wanted the antibiotics for my throat, it was usually better to just go along with the good doctor and confess to an array of questionable sexual proclivities and their subsequent side effects. That way I would leave his office in ten minutes, triumphantly clutching my prescription and only a pharmacy visit away from the antibiotics that I knew would soothe my raging throat. To this day I have more recorded venereal diseases on paper in that man's office than most people have had sexual encounters.

As luck would have it, the one time I needed Dr. J's obvious talent in the arena of venereal diseases would be the one time he wanted nothing to do with me. It happened, ironically enough, at the end of a sustained period of sexual drought.

I'D LIKE TO THINK it was by design that I hadn't had occasion to be naked with a woman for at least three months. I'd like to tell you it was the result of a conscious decision on my part to abstain from sex while I concentrated on more cerebral pursuits. However, it was more than likely just an unfortunate side effect of dumb luck and dumb pick-up lines. It was not, shall we say, for want of trying.

The itching started one night at home, as I was sitting watching the television. I moved to the bathroom to perform a close inspection, out of view from my neighbors, and was horrified to discover that my crotch had become the nesting ground of a vibrant little colony of crabs. Now, it may well defy all accepted scientific belief, but it is with hand-on-heart honesty that I maintain I was not delusional, and that I had not had any sexual contact for months. In the first place, not having sex is not the kind of thing one would willingly boast about. And in the second place, after a three-month humping hiatus, any sexual activity at all would have registered like a beacon in my mind. There was no getting around it. I had the world's first recorded case of immaculately conceived crabs.

Realizing the joy with which Dr. J would greet this news, I made an appointment and walked gingerly around the corner to see him. As per the rules laid out under Murphy's Law, it happened to be the week when Dr. J was doing his bit for the education and training of future venereal disease experts, playing host to a student doctor. And going on the meek reception he gave me as I entered Dr. J's office I concluded he was an undergraduate of that great incubator of international medical practitioners, The Utterly Timid With Absolutely No People Skills School of Medicine.

As I sat in the waiting room, crossing and uncrossing my legs, the young apprentice, awkward in his oversize white coat, kept popping his head out of the examination room to tell me Dr. J would be with me as soon as he had finished imposing an STD upon whichever unwitting soul had come before me. When I finally entered the room, Dr. J shook my hand and urged me to sit down.

"So, what seems to be the problem?" he asked, employing the phrase that doctors the world over must be taught in their first year of medicine. I explained my dilemma, describing the little mites that had taken up residence in my groin and offered to drop my pants to show him.

"No, no, no! That won't be necessary," he said, standing and reeling backward across the tiny room. "I'm sure if you think you have crabs, then you probably have crabs." It didn't strike me as the most professional assessment, but relieved of the need to drop my pants, I didn't argue. The student doctor looked on in fear, quivering quietly in the corner, hoping beyond hope that he wouldn't have to examine my crotch. Identifying *morpions,* as the French call them, apparently fell outside his training duties.

"But how did I get them? Where did they come from?" I asked with genuine bemusement. Setting aside the pen he had been using to write out a seven-page prescription, Dr. J looked at me with what can only be described as abject pity.

"Well, you usually contract them from physical contact with another person," he counseled me in a voice with a rising inflection, obviously reserved only for the most stupid of patients. "You probably picked it up in a back room somewhere. It happens all the time." A back room? Did he mean those fabled blacked-out areas at the back of gay bars where men engage in activity of a decidedly unhygienic nature? Surely not.

"But I haven't had sex for three months," I replied. "Nor am I gay, nor have I ever visited a back room. It doesn't make sense."

Another look of pity, this time mingled with a rising sense of disbelief. Then from under raised eyebrows: "Well, they didn't get there by themselves, now did they?"

But that was exactly the point. They bloody well *had* gotten there by themselves!

"But you don't seem to understand," I began. "I haven't had any sexual contact for three months. I am not delusional. And I have absolutely no reason to lie to you about this. Where did they come from?"

Again, the withering look from under raised eyebrows. "Maybe you just don't remember having sex with someone," he replied, deadpan. "It happens all the time."

I tried to imagine a life in which sexual encounters were so commonplace that you began to lose track of them. But my experience to date had been so contrary, it simply didn't compute. I thought about arguing the point, making a stand for the sake of my dignity and rebuffing his patronizing argument, but finally I decided it wasn't worth the effort.

Exiting the doctor's office, with my prescription rolled up into a scroll, I made my way to a nearby pharmacy, mistakenly believing the worst of this experience was over. But when I handed the prescription to the pharmacist's assistant, she glared at the doctor's unintelligible scribble before handing it back to me.

"Mais c'est quoi ça?" she asked, indicating her complete inability to decipher Dr. J's handwriting.

"C'est pour les morpions," I answered under my breath, looking nervously at the long line that was beginning to form behind me.

"Les quois? Je vous entends pas, monsieur," she said, indicating she hadn't heard my mumble. You could tell it was taking all the patience she had left after a day spent in small talk with lonely pensioners refilling their incontinence prescriptions.

"Les morpions," I repeated, this time more emphatically. *"Les crabs!"*

Suddenly her face lit with recognition. *"Ohhhh. Les morpions,"* she cried, with altogether more volume than I would have liked. *"Eh bien, Pierre!"* she hollered across the pharmacy floor to the pharmacist. *"Le monsieur là, il a des morpions. Qu'est-ce qu'il faut lui donner?"*

I turned a distinct shade of scarlet and concentrated hard on the floor. It wasn't enough that I had immaculately conceived crabs, or that I had falsely admitted to conceiving them in the engagement of wholly questionable sexual activity, I now had to have my unfortunate condition broadcast around my local pharmacy.

As I turned to leave, *morpion*-spray in hand, the line of people behind me recoiled imperceptibly, ensuring I had a clear passage back onto the street. And no, Dr. J, in the event you are reading this, there is no pun intended.

As I was relating the story one week later to members of the Posse over drinks at Au Petit Fer à Cheval, we were joined by Johann, a Swedish colleague of James's. Johann was tall, blond, and like many of his countryfolk, unusually handsome. He was also possessed of a wide-eyed naïveté and an endearing lack of awareness of how strikingly good-looking he was. He had recently moved to Paris from the backwaters of Sweden, taken up residence in the Marais, and through friends of friends he had been given the name and contact details of

Dr. J. He too had had occasion to visit the offices of the good doctor—who diagnosed myriad venereal diseases when all he was suffering from was a cold. Entering our conversation as I was midway through my tale, Johann interrupted.

"Are you talking about Dr. J?" he asked. "He's my doctor too. I went to see him the other week. He's really friendly, isn't he?"

"I guess so," I replied, not entirely sure what he meant.

"Well, in Sweden at least, a doctor would never kiss you on the lips every time you went into his office."

A sudden silence fell among the group. Glasses of wine stopped in midair on their way to meet lips. A couple of guffaws were stifled. Johann must have divined by the look of shock on my face that Dr. J's displays of affection were not a practice endorsed by the French Medical Association.

"You mean he doesn't kiss you when you show up for an appointment?" Johann asked. A shudder of horrible realization seemed to pass through him.

"Um. Not so much," I replied.

Johann sat back in his seat. A haunted look played on his face.

I reached into my pocket and pulled out a pen. On the back of a drinks coaster I scribbled the name of a female doctor I had found in the quartier and slid it across the table to him, giving his arm a supportive squeeze. We were both survivors of Dr. J, after all. Brothers in arms now, I knew his pain. We had to stick together.

Chapter 14

Smelling the Roses

IF THERE IS ONE AREA in which the French have it sorted, it is most definitely the work-life balance. While critics of the Gallic model point to a sluggish economy and hint at a nation of work-shy job-phobics, the French philosophy of working to live, as opposed to living to work, is entirely admirable.

Paris, by virtue of the beauty that lurks at every turn, is a city for gentle contemplation. The term *flâneur* exists only in French, describing a person who spends entire days wandering aimlessly with the express purpose of doing little more than taking in whatever he sees. A French man is never in danger of running too quickly past the roses to ever stop and smell them. A French man is forever lolling about in the rose bed, happily avoiding the rat race and concentrating on the serious business of simply being.

The entire social system in France has been constructed around the idea that leisure time and family time are as inalienable a right for every citizen as free speech and unlimited supplies of cheese. And while at first this proved a difficult adjustment for me to make—coming as I did from Sydney and London, where life seemed to be stuck in a permanent state of thrilling, but exhausting, fast-forward—I soon learned to slow down and savor the gentle pace of my new surroundings.

Nowhere is this determination to savor the good life more evident in France than when it comes to food. The French, as has been widely documented, are fervent foodies.

One of the great joys of living in France is that the table is sacred. Every meal is an event. Food and wine are carefully matched: a good Bordeaux with a fine cut of red meat, a crisp Pouilly-Fuissé with a cut of salmon, or a good Chinon with a *magret de canard*. One complements the other in a beautifully choreographed tastebud tango. There is no such thing as a TV dinner in France, and while McDonald's outlets are opening with greater frequency there than in any other European country, mealtimes are still considered sacrosanct enough to require chairs around a table, a good bottle of wine, and daily practice in the increasingly lost art of dinner conversation.

It's not by accident, either, that during lunchtime in workaday France, it's nigh on impossible to get something as simple as a sandwich. Workers in Paris, be they laborers on a construction site or high-flying CEOs, leave their workplaces at one p.m., take a seat in any of the countless thousands of cafés, brasseries, and restaurants in the city, and settle in for a good hour's worth of quality dining. Where previously I was used to grabbing a sandwich and spending the lunch hour at my desk, Paris forced me to sit at a table with other human beings and choose from a menu that offered such appetizing fare as *salade de chèvre,* wild rabbit with mushrooms, grilled snapper fillet, or steak frites. And all of it would be washed down with a carafe of the house red—usually something light like a Gamay or Brouilly because after all it was only lunchtime.

Such a daily ritual meant that the early afternoon period back at the office was generally a complete write-off. But I figured that the processes of digesting and sobering up were infinitely more productive ways of passing that postlunch, three p.m. office pall than surfing the Web, staring at the clock, or e-mailing friends.

The importance of food to the French national psyche cannot be overstated. It is a subject that they take very, very seriously. Early in my Paris experience I was watching an item during a news report on French television. The report profiled a new breed of "weekend getaway" skiers, French people fleeing city life to spend a weekend schussing in the Alps. The interview featured a thirty-something woman having something close to an orgasm over her lunch.

"So here I have *un bon comté* [a matured cheese from the Savoyard region] with a *petit mesclun de salade! Mon dieu, mais c'est bon!*" Only the French can whip themselves into a frenzy over a plate of cheese and lettuce.

The longer I spent in France, though, the more I learned to appreciate the role that food plays in daily life. Crucial to that education was the market that was held each week not far from the Love Pad, on Boulevard Richard Lenoir, near the Bastille. Over four blocks long, it snaked up the broad stretch of tree-lined pedestrian pavement that ran up the middle of the boulevard. Here grocers jostled with *fromagers*, who tangled with florists, who vied with butchers, who skirmished with fishmongers. There were olive sellers, organic bakers, *charcutiers*, and *pâtissiers*. All of them loudly declaring their wares, screaming to be heard over the hoarse cries of their neighbors. Old ladies pulled shopping caddies, small children sat on fathers' shoulders, and busy mothers pushed strollers through the melee.

Amid the noise and bustle was a finely choreographed dance of hands—chopping, wrapping, slicing, and gutting. Hands reaching out to accept a proffered strawberry or taste-test a dripping morsel of Saint Marcelin cheese.

The fresh produce looked plump and ripe, a vibrant splash of reds, oranges, yellows, and greens against the honeyed-stone walls and slate-gray roofs of the surrounding apartments. The smell of fish, the waft of cheese, and the sound of ruddy-faced vendors talking up *un bon melon* or *un kilo de figues* hung in the air. It was a teeming, vital affirmation of life—one of the weekly joys of my Parisian existence.

I would often linger at the seafood stalls, marveling at the variety of strange creatures dredged from the depths of a foreign ocean. Dorade, bar, raie, and rascasse—lifeless eyes stared out from a bed of crushed ice. I loved to watch the butchers and fishmongers prepare their produce for sale. The deft manner in which they could debone, scale, or gut their merchandise while keeping eye contact and maintaining an uninterrupted stream of conversation with their faithful client never ceased to amaze me. The way they skillfully lopped off heads, thrust their bloodstained fingers into bellies, and ripped out fish gut was an art form in itself—though perhaps not for the faint of heart or weak of stomach.

It was also decidedly not a spectacle for any committed vegetarian. But then, telling a French person you are a vegetarian is like telling them you have the plague. Having been raised on a steady diet of meat and three veggies, and having since faithfully continued my love affair with flesh, I was not in the least inclined toward vegetarianism. I personally have nothing against vegetarians. Some of my best friends are vegetarians. But France, as a nation, is not simply intolerant of anyone who chooses not to eat meat—it is outright contemptuous of them. Most restaurants refuse to even acknowledge the existence of vegetarians, pointedly omitting veggie options from their menus. And woe betide the meat-averse who asks a waiter to "hold the smoked duck's breast" in the chef's salad or leave the *jambon* off the top of the *croque-monsieur.*

"Non. C'est pas possible."

This, after all, is the land of the all-meat restaurant. A country where steak is only ever served while still bleeding, where most chefs are offended when asked to prepare a steak "medium" and would frankly rather commit hara-kiri than cook any cut of meat "well done." It is a country in which one of the favorite dishes, devoured with relish at breakfast, lunch, and dinner, is steak tartare: a mixture of raw ground beef, raw egg, and raw onion. No, vegetarianism is definitely not compatible with French cuisine, and therefore it was not a dietary option that I ever seriously considered. Until the weekend I took a trip to the rural French region of Périgord, in the country's southwest.

CITY SLICKER THAT I WAS, the closest I ever came to making the connection between the slab of cooked flesh on my plate and an actual animal was the occasional glimpse at the market or *boucherie* of a freshly skinned rabbit or recently plucked chicken. In neat rows they would sit, eyeballs disturbingly intact, a startled expression fixed to their bodies. But these cadavers were inanimate; hence my ability to dissociate the motionless, denuded carcasses from creatures that days before may have been hopping or scratching their quiet ways around a farmyard. Rather unfortunately, my weekend sojourn in Périgord served to make me see the connection between fluffy farmyard animal and sizzling roast dinner.

As well as being home to some excellent wines and a large number of English immigrants who had moved there to set up B&Bs in the Dordogne Valley (otherwise known to locals as "Little Britain") the Périgord region is renowned throughout France as the spiritual home of foie gras.

For the uninitiated, *foie gras* translates literally as "fat liver." As its name suggests, it is the fattened liver of a duck or goose and is created by force-feeding poultry and fattening them until their livers bloat. It goes without saying that a delicacy as odd as this is highly prized in French cuisine. It also goes without saying that the force-feeding methods of foie gras farmers regularly come under fire from animal rights campaigners—but they do little to dampen the French enthusiasm for the foodstuff. A slice of foie gras, a chilled glass of Sauternes, a freshly baked baguette, and an onion confiture is many French people's idea of heaven. Served in slices and spread across toast or fresh bread, foie gras has a buttery texture and is so rich, you can feel your arteries harden with every mouthful.

Deciding it would be an important part of our cultural education to see how this most French of French delicacies was prepared, I rounded up a couple of Posse members and trotted off to a Périgord poultry farm. The farm was set in a picturesque valley, all rolling green fields and centuries-old oak trees. The farmhouse was a rustic, tumble-down affair with a big, stone-floor kitchen and an open fireplace. We were led into the poultry enclosure by the farmer's wife, whose job it apparently was to show the tourists the softer face of goose-fattening and -slaughtering.

Contrary to popular myth, the geese's feet were not nailed to the ground to restrict movement and encourage fattening. Contrary to another popular myth, the geese were not crammed into tiny battery cages. They waddled (admittedly with considerable trouble) around a relatively clean, relatively spacious wooden pen inside an airy stable. Not being a goose whisperer, I was unable to tell whether or not the geese were happy to be where they were, much less aware of the fate that was to befall them in a couple of weeks' time. Nor was I able to divine whether or not they enjoyed having a two-foot pipe thrust down their throats three times a day while fat-baked corn was machine-gunned into their gullets. I suspect the answer was no, but who was I to argue with a thousand years of history?

As disturbing as it was to see a goose with a two-foot pipe stuck down its throat, more troubling was the fact that this entire morally dubious act was being executed by a woman who looked like your auntie. That rosy-cheeked, amiable middle-aged lady looked like she should have been making cupcakes and baking pies rather than stuffing geese to the point of explosion. Throughout the *gavage* (French for "stuffing"), the farmer's wife maintained eye contact with us and chatted happily about the weather. The fact that she was able to grab goose after goose by the neck, lock them into position between her knees, and shove a two-foot pipe down their throats without missing a beat of conversation was, I had to admit, impressive. Once sufficiently stuffed, a goose would be released, only to stumble away, distinctly off balance, its eyes in soft focus, punch-drunk from the machine-gun corn experience.

To then enter the farmhouse to try some homemade foie gras seemed somehow a betrayal of our new feathered acquaintances. Only Julien chowed down with any real gusto, showing his true French colors.

"*C'est bon, non?*" he said enthusiastically, as he wolfed down his foie gras. "And you cannot get fresher than this! Straight from the source!"

He motioned with his knife in the direction of the goose-packed stable from which we had just come. That he was as oblivious to our stares of mild horror as he was to the perversity of eating the cured liver of a goose whose offspring were doubtless among the condemned in the enclosure next door was testament to the sanctity of the relationship between a Frenchman and his food.

For make no mistake, food is sacrosanct in France. And the more steeped in tradition its preparation, the more potent a symbol it is of the country's proud gastronomic tradition—and therefore the more proudly it is consumed. To a French man, foie gras is much more than a process of inflating livers by force-feeding poultry. To reduce it to such a base level is to miss the point. Foie gras is a French national institution. It is a rustic, time-honored product of the countryside to which French people (even if they have seldom actually been out in it) feel intimately attached. It is a vital affirmation of their pure idiosyncrasies—to which, as the world becomes more globalized and homogenized, the Gauls appear to cling with added fervor. It is as much a part of the French gastronomic heritage as Camembert cheese, crème brûlée, and Champagne. And for the same reason vegetarianism had never really taken hold in France, foie gras, I concluded, will never be phased out of the popular French diet. Any animal that happens to be born on a French farm exists solely to feed the national appetite for handcrafted, artisan-oriented, quality foodstuffs.

While the rest of us nibbled politely on the proffered morsel of foie gras, desperately trying to shut out the muffled sound of forlorn honking filtering through the wall, Julien wolfed his down in minutes. We would all return to Paris, and within the month we would all happily devour a plate or three of foie gras. But on this afternoon, and out of deference to our feathered friends on death row next door, we felt just the slightest bit guilty.

Chapter 15

Tomatina

THERE COMES A TIME in every young man's life when he is brought face to face with mortality. For some, it can be the result of a near-death experience. For others, it can rear its ugly head when a loved one passes on. But for a narcissist such as myself, all it took was the prospect of an imminent thirtieth birthday.

Doubtless there are men in the world for whom the passage of something as insignificant as a thirtieth birthday would barely register. So busy are they with the daily struggle of keeping themselves, their wife, and their seven children fed, clothed, and sheltered, they cannot afford the luxury of spending whiskey-fueled, angst-ridden hours in smoky Parisian bars analyzing exactly what they have achieved in the time they have been on the planet. Sadly though, without seven children to otherwise occupy my waking hours, I had plenty of time to reflect on my achievements over three decades of existence. I've long been of the opinion that when it comes to birthdays, you really have something to worry about only if, while performing a birthday-inspired stock-taking of your life, you are unhappy with where you are at or what you have done to get there. Otherwise you must be in pretty good shape.

By that measure, I certainly had no complaints. Here I was living in Paris, having just spent eighteen of the best months of my life surrounded by amazing friends, blessed with a high-paying ultimately cushy if uninspiring job, good health, intact faculties, and occasional luck with the ladies. Yet there was no denying that with the slow crawl to forty under way, I had better start making more of a concerted effort to behave like a juvenile.

The Tomatina festival in eastern Spain struck me as the perfect place to start. Originally conceived by superstitious tomato farmers as a thanksgiving ritual, dedicated to the gods of ripe vegetables, the festival has become renowned around the world, largely thanks to the dramatic images of red-stained revelers it annually yields to the international news media. The festival is centered in the otherwise nondescript village of Buñol, a half-hour train trip from Valencia. Each year it requires the participation of all the tomato farmers in the region, plus several truckloads of tomatoes.

The concept behind the festival is simple. Local farmers get tanked on local moonshine, tons of tomatoes are dumped in the town square, and several hours of tomato-inspired chaos ensues. What started as a relatively small, decidedly local harvest festival has in recent years transformed into a no-holds-barred, internationally renowned tomato-chucking contest. It was, as far as I was concerned, the perfect location for juvenile behavior on the occasion of my thirtieth birthday.

Surprisingly enough, it didn't take too much to convince the Paris Posse of the merits of traveling all the way to Spain to stand in a town square, drink a large amount of alcohol, and throw tomatoes at one another. And so, after packing clothes we would be happy never to see again, we traveled en masse from Paris to Valencia.

We arrived in Buñol two hours before the festivities were scheduled to begin. We were a party of seven: myself, Fiona, Sylvie, James and his girlfriend Victoria, Charlotte, and the delightful Silvia Picotti, a recent Italian addition to the Posse ranks. Victoria, skilled at all things creative, had thoughtfully hand-painted team T-shirts especially for the occasion. Emblazoned across the chests of the female members of the party were the words "Bryce's Babes." For the blokes, "Bryce's Bruisers," and for me, a simple, no-nonsense "Bryce." The effort and inherent artistic talent involved in the creation of the T-shirts would doubtless be lost on the tomato-hurling masses, but we were uniformed to the hilt and ready to go into battle.

Employing the organizational foresight for which I had by now become famous among my friends, I had included in our Tomatina kits a pair of safety goggles for each member of the team. Granted, participating in a tomato-throwing festival wearing safety goggles—of the sort usually worn by white-coated chemists or band-sawing carpenters—was a little like running with the bulls in a sumo suit. It screamed "nerd," no question. But I was a cautious lad at heart and had been well raised by my mother to ensure that all risk-taking activity was mitigated by a hefty dose of good old common sense. "You'll have an eye out!" I could almost hear my mother saying, long before we even arrived in Spain. Better to look like festival geeks, I figured, than come away with tomato-impeded eyesight.

Once we arrived in Buñol, the drinking began in earnest. Chugging back extralarge cans of beer, we entered the narrow streets of the tiny village and were almost instantly in the center of the madness. Some twelve hundred people had crammed into the narrow main street, most of them young, shirtless Spanish males, whose average age was seventeen and who were, to a person, high on the combination of underage alcohol and adrenaline.

The street measured barely three yards in width and was hemmed on both sides by three-storied apartment buildings. Hanging from balconies above and taking great delight in the spectacle below, grannies in simple black frocks and with their gray hair tied in buns poured bucket after bucket of cold water over the crowds below, sending up screams from street level. Garden hoses connected to kitchen taps rained more water down on the masses, creating a progressively drunken, gloriously soaked impromptu wet T-shirt competition.

Just when it seemed the street could hold no more people, the rumble of approaching trucks heralded the arrival of the tomatoes.

Three trucks, piled high with tomatoes of every shape and hue, lumbered into the street, making painfully slow progress as the crowd gradually parted to let them pass. Not content to wait for the trucks to deliver their load, some enterprising young things clambered atop the vehicles and starting hurling armfuls of tomatoes into the crowd. The madness began.

By inching their way down the hundred-yard main street and depositing a two-yard-high pile of tomatoes at every ten-yard interval, the trucks soon managed to turn the street into a heaving, writhing, red-stained war zone. Intoxicated Spanish youths mercilessly pelted tomatoes of varying ripeness at the geeky band of safety-goggle-sporting, uniformed tourists. The girls took cover in the nook of a garage door, while we men, half-drunk, beers still in hand, valiantly attempted a counteroffensive. The safety goggles, much mocked by other festival-goers ten minutes previously, were now the only thing between us and premature blindness, as tomatoes—some of them green and decidedly hard—thwacked against our temples.

At our feet a tomato quagmire was developing at an alarming rate. Wading knee-deep in a fleshy soup, covered from head to toe with the red remains of a hundred well-aimed missiles, and making futile attempts to clear tomato seeds and flesh caked to our safety goggles, we entered the fray and started chucking. Great handfuls of semisquashed tomato were heaved from the ever-diminishing pile in the center of the street and squished unceremoniously into one another's scalps.

Realizing the futility of trying to keep even relatively above the fray, Charlotte, Sylvie, and I dove headlong into the soup. We discovered that by lying on our backs, with the filth of the main street cobbles rubbing coarsely on our arses, we could completely immerse ourselves in a bath of stinking tomato juice. A rough attempt at a breast stroke was interrupted by an all-in pile-on by my brothers and sisters in arms. While above us the air was thick with flying tomatoes, we wrestled in a sticky gumbo of tomato and street filth—laughing hysterically.

And then, just as quickly as it had started, it was over. With the supply of tomato missiles exhausted, the youths lost interest and the chucking ended, giving us a chance to assess the damage. The battle, from first dump to last chuck, had taken all of twenty minutes. How then was it that an entire village could be so utterly transformed in such a short time? In the aftermath red-stained survivors waded slowly through the soup, clinging to one another for support and nursing heads that had been pummeled by flying fruit. The walls of the buildings were splattered red with the detritus of a thousand exploded tomatoes. It looked, for all the world, like something out of a war movie—an apocalyptic scenario whose seriousness was only tempered by the stubborn presence of beer cans and continued fits of hysterical laughter.

The local council, obviously experienced in such events, moved quickly to start the cleanup. Before you could say, "I pity the fool who has to clean this up," an efficient convoy of purpose-built trucks was crawling up the main street, high-pressure-hosing everything in sight. Within half an hour the soup had been hosed away, the walls of the buildings were returned to their former pristine state, and the main street cobbles were once again baking in the midday sun. I took a mental note to ask a Spaniard the next time I needed help removing a tomato stain from clothing. The only evidence left in the street that a tomato-hurling festival had just taken place was us.

After the staining came the smell. If you think about, it should not have come as a huge surprise to us that the combination of harsh, midday summer sunshine in eastern Spain and tomato pulp would make for a stinking cocktail. But nothing could have prepared us for the full discomfort of feeling like human pizzas as we trudged out of the village.

As per Tomatina tradition, we were bound for a waterfall and swimming hole on the outskirts of Buñol. A thousand tomato-stained humans squelching along the country road from Buñol to the waterfall must have looked like a procession of bloodied refugees escaping a war zone. We looked like survivors of a bizarre vegetable holocaust, baking slowly in the midday heat and picking tomato seeds from our ears and hair as we walked. Once at the waterfall, we realized too late the pitfalls of arriving toward the end of the exodus. The surface of the water in the small lake at the base of the waterfall was thick with a churning layer of tomato seeds and had taken on a soft pink hue. Desperate to wash at least some of the caked mess from our matted hair, we nonetheless dived in and started scrubbing.

On the train back to Valencia some two hours later, we sat, exhausted, in a carriage filled with fellow revelers. No amount of waterfall bathing had been enough to fully remove either the stain or the stench. It was only after the train had rolled into Valencia station and we had stepped out onto the platform that we realized the pungent odor that comes from mixing sweaty humans with the juices of countless tomatoes.

From Valencia we headed straight onto a ferry for two nights of excess in Ibiza. I spent the actual night of my thirtieth birthday on a podium in the vast, heaving cavern of Pacha nightclub, surrounded by eight hundred of my close personal friends. Well, at least they seemed like close personal friends at the time—but maybe that was just the drugs.

Back in Paris a week later, I was still picking tomato seeds from body creases I never knew I had. If I was going to undertake the crawl to forty, I could now do so secure in the knowledge that I had given immaturity one last, tomato-soaked fling.

Chapter 16

Lesson in French Love 2:
Le Bonheur

WHEN IT COMES TO LOVE, there is no gray area in France. If French love were a set of traffic lights, it would have no yellow. Green or red—it's either all or nothing.

I had been observing the French in their natural habitat for almost two years now and had come to the conclusion that as a people, they are genetically conditioned to always be somewhere in the vicinity of love. Love, or the cruel deprivation of it, is like oxygen to the average French person—and life is simply a series of stages of either falling into it, being up to your eyeballs in it, or falling out of it. Give a French person half a chance, and they'll act as if they invented love. As if, for some cosmic reason, they were the only race capable of truly understanding and experiencing it.

The French belief that they have a heavenly ordained monopoly on love is best illustrated by their collective pursuit of the heightened state of emotion known as *bonheur*. *Bonheur* is a state of being that you can apparently experience only if you are French. Translated literally, it means, quite simply, "happiness." A common enough condition, you might think, but for a French man the symptoms range from impaired reason and a sudden complete neglect of your male friends to an impulsive desire to spend ridiculous amounts of money on a range of state-approved love accoutrements (like an expensive dinner, a gaudy piece of jewelry, or a vacation for two in Corsica).

When a French man is experiencing *bonheur*, it's best to quickly acknowledge the inferiority of emotional range inflicted upon you by virtue of your birthplace (namely, any country outside France) and sit back and take notes. He'll tell you he is in love and that, despite the fact this is his third time in as many months, it has never been like this before. He'll confidently maintain that this is it, the real thing—and that you, as a foreigner, couldn't possibly understand. Then, like a new member of a secret club, he will suddenly find himself invited to a slew of dinner parties—strictly couples-only affairs—where he will bask in the unique, smug comfort that comes from being a member of a self-selecting community. He will happily, willingly throw himself headlong into the labyrinthine, hazardous obstacle course that is the French woman's psyche and prepare to thrash about in an orgy of emotional self-flagellation. It is his birthright, after all.

There will be an initial bout of passionate, spontaneous sex. He and his paramour will devour each other in a carnal cornucopia of bedroom antics, pausing only for the occasional cigarette or to pop outside to a crowded café to indulge in a half hour of heavy petting—because God knows, it's not worth petting heavily if it doesn't offend the sensibilities of at least ten people sitting in close proximity.

All of this behavior will only be compounded by the French man's unshakable belief in the persistent myth that he and his countrymen are the world's greatest lovers, a misguided belief only encouraged by Paris's worldwide reputation as a city for lovers. And once the French man and his lover have executed their public displays of affection, they will concentrate on the serious business of making public displays of aggression and melodrama. For a Parisian couple will not have an argument, will not fall into a passionate embrace—will not, in effect, indulge in any display of serious emotion—unless they have an audience. It is almost as if the audience legitimizes the sentiment. Why snog in the privacy of your own squalid studio apartment when you could do it on a heavily touristed bridge over the Seine? Why argue vociferously in the privacy of your own home when a packed café or restaurant would ensure a heightening of the melodrama?

As a stitched-up Anglo-Saxon in a land full of Latins, I soon stopped being charmed by public displays of affection and started to be repulsed by them. Whatever the reason—whether I was reacting against the contrived emotion behind them or felt I wasn't getting my fair share of the loving that appeared to be on every corner—I wandered the streets of Paris willing the snoggers to take a cold shower and the heavy petters to get a room.

It was left to Julien, as my token French friend, to educate me on the complex relationship that your average French man has with love. Julien has almost been married on more than one occasion. In one instance he came perilously close to the altar. I know because I was supposed to be his best man.

It all began while our hero was on the rebound from a bruising romantic encounter with a feisty Italian *principessa*. His love interest this time round was Claire, the new girl in his law office. She was a young lawyer with a bourgeois Paris pedigree. He was the dashing young Parisian *avocat*, passionate, committed, and bearing more than a passing likeness to Olivier Martinez (albeit a distinctly smaller version). They started seeing each other outside the office, careful to hide their budding romance from colleagues. True to French form, it took barely a month before Jules had fallen hard. Within two months he had packed up his belongings from the apartment he shared with Will and moved in with Claire.

One blustery February afternoon, four months after the pair had started dating and hence disappeared from our lives into the vortex of dinner parties that is the fate of coupled-up Frenchies, Jules invited me for lunch. Given that we often met for lunch, I figured it was just one of our semiregular bloke's lunch dates, a chance to catch up, check in, and swap notes. But he had an entirely different motivation for the encounter.

"Mate," he said in heavily accented English, employing one of the few Aussie words I had managed to slip into his vocabulary, "there's something I have to tell you." The waiter arrived and delivered our lunch. "I have asked Claire to marry me, and I want to ask you to be my best man."

It was all I could do not to choke on my steak frites. "Oh," I exclaimed, scrambling for the right words, desperate to hide my complete and total shock. "Wow. Gosh. Yeah. I mean. Of course! Of course I will be your best man. It would be an honor."

We sat there in the café nodding and grinning stupidly at each other. He was genuinely excited about the decision he had impetuously made. I was uncharacteristically lost for words.

Why? It wasn't the fact that the courtship had been so short. It was more a conviction, shared by most of our circle of friends, that on a very basic level the couple were not well suited. Julien was never himself when he was around his bride-to-be; he seemed to spend the whole time they were together tending to her, fetching her things, worrying about whether she was too hot or too cold—and always tiptoeing around her on eggshells. There's thoughtful attention, and then there's mollycoddling. This, we all agreed, was definitely doing the latter.

And so he and I sat opposite each other, eating in silence. Every now and then I would utter a "Wow, marriage, eh?" or "I must say, I didn't see that coming." Then finally I could stand it no longer.

"Look, I'm going to say this once, and then I will never say it again. You have to promise me you won't be offended. I am only saying this because we are good friends, and good friends should be able to say these sorts of things without offending each other."

He put down his knife and fork and looked at me with concern.

"Well. It's just that—are you sure you know what you're doing? I mean, are you sure you've made the right decision? The thing is, it's just that, it's all been rather quick. Why the rush? Why not give it a few more months and then get engaged?"

He stared at me in disbelief.

I looked at my plate. I had said what I felt needed to be said, and now I couldn't make eye contact with him.

His expression turned from concern to abject pity.

"Mate," he said in his best benevolent tone. "One day you too will

fall in love. And then you will know that I am making the right decision."

It was official. The man was a lost cause. The wedding was on, and
as best man, my role from here on in was to be chief cheerleader.

"Right," I replied, trying to hide my sense of rising indignation.
"Of course. When I fall in love, I guess I'll understand."

And so the wedding preparations took place. A ring was purchased, a dress was selected, a venue for the reception was booked, and
cases of Champagne were ordered. I had all but picked out my suit and
prepared my best man speech in French—before, three months shy of
the big event, he pulled the plug. With the benefit of hindsight, I suppose I should have seen it coming. After all, during a bachelor party
weekend in Barcelona I was privy to an early-morning conversation
with Julien that ought to have set off alarm bells.

The male members of the Posse had trooped en masse to the
northern Spanish city for Julien's bachelor party.

Following an evening of sustained substance abuse, Julien and I
found ourselves unable to sleep and so left our hotel in search of breakfast. After a good hour at a café, most of which was spent in silence,
sipping a single orange juice and staring dully into the middle distance, we decided to take a walk. Experiencing a moment of clarity of
the kind normally reserved only for recreational drug-takers and the
truly psychic, we spotted a double-decker, open-topped tourist bus
making the day's first tour of the city and decided to hop aboard.

It was nearly empty. We had seats to stretch out on, fresh air to
breathe, and there would be a passing parade of Gaudi-inspired archi-
tecture to aid our passage back to the realm of the clearheaded. Or so
our reasoning went. Of course, five minutes into our tour—when the
pair of us were stretched out across a bench seat on the top deck at the
back of the bus, staring blankly up at the cloud-spattered sky—every
early-rising tourist and his annoying band of children clambered
aboard, ruining our idyll. Forced to sit up (a challenge in and of itself),
we spent the remainder of the two-hour journey hanging listlessly over
the edge of the bus as the wonder of Sagrada Familia cathedral was explained to us in no fewer than five languages.

As we rounded up the tour with a wholly unnecessary turn

through Barcelona's more unsightly light-industrial areas, Julien suddenly sat upright.

"Mate," he said, opening our first verbal exchange in two hours. "What do you think about monogamy?"

Tearing my eyes away from the riveting spectacle of a passing tire factory, I looked at him with disbelief. Surely, knowing my current state, he couldn't expect me to hold forth on the relative merits or otherwise of having sex with the same woman for the rest of one's life. If he was seeking reassurance for the decision he had made to chuck in his freewheeling single days and get hitched, his timing couldn't have been worse. On any normal day I am the fount of all emotional knowledge. But today I was no good to either man or beast. I knew what I was supposed to say. I knew that this sudden outburst was indicative of a deeper malaise in my little French buddy's soul—that it was, in effect, a cry for help. I mustered all the sensitivity I could find, straightened myself in my seat, and looked him square in the eye.

"Jules, it will all be okay," I said. "You have made one of the biggest decisions of your life. It's perfectly normal for you to be questioning it. If you truly believe you have made the right decision, then I am sure everything will be fine."

Three weeks later the wedding was off.

Apparently it had all come to a head one night when he was at home with his fiancée. She had drifted off to sleep in front of the television. It was nine o'clock on a Friday night, and outside the window of their stylishly bourgeois apartment, the sleepy streets of the interminably dull sixteenth arrondissement were deserted. Julien stood at the window, poured himself a whiskey, and stared out across the lights of Paris, imagining where his single mates might be—which bar they were in, what mischief they might be getting up to.

He looked back at the couch, saw his future, and decided, quite simply, that he didn't want it after all. Even in the City of Light, the path to *bonheur* is not a straightforward one.

Chapter 17

Desperately Seeking Plumbing

PARISIAN PLUMBERS, like the majority of people in France's so-called service industry, are a recalcitrant mob. They will work only the hours they want to work, keep a careful cap on the number of certified professionals they will allow into the industry, and remain supremely indifferent to the greater populace's need for such basic sanitation requirements as a properly flushing toilet.

In my first two years in Paris, ranks of Polish plumbers had piled across the French border desperate to find work and keen to get their hands on Paris's sewer system. But the French plumbers' union and the French government seemed to expend an inordinate amount of effort on keeping them at bay—a cruel irony, it seemed to me. Their argument, as best as I could understand it, was that Polish plumbers had no right to practice their trade in France because they did not overcharge, were prepared to work at all hours of the day or night, and hence were about to ruin what was an otherwise finely tuned industry. It was an argument that found little favor with me at the best of times, and one that I came to disagree with violently when the pipes in the bathroom of my seventeenth-century apartment decided to pack it in.

My close encounter with the Parisian plumbing fraternity came one mid-September morning. I was rudely awakened by a loud knocking on my door. My neighbor from downstairs—a woman who, despite having lived downstairs for over two years, had never seen fit to share more than three words of conversation with me—now stood on my doorstep speaking rapid-fire French and gesticulating wildly. Still dazed from my exertions on a Petit Fer à Cheval barstool the night before, I stood in my boxer shorts, scratching my stomach and yawning, trying to take it all in.

Previous experience with random French people banging down my door to scream at me in rapid-fire French had taught me simply to thank them very much for dropping by, close the door, and crawl back into bed. However, Madame Downstairs was not to be so easily deflected. A strange brown stain was forming on her living room wall, she said, and she wanted something done about it. Fast. It only took a relatively brief, and wholly reluctant, walk downstairs to her apartment to see that something of mine—most probably my toilet, given the color of the stain—was leaking into her living room.

Time to call the plumber, I thought to myself.

MY LAST ENCOUNTER with the French plumbing profession had been almost a year before—and the scars had only just healed. On that occasion my water heater had given out completely. It was midwinter, and as a reasonable, albeit relatively naïve, human being, I expected the problem would be fixed posthaste. I called the plumber. After a one-sided conversation in which he explained to me how busy he was, how people couldn't just expect him to drop everything and come running every time they had a plumbing problem (I thought it best not to point out that in fact, technically, that was his job), we managed to find a time and date in his work calendar that apparently did not interfere with his busy social life. The rendezvous was set for ten days hence.

I was gobsmacked. How could anyone be expected to live in an apartment, in the middle of a Parisian winter, with neither heat nor hot water? It was beyond me. Surely the UN Commissioner on Human Rights had been called to intervene in lesser crimes. But neither the plumber nor my landlady could comprehend the urgency of my situation. Apparently it was perfectly acceptable for a tenant to go for two weeks without heat or hot water. And no, ôf course there was no question of a reduction in rent. The hot-water heater had broken down because of misuse. It had nothing whatsoever to do with the fact that it hadn't been replaced or serviced since Napoleon got his comeuppance at Waterloo.

During the ten days of personal hygiene purgatory that ensued, I joined the relatively large community of fellow showerless souls at the local gym. We would gather there immediately after work, make no pretense of the fact we were in the gym only to avail ourselves of the showering facilities, and give each other a nod of solidarity as we went about our ablutions. Brothers in filth.

When finally the happy day arrived for Monsieur le Plombier to come and assess the parlous state of my water heater, he arrived at my door without so much as a wrench in hand. Standing before my dormant water heater, he folded his arms and nodded sagely, before telling me it was broken.

"So can you fix it?" I asked, in what I assumed was a redundant question.

It was all he could do not to laugh. He gravely informed me that to fix the water heater he would require his tools, which he patently did not have upon him. I was too confused to be able to openly wonder exactly what was the point of a plumber coming to visit a client without his tools. What did he think he was coming to do? Shoot the breeze? Have a quick cup of coffee before moving on and imposing his impotence on the next unsuspecting victim? As it was, ten days of risking athlete's foot in the gym showers had drained me of energy. I was dirty and broken. He had me exactly where he wanted me.

When finally he did return, one whole week later, it was with his tools and a hefty invoice for services barely rendered.

AND SO HERE I WAS AGAIN. Almost one year since my last encounter with the French plumbing industry, I was about to throw myself at its mercy once more. Given the speed with which the rest of the country embraced progress and change, I was fairly confident that this impending brush with French plumbers was once again going to leave me in the shit. The fact that we were on the cusp of one of France's infamous stretches of public and religious holiday marathons would serve only to alter the depth.

True to form, all three of the so-called "emergency" plumbers I called professed an inability to attend, each of them citing a too-heavy workload. While I was on the phone to one of them, listening to him tell me how he was up to his elbows in attending an emergency call outside Paris, I couldn't help but hear in the background the final boarding call for the Air France flight to Nice. The slimy bastard was scarpering to the seaside like the rest of Paris, leaving me *sans toilette* for at least six days.

There was nothing for it but to draw up a strategic pooing plan. Number twos would be restricted to lunchtime and late evenings, when I was most likely to find myself at work or at a café or bar. Number ones would have to be spread carefully around the neighborhood, at any one of the several cafés in my immediate vicinity. I had it down to a tee. By rotating the cafés I frequented over the six-day period, and by carefully selecting only those whose facilities were at the back of the establishment and hence far removed from the prying eyes of suspicious service staff, I managed to evade detection. Not so among my friends, however, to whom I soon became known as the "phantom pooer." My plight became so well known in my close circle that inquiries would be made at dinner parties as to when I had last had a movement. Perhaps not surprisingly, invitations to dinner dried up noticeably around this period.

Just as I was starting to run out of accommodating café owners, the plumbers of Paris returned en masse from their mid-June sabbatical. Relaxed and tanned from their sojourns on Côte d'Azur beaches, they suddenly found time in their busy schedules to attend to my broken pipes. By the time a hulking mass of conspicuously tanned plumbing expertise finally deigned to pay a visit to my apartment, I had been *sans toilette* for a grand total of fifteen days. I had spent more than two exhausting weeks strategically planning every call of nature.

It took him all of seven minutes to arrive at my apartment, saunter into my bathroom, and change a washer on the cistern. That he charged me a hundred euros for the privilege and then sauntered back out was almost more than I could bear. As he closed the door behind him, I stood dumbstruck in my living room, unsure whether to feel shame at having not had the wherewithal to change a washer (what would my DIY-obssessed father say?) or anger at having had to wait two weeks for it to be done. Finally I figured there was nothing to do but laugh. If nothing else, the experience had allowed me to get to know the proprietors of every café within a fifty-yard radius of my apartment.

Besides, it was not as if I had come to expect anything else from that great oxymoron, the French service industry. In a country where shop assistants could rarely be bothered to look up from whatever magazine they were reading, much less serve you, a two-week wait for a flushing toilet was probably not unreasonable. In a nation where subscribers to an Internet service provider were regularly overcharged, arbitrarily denied access to the Internet, and then expected to pay an exorbitant per-minute rate when they phoned to complain, it was probably to be expected. And in a city where you were expected to pay a princely sum for a stuffy waiter at an overpriced café to treat you like dirt, it wasn't the least bit surprising.

I was fast learning that when it came to customer service in France, I could either accept that the customer was never right, or I could go slowly, painfully mad. Launching a one-man campaign to try to re-educate an entire country was fruitless and foolhardy.

"Do you understand what is meant by the expression *customer service*?" I would scream down various phone lines. "I am the client, you are the service provider. You are supposed to be providing a service to me." This regular rant was almost always met with indifferent silence on the other end of the premium-rate line. They were, after all, paid handsomely to be infuriatingly unhelpful. The longer you stayed on the line fuming, the more money they made. You could almost hear them filing their nails out of abject boredom on the other end of the line.

Quiet acceptance of the utter inefficiency and infuriating illogicality of it all was the only way forward. France had been here longer than I had, and it wasn't about to change its habits—no matter how unhygienic—just because I didn't like them.

Chapter 18

Come On Down!

I HAVE LONG BEEN of the opinion that you cannot truly claim to know a country until you have been on at least one of its game shows. Anyone can move to another country, learn the language, take a lover, and eat the local cuisine, but can they really claim to know what makes that country tick? Can they really say they have an unrivaled insight into the machinations of its people? Only a locally produced game show can proffer that kind of insight.

So when the producers of a well-known French game show, *Attention à la marche,* invited me to appear as a special guest, I accepted with barely a second's hesitation. It was late autumn in the second year of my Paris stint. Life in my adopted city had become happily comfortable. The nocturnal antics of the Posse continued to amuse me, the occasional weekend trips to other European capitals never ceased to entertain me, and life in my orange-walled abode had never been better. And yet it had been a good long while since I had done something utterly random simply because it could be done. Appearing on a French TV game show seemed as random an activity as any other to break that dry spell.

The show's producers were recording a special Christmas edition. They wanted a selection of Paris-based foreigners to appear as contestants and relate, during the course of the show, how Christmas was celebrated in their respective countries. The fact that I had never seen or heard of the show and therefore had no idea what it entailed was of little consequence to me. The fact that it would require French language skills far more advanced than any I happened to possess was also not a consideration. As far as I was concerned, this rare opportunity to appear on prime-time French TV satisfied two very important criteria in my life. First and foremost it was an opportunity to be in the spotlight. Secondly, it would make for a fantastic story to tell at my next dinner party.

The producers of *Attention à la marche* had gotten my contact information from an English production company that had similarly solicited my services some months earlier for a pilot game show they were shooting in Paris, in English, for the BBC. On that occasion I had left the TV recording studios under something of a cloud for having ruined the pilot.

That game, called *Try Your Luck* or something equally inane, required contestants to hit a buzzer if they knew the answer to a quiz question. If they were right, they got to choose and take possession of one of eight oversize playing cards that were displayed, face down, on a stand on the opposite side of the studio. The two contestants with the two highest playing cards at the end of round one would advance to round two.

As it happened, I knew all the answers and wasn't afraid to show it. It also happened that thanks to a poorly positioned studio light, I could see the underside of all the playing cards reflected in the Plexiglas stand on which they were positioned. Neither of which—namely my propensity to retain lots of useless information nor the failure by a lighting engineer to do his job properly—was technically my fault. By the end of round one I had answered all the questions correctly and was in possession of all the playing cards, meaning I was the only one eligible to proceed to round two, meaning the game had to stop and the recording had to be interrupted.

Despite having told us at the outset to test the limits of the game, to see if there were any flaws in its logic, a rather stern Dutch producer from the Endemol production company now stormed onto the set to take me to one side. Apparently nonplussed that her show had been proven flawed, stressed by how much more overtime she was now going to have to pay the camera operators due to this unscheduled break in the proceedings, and perhaps a little embarrassed that it was all taking place in front of a full studio audience, she lowered her voice into a mean little whisper and dressed me down.

"Now Bryce," she said, "we all think it's very impressive that you know the answers to all of these questions, and you are obviously a very intelligent young man. But the game isn't going to work if you answer all the questions and take all the cards. Do you think maybe you can hold back and let someone else answer a couple of the questions?"

It had struck me at the time as being distinctly unfair. Here I was being punished because some moron employed to conceive game-show formats had failed to account for a Smartass-in-the-Studio scenario. But I pulled my head in as requested, let others answer questions, and consequently did not win the game. As I left the TV studio two hours later, not even my thirty-eight-euro participation fee, plus lunch expenses, was enough to soften the distinct sensation of having been cheated.

BUT THAT UNFORTUNATE game-show experience was in the past and here I was, on this bitterly cold and wet November morning, making my way through Paris's drab northern suburbs on the train for my second close encounter of the game-show kind. The TV studios were located on the outskirts of the city. Arriving wet, cold, and just the slightest bit anxious about my upcoming French TV debut, I announced myself to a security guard manning the entrance gate, struggling to be heard over the noise of six lanes of traffic speeding along the highway beside me. He checked me off on a list on his clipboard and waved me through. As I picked my way around puddles toward Soundstage 21, a colony of butterflies materialized in my stomach. For unlike the ill-fated *Try Your Luck,* this game show was not a pilot.

Attention à la marche was a bona-fide, ratings-winning, prime-time French game show. It was being recorded. It would go on the air. Its host, a man I had never heard of, was apparently a household name in France, and its Christmas special was one of the season's TV highlights.

I found the soundstage where my game show was being taped, and another security guard promptly sent me to wait in the studio cafeteria. Suddenly I was surrounded by Frenchies of a type I had only ever read about before. Bussed in from the nearby French countryside for the express purpose of being a studio audience, they all hailed from what snobbish Parisians call *la France profonde*—provincial France. The young men wore tracksuit pants, baseball caps, and too much hair gel. The young women were pierced to within an inch of their lives and wore puffer jackets, a sullen look, and too much eyeliner. The older folks looked as if they had stepped straight from a French-countryside tourist brochure, all cloth caps, plaid skirts, ruddy complexions, and sensible shoewear. It was a Tuesday morning, a midweek workday. Yet here was a cafeteria filled with able-bodied men, women, and children preparing to sit on bleachers in a TV studio for the next six hours and cheer nonsensically at complete strangers. No wonder the country was in a mess.

My fellow contestants were an older English gent who was married to a French woman and had spent twenty years living in Paris; a young Spanish woman whose mother was French; and a beefy professional bouncer from Montreal—where they speak French. Only as we took our places on stage for the taping to commence did I realize what a monumentally stupid idea it was to think that I could pull this off. My French was okay. I could hold my own at a dinner party, conduct myself in most social situations, and had even started to master the art of cutting putdowns when affronted by surly waiters or difficult shop assistants. But standing in a TV studio with lights and cameras trained on me, performing in a game-show format I had never seen before, and answering questions whose meaning I could only hope to guess at—it was sheer madness. While standing off-set having makeup applied, I barely understood a word the makeup artist said to me. How was I going to cope with forty-five minutes of rapid-fire, slang-infused, game-show French? I was doomed.

Suddenly the studio lights began swirling frenetically to mark the arrival of the game-show host. I stood in the dark, frozen to my spot backstage. My heart was pounding. Was it too late for me to sidle quietly off stage, hotfoot it back to the train station, and disappear into the anonymity of the Paris streets? Yes, it was too late. Through the wild applause of the rent-a-crowd, I discerned what sounded like shouts of *"Australie," "kangarou,"* and *"je vous présente Bryce!"* And then a gentle but firm push in the back from a clipboard-bearing producer sent me forward and into position behind a set of sliding doors. They pulled back to reveal a set of garish colors, a wildly applauding audience, and a game-show host with a maniacal grin pasted to his face. The lights were blinding as I picked my way gingerly down a set of illuminated, flashing stairs. On either side of me the set was piled high with Christmas paraphernalia. Enormous boxes wrapped in gold, red, and green reflective paper. Christmas trees ablaze with flashing lights, Santa sleighs and bags of toys and oversize candy canes. And all of it covered in a thick layer of fake snow. Glancing furtively to my left and right, I realized there was no escape. The show had begun, the cameras were rolling, and forty-five minutes of uninterrupted humiliation now lay between me and salvation.

People watching at home later told me I looked like a deer in the headlights. All I recall is a sensation of pure terror, the terror of the soon-to-be-monumentally-mortified. I took my place at the contestant console and pasted a pained smile to my face. *Dear God, please let this be over soon.* With all the contestants in place, it came time for the host to introduce us all.

"Bryce!" he intoned in that excitable game-show-host way. Tall, gangly, and forty-something, apparently incapable of expressing a sentiment that wasn't overblown, he had all the hyperactivity typical of his profession. Now he was looking at me and asking me a question. I could see his lips moving, I could hear a series of words, and I could tell that put together they formed an inquiry. But under the glaring studio lights and over the din of the studio audience, I couldn't make out a word of it.

I smiled, laughed nervously, nodded, and even uttered a noncommittal *"Ah, oui!"* then realized it wasn't sufficient and so added: *"Oui, oui, c'est vrai, en Australie il fait toujours beau."* The spontaneous peals of laughter from the studio audience suggested my answer had nothing to do with the host's question. The die had been cast, my role had been assigned—for the next forty-five minutes, I was to be the funny foreign game-show buffoon.

As the game (if indeed you could call it that) got under way, the questions ranged from the frankly bizarre to the truly ridiculous: "What percentage of French people can pick up their bath towel with their toes?" and "Imitate the noise people make at the point of love-making ecstasy." As if it weren't bad enough that I was being made a complete fool of on national television, I had to do it by faking an orgasm. To say I was embarrassed would be an understatement. Two rounds, six questions, and twenty-five minutes of complete incomprehension later, I was unceremoniously knocked out of competition and, much to my relief, sent packing.

The only consolation, I reasoned as I scurried back into Paris, was that no one would ever see it. But that's the thing about crap television. People watch it more often than they admit. For weeks after the program aired friends and friends of friends and former colleagues and bartenders at the Petit Fer à Cheval would ask if I was *le kangarou fou* they had seen on TV. At a rock concert some months later I was minding my own business postgig, preparing to disappear into the night, when I was approached by a complete stranger.

"Excuse me," she said in an unmistakable Australian accent. "Um, this might seem kind of odd, but is your name Bryce?"

I nodded.

"Oh wow. I've been standing over there wondering if it was you," she said. "My husband is French and saw you on that game show. He taped it for me. I watch it all the time, whenever I'm homesick—or whenever I need a laugh."

Excellent. My status as an object of derision had gone cross-cultural.

Chapter 19

Get 27

I T IS A FACT universally acknowledged that a young man in a foreign city, with a healthy ego and too much time on his hands, will eventually find himself fronting a rock band. Whether we sing in the shower, air-guitar around the living room, or use a hairbrush as a microphone in front of the mirror, there's a rock star lying dormant in all of us. All it takes to wake the sleeping beast is an unusual amount of self-possession and a whole lot of chutzpah: two qualities that James and I had in spades.

It was a Thursday evening in February, just after my third anniversary in Paris. James and I were propping up the bar at the Connétable, sipping whiskeys while the greater population of Freaksville, Paris, stumbled around us. Marie was tending bar in her inimitable Gallic fashion—cigarette in hand, look of abject boredom on her face, pointedly ignoring customer requests for a beverage. As the night wore on and the whiskeys took hold, the banter turned to bravado, and we revisited a favorite, recurring drunken conversational theme: the formation of a band.

Possessed as we were of an unshakable belief in our own musical talent, we reasoned that it was not only possible to create a band for the public performance of what my mother calls "young people's music" but more crucially, it was our sworn duty to do so. We owed it to Paris to foist our complete lack of musical ability upon the city. We owed it to France to liberate the country from the grasp of the awful music it seemed determined to consume. And by god, one day, we were going to make it happen.

In her most expressive gesture for probably the entire week, Marie rolled her eyes. She had heard it all before. How many more bottles of whiskey would be consumed, she wondered, before these big-talking foreigners put their questionable musical talent where their mouths were and actually formed a band? Bored by the drunken gibberish, she took the Connétable booking schedule from a shelf behind the bar, opened it to April 18, and scrawled at the bottom of the page, *"Bryce et James—concert."*

The gauntlet had been thrown down. The die had been cast. And even through the Johnnie Walker haze, we both knew that once the Connétable publicity and promotions juggernaut had been set in motion (a poster on the door and a few flyers on the bar), we would be powerless to stop it. Le Connétable, by virtue of its popularity among long-haired musical types, had already played host to some of our earliest drunken performances. Invariably comprising a tunelessly rendered version of Robbie Williams's "Angels"—James on acoustic guitar, me on the stairwell with vocals—our performances had never failed to inspire total silence among our audience. We took this to be quiet contemplation of the raw power of our musical talent. Now it was time to take our act to the next level.

Finding other members for the band proved relatively easy. Prerequisites for band membership included: vague musical ability, an oversize ego, and an unquestioning belief in one's own attractiveness to the opposite sex. Claudio immediately sprang to mind.

Hailing as he did from Conegliano, in the northern Italian hills above Venice, Claudio, like many of his countrymen, dedicated a large amount of his time and energy to the dual activities of pursuing women and preening. Employing a Latin charm that we Anglos could only look on with envy and awe, he could woo a woman at twenty paces. And in the odd instance where his Italian charm failed, his flawless sense of humor and his propensity to perform usually picked up the slack. Claudio was such a comic, such a natural ham, and so effortlessly charismatic, he had earned the nickname Coco—as in "clown." If for no other reason than to entertain us during rehearsals, he would be a perfect addition to the band.

Since I had already selflessly claimed the lead singer role (an uncharacteristic gesture of narcissism on my part) and James had declared an interest in the lead guitarist role, Claudio's rudimentary ability to pluck a guitar string made him an excellent choice for rhythm guitarist. It took little in the way of persuasion to convince Claudio to join the band. The prospect of what he confidently predicted would be screaming hordes of panting groupies appeared to sway his decision.

The recruitment of a bass guitarist and drummer was less straightforward. Stefan was a highly accomplished computer geek from Indiana whom I had recently hired as the "webmaster" at ICC. Renowned for his higher-than-average intelligence and a firm conviction that just about everything in life was part of a CIA conspiracy, Stefan was also a dab hand on the bass guitar. If we could distract him long enough from his Noam Chomsky and Michael Moore dogma, I figured, he might just be able to provide the all-important bass lines to the ragtag cover tunes we were planning to massacre. He also appeared to have an unlimited supply of very powerful dope, which was going to be vital to the rehearsal process.

So that left only the recruitment of a drummer. Anyone who has ever had anything to do with a band will know that the drummer is by far the most important member. A drummer's syncopation, sense of rhythm, and ability to maintain a beat are the foundations upon which the band relies. Our drummer, we decided, would need to have the added ability to play loud enough to drown out the rest of our questionable musical talents.

Enter Maurizio. Though he was in his early forties, Maurizio, also of Italian origin, exuded the enthusiasm and lust for life of a teenager. Unfailingly generous, gentle, and polite, the perpetually happy proprietor of his very own Italian restaurant, Maurizio was one of those Latinos who made you feel warm just by being around. He also happened to be a convicted criminal, a political exile, and was wanted in his home country for crimes he committed as a teenager in the service of the Red Brigade, a Communist terror group. In the mid-1980s, as one of some twenty former Red Brigade members who had been granted asylum by French president François Mitterrand, Maurizio had arrived in France as an asylum-seeking fugitive. He had previously served six years of an eighteen-year prison sentence in Italy for his role in several bank robberies in the late seventies, and faced certain prosecution should he ever set foot back in his homeland.

Now he and his wonderful wife Concetta carved a hardworking, honest living out of a small restaurant, La Baraonda, in the tenth arrondissement. Purveyors of delicious homemade pasta, seafood, and tiramisu, they spent almost as much time plying their trade as they did receiving random members of their neighborhood for long chats over espresso coffees.

With Maurizio on board, the band was complete: a self-obssessed Aussie, a preening English bovver boy, a philandering Venetian, a conspiracy theorist American, and a bona-fide Italian terrorist. We were ready to make music.

Rehearsals were initially staged in the tiny basement bar of Le Connétable. A dank, stone-lined hole under the main bar area, the basement stank of mildew and stale cigarettes—perfect conditions for the gestation of a rock phenomenon. James and I would meet there after work, take off our ties, plug in his guitar and my microphone, and work through a collection of randomly selected songs. From Oasis to Van Morrison, Radiohead to the Strokes, Robbie Williams to R.E.M., Beck to Britney—we left no musical stone unturned in our quest for the perfect cover tune playlist.

As the weeks ticked by and the inaugural gig fast approached, we toiled away in the dark. With each passing day we became ever more acutely aware of how supremely lacking in natural talent we were.

The additions of Claudio and Stefan, rather than bolster the rehearsal sessions, only seemed to confuse the issue, invariably ending in argument and bruised egos all round. Whether a song was in C or G, whether one of the guitarists was playing out of tune, whether we should stick to the song as it was originally recorded or play it with our own signature twist, all became the subject of heated debate. In composing the playlist we had to constantly, delicately compromise between Claudio's insistence on including bossa nova classics and James's preference for belting Brit rock. And all the while the great unspoken truth that all of us felt but none dared mention was that whatever that noise was we were making each week, it was patently unsuitable for public consumption. Still, the concert was locked in. What we lacked in musical prowess, we would simply have to make up for in bravado.

A week before our concert night, the dingy rehearsal studios where we had moved in the grungy twentieth arrondissement began to resemble a war zone. In broken French (the only language we all spoke in common) a hypersensitive Italian clashed with a no-nonsense Englishman who snapped at a bossy Australian who picked on a guileless American. It was like trying to build the Tower of Babel without bricks and mortar.

We wrestled with the finer nuances of the Britney Spears classic "Baby, One More Time" and rendered barely recognizable such worldwide hits as Michael Jackson's "Billie Jean." With increasing frustration we tripped clumsily over the chords, breaks, and melodies of such guaranteed crowd-pleasers as Oasis's "Wonderwall," Van Morrison's "Brown-Eyed Girl," Radiohead's "Creep," and the Strokes' "Someday." While the rhythm guitarist pouted, the lead guitarist belted out long-winded solos. While the singer missed his cues, the perma-stoned bass guitarist plucked happily away inside his own noxious smoke cloud. The drummer, for his part, spent most of the time looking on in total bemusement. Yet for reasons that still escape me, we would emerge from each session fantasizing about the size of the check Sony Records would undoubtedly throw at us the minute we were unleashed on Paris's unsuspecting public.

But before we could attain rock supersuperstardom, we needed to come up with a catchy name. Choosing a name for a band is a delicate exercise. You have to pick something that's clever without being smart-ass. Obtuse without being pretentious. Accessible without being obvious. It has to appeal to your audience, say something about your style of music, and look good on the cover of *Rolling Stone* when inevitably you are featured there. In our case, it also had to be bilingual—and preferably serve as a sufficiently witty or enigmatic distraction from the fact that none of us could properly play musical instruments. We settled on Get 27 (or *jet vingt-sept,* as it is pronounced in France). It was a name that rolled easily off the tongue, borrowed heavily from the Blink 182/Matchbox 20 school of word-number band name combinations—and happened to also be the name of a foul-tasting mint liqueur often to be found gathering dust on the top shelves of French bars. None of us particularly liked the liqueur, but we all liked the fact that it was favored by aging professional alcoholics, the kind of men whose bent frames could often be seen hunkered at the bar of the Connétable. The kind of men we all feared Paris would eventually turn us into.

Working on the smoke-and-mirrors principle of rock goddery—namely, that any old tripe will pass as music as long as it is marketed properly—I set to work straightaway on creating a Get 27 website. Within three days, thanks to the Web-manipulating skills of a friend at the OECD (whose international civil servant job seemed to entail little more than watching the clock, making coffee, and not paying tax), the World Wide Web became just that little bit wider with the addition of the Get 27 homepage, complete with detailed biographies that almost made us sound legit.

A website was fine and well, but no amount of online verbosity would disguise the fact that when the day of our debut performance finally arrived, we were spectacularly unprepared.

That day our final rehearsal only served to emphasize how much more polishing our act needed. A playlist that ran the musical spectrum from Gloria Gaynor to the Libertines was only half-formed. The break between choruses in our rendition of AC/DC's "Highway to Hell" was an unmitigated disaster, and despite our best efforts, we hadn't even come close to nailing the ending of at least six of our thirteen songs. The hours ticked by as we strummed and toiled. When night rolled around, we were, to a person, a bundle of nerves. Sure we were only playing the tiny basement bar of the Connétable, and yes, the audience would consist exclusively of supportive, drunken friends. But so successful had we been in convincing those friends that we were actually "not that bad," we now had to pull something special out of the bag.

Invoking a strategy that had served countless rock bands before us, we realized there was only one thing to do. We had to get stonkingly, irreversibly drunk. At a pregig dinner upstairs at the Connétable, the five band members were notable for their terrified looks and propensity to drink entire glasses of fine red wine in one furtive gulp. While downstairs the crowd was swelling—causing Marie, the bartender, the distinct inconvenience of actually having to serve drinks—upstairs our stomachs were churning. What were we thinking? Who were we kidding? Did we really believe we could pull this off?

Chapter 20

It's a Long Way to the Top

UNDER NORMAL CIRCUMSTANCES, stepping into a room packed to overflowing with inebriated friends would be near the top of my list of favorite ways to spend a Friday evening. So why then, on this particular night as I followed my bandmates from the first-floor restaurant to the basement bar area of the Connétable, did I feel like I was walking toward my own execution?

A loud scream of approval greeted us as we appeared at the bottom of the stairs. A rhythmic clap started up, and a chant of "Get 27! Get 27!" echoed off the walls of the tiny underground space. The basement bar of the Connétable, it must be said, is no Madison Square Garden or Wembley Stadium. A damp cavern hacked into the limestone beneath the restaurant proper, it measures no more than twenty yards long by eight yards wide. It is a narrow, stunted tunnel with leaching walls and appalling acoustics. Most nights you would be hard-pressed to squeeze forty people into the space with any comfort. Tonight at least eighty people were crammed into the dirty grotto. The drum set, guitars, amps, and microphones were wedged awkwardly at one end of the dirty cave. I picked my way through the drunken crowd—running a gauntlet of back-slapping, cheek-kissing friends—and arrived at the microphone stand. All of two feet separated me from the first row of enthusiastic groupies.

We picked up our instruments, took a collective deep breath, and launched into an hour and a half of dubious musical entertainment. The first two songs passed in a blur. With eyes either firmly closed or focused on the back wall, I warbled and screamed my way through the Cure's "Boys Don't Cry" and "Someday" by the Strokes. I didn't dare make eye contact with anyone, lest I see a look of horror among the familiar faces or, worse, a patronizing smile of indulgence, the kind a mother might give on school concert night to a desperately untalented child. For their part, the guys in the band were racing through each song in record time, heads firmly hung, eyes fixed on feet or concentrated nervously on guitar frets.

Halfway through the show, we dared to look up—and saw the room heaving. People were dancing, jumping, whistling, and singing along. Whether it was the alcohol, the distinct lack of oxygen, or just plain politeness, the audience appeared to love us. We started to warm to our rock star roles and relaxed into the remainder of the set. In no small part thanks to the industrial quantities of alcohol we had imbibed at dinner, we managed to rock our way through a playlist of some thirteen songs. Most of them, surprisingly enough, managed to be just about passable imitations of the originals. It was, as debut performances of small-time amateur cover bands go, an unmitigated triumph. The crowd refused to let us finish, demanding no fewer than four encores—all of which we were forced to draw from the original playlist of thirteen, since that was all we knew.

A WEEK LATER, buoyed by our subterranean success at the Connétable, we decided to take our music to the streets. We started rehearsing for Paris's annual Fête de la Musique outdoor music festival. Held every year in June on the evening of the summer solstice, Fête de la Musique has become a highlight on the city's cultural calendar. The streets are closed to traffic while bands running the gamut of musical style and talent set up on street corners and entertain the wandering crowds.

Our chosen corner was a patch of pavement just opposite the Connétable, on the corner of the Rue des Haudriettes and the Rue des Archives. Selected for its easy access to the free-flowing beer taps of our favorite bar, plus the dramatic backdrop provided by a massive stone water fountain, the corner was also two blocks from the gay bars of the Marais, whose techno DJs traditionally pulled the biggest crowds each year. We were unashamedly going for the spillover audience. A complicated and dangerously precarious system of electrical equipment connected our amps, lights, and microphones to a single power point in the Connétable. As the sun waned and the sky turned that soft pink for which Parisian summers are renowned, the crowds began to gather. Two hours, thirty songs, several gallons of sweat, and three encores later, the streets surrounding the Connétable were standing room only. A crowd of some five hundred people had gathered to variously dance, sing, or gawp with bemusement at the hyperactive foreigner with the blond afro and his band of mismatched amateur musos. People were scaling traffic lights, shinning lampposts, and clinging precariously to the walls of surrounding buildings just to catch a glimpse of us. It was a true rock-star moment.

For us, the entire exercise was one great vanity project—conceived as a joke and executed as a dare—but we couldn't help noticing that we appeared to have struck a chord (no pun intended). Working the crowd from behind my microphone, indulging my every rock-star desire, and throwing myself shamelessly about the makeshift stage, I became slightly unnerved at the number of attractive young women making meaningful, persistent eye contact. I was sweating like a pig, making an spectacle of myself, and battling to hold a tune on a clapped-out sound system with a ragtag bunch of musicians. But the ladies were loving it. It was then that I had a rock-star epiphany. When it comes to fronting a band, it doesn't seem to matter how unremarkable you are in the looks department. Grab a microphone and belt out a ballad, and women are putty in your hands. Just ask Mick Hucknall.

And so began one of the most formative chapters of my Parisian experience: a period of my Parisian life in which late-night bars were frequented, loose women were courted, and general loucheness became a lifestyle choice. In sum, it was not a whole lot different from the life I had been leading up to that point. I never *really* believed that this little flirtation with amateur warbling would morph into anything permanent, but postgig and high on a mixture of adrenaline and illicit substances, with the cheers of the crowd still ringing in my ears, I found myself entertaining Learjet fantasies. Next stop, a million-dollar recording contract, a breakthrough single, and a massively successful world tour.

Waking the morning after the Fête de la Musique with a sore throat, a sore neck, and muscular pain in limbs I had forgotten I owned brought me face to face with a crushing reality. At thirty-one years old, with no musical training or skills, and the master of only a couple of cover tunes, the chances were I had embarked on my rock-star run too late. But the prospect of sustained public humiliation was too great to resist—and besides, we were on a roll.

And so a two-year touring schedule began in earnest. No wedding, party, or dingy venue was too small for us. No payment was too meager. If a room had a stage, an electrical outlet, and a collection of more than four people, we would wield our instruments without fear or favor. Our gigs veered from the mildly prestigious to the frankly ridiculous. One week we would play to a crowd of six hundred at the Australian Embassy, supporting platinum-selling Aussie songstress Delta Goodrem; the next we would be playing to bemused aunties, uncles, and cousins at a wedding on a boat. A gig at the renowned Paris jazz venue New Morning before some three hundred people would be followed a couple of weeks later with a performance in a community hall in provincial France—the hall empty but for us five noisy *étrangers* on stage and four septuagenarian farmers in the audience (one of whom had his hearing aid turned off especially for the occasion, allowing him to sleep through the entire performance). As self-appointed band manager, I never refused an engagement, working on the principle that we needed all the onstage experience—and all the musical practice—we could get.

We held rehearsals consistently for two years as we changed and refined the playlist. You could always tell when a gig was imminent (for
which we were consistently underprepared) as relations between the
band members became increasingly strained. Tantrums were thrown,
stern words were exchanged, and threats of quitting were bandied
about, as the gig grew closer and the utter embarrassment we were
about to make of ourselves—again—became more apparent. And yet
we persevered, inspired by the continuing delusion that our ham-fisted
attempts at creating a melody were somehow contributing to the musical canon.

The grotty Studio Bleu rehearsal studios in the colorful tenth arrondissement became the staging ground *du choix* for our sporadic
attacks on the unsuspecting world of live musical entertainment. We
would gather there most Saturday afternoons, having negotiated the
crowds of milling Turkish men on the corner of the Rue des Petites
Ecuries, climbed the stairs to the first floor, and squeezed past the smil-
ing black faces of the gospel choir that rehearsed in the studio next
door. Once there we would spend up to four hours at a time, trans-
forming works of internationally recognized musical accomplishment
into pale shadows of their former glorious selves.

This weekly exercise in artistic assassination required as much
diplomacy as it did actual musical talent. When we weren't juggling
the delicate ego of an Italian rhythm guitarist who never seemed to
practice, we were keeping in check the inflating sense of self-importance
of an Australian lead singer who was showing distinct signs of starting
to believe his own publicity.

The self-delusion reached a peak when we went into a recording
studio to "lay down some tracks," as industry parlance goes. The fact
that the recording session took place in a studio in the backyard of a
friend of Maurizio's, in an outlying Parisian suburb whose existence I
had never before registered, did little to disabuse us of the perception
that we were about to make a little bit of musical history. The studio
control room—if indeed you could call an out-of-service refrigerated
shipping container a studio control room—featured a collection of
old-school sound-recording equipment. While the lads played their

instruments in a dilapidated barn on one side of the yard, I sang into a microphone in a garage on the other side. Crackling headphones kept us all in aural contact, but nothing could keep us in tune. Nevertheless we had become recording artists—a fact we bandied about with as much abandon as the fallacy that we had performed a "world tour."

In reality, the Get 27 world tour was a piecemeal collection of half-baked, purely opportunistic musical performances at a variety of international social events that we were to attend that year. The wedding in Brazil of two good friends, Alex and Niki, became a chance for James and me to display our tenuous grip on musicality to a whole range of new people in the tiny Bahia township of Praia do Forte.

On a visit to his hometown of Conegliano, Claudio and I managed to suppress the inner shrinking violet in both of us long enough to offer an unsolicited half hour's entertainment to a group of diners in a mountaintop restaurant, then again at a nightclub later that night. In both instances we shamelessly sidled up to bands that had actually been hired to provide musical distraction for the evening and told them we were available to play should they need a break.

It got to a point where whenever two or more of the Get 27 band members were out together, a PA system left carelessly unguarded ran a fairly good chance of being hijacked. Charlotte's thirtieth birthday party in the frightfully English town of Henley-on-Thames provided another date on our international tour schedule, as did the thirtieth birthday of a sweetly indulgent friend of James's new girlfriend, Stéphanie. This latter gig took place in a poolside bar in Marseille. Either inspired by our performance or desperate to escape it, a bevy of beautiful young things started removing clothing and throwing themselves into the pool. And in a show of pure professionalism, we abandoned our instruments midset to follow suit. Rock and roll.

When the three-year anniversary of Get 27's debut performance at Le Connétable rolled around, I took stock of my journey on the road to rock superstardom and concluded that it had definitely been more flatline than meteoric. We had no Sony Records contract, nor would we ever. My ability to render popular tunes recognizable had undergone no visible improvement. Moreover, I had not a single original composition to my name. Instead of being featured in the pages of *Rolling Stone,* the only writing about my budding career as a rock star was that which was on the wall. The ruse was exposed, the jig was up. And so it came to pass that almost three years to the day since we had rocked the foundations of the Connétable, Get 27 performed its farewell gig.

Using Fête de la Musique as the backdrop for our last musical hurrah, we set up on a strip of pavement next to the Canal Saint Martin. Before a five-hundred-strong—and politely appreciative—crowd we worked through three years of repertoire. Under an indigo Paris sky, and in a performance that lasted just under two hours, we bade adieu to and gently let go of our respective rock-star fantasies.

As the last refrain of our final song echoed off the walls of the surrounding buildings, two of our loyal male fans climbed a nearby pedestrian bridge spanning the canal, stripped naked, and threw themselves in. As they hit the water and plummeted into the stagnant depths of the fetid canal, I reflected on what a fitting final metaphor they provided for my brief foray into music. Their alabaster buttocks had been foisted upon an unsuspecting public thanks to a similar conceit that had years previously convinced me the world was hankering to be exposed to my questionable musical talent; both enjoyed a brief, showy display before disappearing into the murky depths of obscurity, where they rightly belonged.

Chapter 21

Because I Cannes, Cannes, Cannes

WHEN MY LIFE IN PARIS was well into its third year, and Get 27 was still going strong, my job, on the whole, continued to prove an inconvenient intrusion into my social life. Moreover, it was a gig that really didn't rock my professional boat.

I was in a city I loved, earning a salary that afforded me a lifestyle that was sweet by anyone's reckoning, yet I missed the dynamism of my former professional incarnation. And so I found myself yearning to get back into the journalism caper. I started writing freelance articles for a variety of Australian newspapers and magazines, keen to not only keep my hand in, as it were, but also to relieve the deep-seated feelings of guilt I experienced working as a PR flack.

The timing of this first foray into the world of Paris-based freelance journalism happily coincided with the Cannes Film Festival. And following an introduction by a Paris-bound TV producer friend, I soon found myself negotiating with the American television network NBC to work as their man in Cannes—producing nightly reports for their flagship nightly entertainment program, *Extra!*

It is fair to say that the international calendar contains few more pointlessly vacuous occasions than the Cannes Film Festival. With the possible exception of the Oscars and the Golden Globes—which, let's be honest, are little more than extremely high-profile fashion parades—there's no other annual event whose hype so far outstrips its actual importance. Each year a hoary collection of movie stars, movie producers, movie distributors, and studio executives descend on the French Riviera for a weeklong orgy of self-congratulation. Each year a phalanx of freebie-hunting entertainment journalists follow them there to pay homage at the shrine of meaningless celebrity. And each year the Eurotrash jet set in their multi-million-dollar boats order their hired crews to set course for Cannes, where they moor in the Vieux Port to spend ten days sipping Champagne and hoping beyond hope to be asked to pose for the *Hello!* magazine photographer. It is mindless, meaningless, inconsequential pap, a heinous waste of time and money. And there was no way I was not going to be a part of it.

Now I'm not a star-stalker, by any stretch of the imagination. Indeed, having spent the better part of my early years as a newspaper reporter writing a gossip column, I've met my fair share of so-called beautiful people—and most of them leave me cold. But I absolutely hate not being a part of the action. And as anyone who has ever attended Cannes will tell you, for two weeks in May everything else in France ceases to exist. That year *The Matrix Reloaded, Terminator 3,* and a dreadful remake of an equally awful French *classique, Fanfan la tulipe,* were among the films being presented at Cannes. The film fest therefore held out the promise of close encounters with such titanic cinematic talents as Keanu Reeves, Arnold Schwarzenegger, and Penelope Cruz. It was going to be a doozy.

SO IT WAS that I arrived with my trusty camera crew on the famed Croisette, ready to tackle Cannes. For the two weeks that picturesque stretch of the French Riviera is transformed into a seething mass of showbiz froth and bubble. Beautiful old beachside hotels like the Majestic and the Martinez, while hinting at the resort town's glamorous history, seem to stare down with disdain upon the spectacle unfurling in the streets below. Every billboard in town is plastered with the poster for some upcoming film. Flashy sports cars rumble up and down the narrow stretch of road running beside the beach. In a parade of plastic surgery and peroxide, the aging wives of movie moguls compete with one another to see who can put on the most ostentatious display of jewelry. Conspicuous consumption keeps the Gucci, Chanel, and Dior boutiques crowded at all hours of the day and night, while just offshore, floating in boats the size of cruise liners, Arab sheikhs, Greek playboys, and IT geeks-made-good play with their turbo-cruisers, Jet-Skis, and helicopters.

Down on the beach a row of hastily erected marquees host a string of open-air bars—each one fitted out with a pair of hulking security guards and a velvet-roped VIP area in the vain hope that a stray film star might drift their way. The Croisette—the long stretch of beach-side promenade—is crammed with wannabe directors hawking their latest opus, aspiring young actresses wearing next to nothing, and wave after wave of excitable star-spotters, digital cameras in hand and autograph books at the ready. And everywhere you look, harried publicists, stressed-out producers, and frantic sales executives run from hotel meeting to lunch date to film screening to press conference.

Nestled among the palm trees is the Palais des Festivals, where all the film-screening, press-conference, and red-carpet action takes place. On every night of the festival, at least one major international film is premiered—and that is when the stars come out to play. Stepping from limousines in dresses worth thousands, they make a carefully choreographed entrance, parading slowly in front of the several hundred photographers, cameramen, and reporters jostling for an exclusive shot or soundbite. The media pit is a no-holds-barred celebrity feeding frenzy. All normal rules governing human interaction are thrown out the window and replaced by the overriding film festival law: survival of the pushiest.

I was working as a producer for *Extra!* which meant I did all the hard work so that my preening reporter could look good. I would wait in line to attend press conferences and ask the questions that he would then splice into his TV package for that night's program. I would get up at six a.m. to scramble for the media passes to access the red-carpet area and stand in the blazing sun for hours to hold the spot so that he could swan in at the last moment, do his hair, and take the glory. It was sweaty, exhausting, thankless work that not even close encounters with big movie stars could make up for.

When I wasn't fighting for my life on the red carpet, I was running up and down the beachfront with my trusty camera crew in tow, careening in and out of hotels to attend press conferences and cover what are known in the film industry as "junkets." Junkets are so called because every journalist who attends them is massively compromised from the outset. These highly contrived encounters with the stars of a film are conceived to give the TV viewer or newspaper or magazine reader the impression that these Hollywood giants have given generously of their time to discuss their latest project. In reality, it is a forced, hurried encounter, comprising three parts ass-kissing and one part actual journalistic inquiry.

One of our first junkets was for the film *Terminator 3*. On the top floor of a beachside hotel, fifteen TV crews gathered and set up their equipment in preparation for the arrival of the film's star, Arnold Schwarzenegger. A veritable aviary of flapping PR flacks flew frantically about the room, making sure everyone knew "the rules." Arnie, we were told (renowned in showbiz circles for being a control freak), would be available for only a total of thirty minutes. He would give each camera crew a two-minute interview—just long enough for him to repeat, for the thousandth time, the same platitudes he had uttered to every other journalist in Christendom. Some subjects, of course, were strictly off-limits. "Thou shalt not ask about his presidential ambitions" and "Thou shalt not mention the various sexual assault lawsuits" that were pending at the time, following his announcement that he would run for California governor. Instead, Arnie's flunkies proposed a series of "suggested questions," including the probing "How did you manage to get back into such fantastic shape for the movie?"

As he entered the room, a deferential hush descended. Resplendent in a camel blazer, Cuban heels, and sunglasses, he walked to the center of the room, sucked contemptuously on his stogie, and barked a grumpy "All right, let's go." I noted with no small amount of satisfaction that he was short. A short orange-fake-tanned Austrian.

My crew and I were told we were fifth in line to speak with Arnie. In addition to preparing ourselves for our allotted audience with the big fella, we had to juggle simultaneous interview opportunities with the delightful Claire Danes (the thinking man's starlet) and Nick Stahl, who had been plucked from obscurity to play Arnie's charge in the film. Thanks partly to the fact that she actually had something halfway intelligent to say for herself, my crew and I spent too much time interviewing the delectable Ms. Danes, meaning that when Arnie was ready to receive us, we were not ready to receive him.

The Terminator was not a happy bunny. The fact that *he* had to wait for *us* to reset the camera and rebalance the sound levels was bad enough. But once the camera was rolling and he was midway through rote-replying to one of my reporter's sycophantic questions, I stepped on the sound technician's foot, causing a tiny distraction that was apparently more than a Terminator can bear.

"Stop the camera," he ordered, terminating the interview and staring straight at me. "I'm not going to continue until *you* stop messing around and concentrate on the job at hand. Are you finished?" I was stunned. I had copped the brunt of a Terminator tantrum. My reporter laughed nervously and tried to smooth over the awkwardness with a probing question about how exactly Arnie had managed to get into such sensational shape for the new film. Meanwhile, I stood there making dagger-eyes at the man who, seven months later, would be sworn in as governor of the State of California—the world's eighth-largest economy.

The junket with the stars of *The Matrix Reloaded* was a walk in the park by comparison. As the only Hollywood blockbuster among the otherwise shamelessly arty fare that was in competition at the festival, the *Matrix* gang knew better than to try to mix with the pretentious types clogging up the Croisette. Instead, they decided to go slumming at the famous Hôtel du Cap. Arriving at the hotel, at the end of a winding private road, we were struck first by the elegance of the main building, a beautifully restored château set in carefully tended gardens.

Meticulously groomed lawns rolled like green velvet toward a small cliff that fell into turquoise water. Everything about the place was exquisite, from the marble-floored reception area to the pristine blue-and-white-striped sun lounges by the pool. Even the trees appeared to have been artfully trimmed into pleasing uniformity.

Under instructions from the army of security guards, we followed the path from the main hotel building down toward the water's edge. There we came upon a series of wooden bungalows, in which the principal cast members of *The Matrix Reloaded* had taken up court and were preparing to receive the world's television media. We needed no camera equipment for this job—each bungalow had its own camera already set up. You just took a number and waited to be called to take your place in the hot seat opposite one of the cast members, ask your three questions, and move on.

Perhaps unsurprisingly, star Keanu Reeves was the least interesting. In a desperate attempt to give the film more meaning than it had, and using words he appeared to have picked up from a skim-read that morning of *Nietzsche for Dummies,* the heartthrob gave the distinct impression that his casting as the village idiot in *Bill and Ted's Excellent Adventure* was no accident. In the eyes of Reeves, *The Matrix Reloaded* was a dystopic vision of a consumerist society gone mad. In its dark evocation of a future in which reality and surreality blurred, life as you knew it was in fact a simulacrum of life as it used to be, as opposed to how it is—in the conventional sense of being, and taking into account the philosophical question of place, sense of place, and how it is determined by individual perception—the film was really a natural extension of theories of the French philosopher Jean Baudrillard.

"So it's not just a movie about guns and computers then?" I asked.

As the week drew to a close, I paused between frantically rushing from celebrity interview to satellite feed to reflect upon the absurdity of what I was doing. I was ricocheting from one Hollywood A-lister to another, creating "stories" where there patently were none, and scrapping with the competition over manufactured "exclusives with the stars," all for the edification of and nightly consumption by an American TV audience who had long ago surrendered themselves to the cult of mindless celebrity. It was enough to make me throw my media pass into the Mediterranean and hightail it back to Paris.

But not before I availed myself of one last festival perk: the MTV Cannes Closing Party. Unlike many of the luminaries strutting the boardwalk that week, local resident and French fashion icon Pierre Cardin was anything but vulgar. So it came as somewhat of a shock to learn that he was going to host the MTV booze-up at his architecturally splendid Côte d'Azur property. In the high-voltage party world of the Cannes Film Festival, this was the one invitation that everyone coveted. Sponsored by the world's premier youth music network and holding out the promise of more film stars per square foot than any other patch of the French Riviera, the shindig—and getting access to it—became the singular obsession of all serious social climbers in Cannes that week. I had an invitation to the party by virtue of the fact that I was covering it for NBC.

When the big night arrived, invitees were all bussed twenty-five miles along the coast to Cardin's emblematic "bubble-house." Designed by Russian architect Antti Lovag, this multileveled collection of modular concrete and glass bubbles spills down the coastal cliff face toward the ocean. Like a spaceship clinging to the mountainside, it is at once stunning and bizarre. But then it was certainly no more bizarre than the fashion guru giving his beautiful home over to MTV so it could invite a thousand freeloaders to deface it.

As the crowd grew and the free alcohol flowed, revelers began exploring the sprawling residence, a labyrinth of artfully lit rooms connected by a warren of narrow concrete corridors. Arnie and crew—fresh from intimidating a whole new host of camera crews—took up residence in the roped-off VIP area, while Keanu and the *Matrix* kids mixed it up down in the garden with the plebes. For his part, our octogenarian host, the navy-blazer-sporting Monsieur Cardin, appeared to float aimlessly about his home, seemingly wondering who these people were and exactly what they were doing in his house.

Before long the alcohol began to have its diuretic effect, swelling the bladders of the thousand-strong crowd. In their infinite wisdom, the party-planners had provided only six Portolets, the lines for which stretched around the corner, past the live band, and up the driveway. The women mostly stood patiently, shifting nervously from foot to foot, but the men took one look at the lines and headed for the shadows of the nearby terrace. A row of alabaster buttocks stood in line on the bulbous roof above Pierre Cardin's living room. With heads thrown back to the stars, and looks on their faces that can only be inspired by a long-overdue piss, they relieved themselves. Rivulets of urine cascaded down the modular concrete of the home of one of the world's most stylish fashion designers. And as I added my trickle to the deluge, all I could think of was the stench that would greet our host the next morning as his home baked under the midsummer Mediterranean sun.

As I stood emptying my bladder over Pierre Cardin's celebrated designer home on the French Riviera, the scene unfolding around me seemed an appropriate metaphor for the entire Cannes enterprise. Though it was all dressed up in designer frocks and red-carpet carryings-on, the film festival was little more than an exercise in vulgarity: a bunch of common-as-muck freeloaders incapable of holding their piss.

Chapter 22

Get Your Motor Running

I T WAS THE FRENCH PHILOSOPHER Jean-Paul Sartre who once famously opined that "hell is other people."

You don't have to live long in Paris to see where he was coming from. Sartre must have coined this enigmatic phrase almost immediately after taking a ride on the Paris Métro during peak hours in summer. I have nothing personal against the city's extremely efficient public transportation system. It is reliable, practical, and (but for a semipermanent stench of urine) relatively clean. The infrastructure itself is fine. It's the people who use it—and their collective aversion to showers or deodorant during Paris's steamy summer months—that finally pushed me onto the seat of a motor scooter.

The epiphany came one morning as I boarded my train for work on the populous line one of the Paris Métro. Freshly returned from the Cannes Film Festival, and with the whiff of the sea air still in my nostrils, I was almost bowled over by the pungent aroma of unwashed armpits. Summer was almost upon the city, and when it arrived, I knew from experience it would bring with it the Métro commuters' aversion to deodorant. The short train ride from the Hôtel de Ville to the Champs Elysées was enough to make up my mind. I resolved then and there not to spend another summer in the company of criminally neglected body odor. Calling the office from my cell phone, I told them I would be late for work. I emerged from the Métro at L'Etoile, in the shadow of the Arc de Triomphe, gasping for fresh air. It was nine in the morning, but already the large roundabout surrounding the monument was a furious mass of surging traffic. Like a colony of angry ants, innumerable cars, trucks, buses, and scooters crisscrossed, cut off, cut in, and otherwise forced their way in a frantic, clumsy, counterclockwise dance around the famous arch. The figure of La Marianne, the warrior-woman of France carved into the facade of one of the arch's supports, looked down on the scene with an expression of wide-eyed horror. She knew, from years spent witnessing it firsthand, what I was about to discover: French drivers are certifiably mad.

But now, blissfully ignorant of the pact I was about to sign with the driving devil, I marched into the first of the row of scooter shops that line Avenue de la Grande Armée and started perusing. It's a curious thing about Paris retail outlets: purveyors of the same product all tend to congregate in the same street. If you want a computer, go to Avenue Daumesnil in the twelfth arrondissement, where you will find every computer store in Paris. If you need a guitar, Rue Victor Massé in the ninth is where you'll find all the music stores. If it's a water heater you need, every one of those shops is crowded along Boulevard Richard Lenoir. I've never understood the logic behind this situation. Do they all share the same supplier, who has cleverly convinced them to stick together to simplify his delivery schedule? Is it a throwback to the days of blacksmiths and artisans, when guilds were formed and alliances between like-minded professionals forged? Or is it simply another example of the remarkable lack of *nous* the French display when it comes to entrepreneurship and competition? While it certainly made life easy for the consumer—having all of the competition crammed into the same street for easy comparison—it makes no economic sense whatsoever. But then, little in France does.

As I waltzed into the scooter shop, I clapped eyes on the bike I knew I would make mine. She was black, she was sleek, and she had fancy alloy trim and a distinctly retro design. It was love at first sight. She was an Aprilia Mojito—and she was as good as sold. When it comes to significant purchases like this one, I have always subscribed to the personal motto "Style over substance." So as the salesman enumerated the many mechanical benefits of my new steed, I politely feigned comprehension. He talked of carburetors and brake fluid, mentioned something about gasoline consumption, and said something crucial about the oil levels that I absolutely had to remember. I nodded gravely and gave the front wheel a little kick for good measure, just to complete the fraud. Even if he hadn't been speaking rapid-fire French and using vocabulary that even in English I don't fully understand, I still wouldn't have taken in a word. I was busy with a daydream that had me flying down the Champs Elysées on my Mojito, wind tousling my golden locks, Gitane hanging in a devil-may-care fashion from my bottom lip, stopping traffic with my derring-do and causing beautiful French maidens to swoon.

Jolted out of my reverie when the earnest grease monkey demonstrated the kick-start feature, I refocused momentarily to assure him that I knew exactly what I was doing, that he need not worry, and that there was no way I would forget whatever that crucial thing was with the oil levels.

I handed him a check, and he handed me the keys.

Now, I had never before ridden a motor scooter, nor any vehicle from the motorcycle family for that matter. Nor was I in possession of a motorbike license. But neither fact seemed to be an issue. He handed me a helmet and wheeled my new toy out onto the busy street. Suddenly I began to wonder about the wisdom of my impulsive decision. Traffic was surging down the Avenue de la Grande Armée toward La Défense at an alarming speed.

Jolting away from the curb and merging gingerly with the manic morning traffic, I felt my heart rate leap as the utter vulnerability of my situation suddenly became apparent. As it dawned on me that I was fast approaching the angry melee at the base of the Arc de Triomphe, I began to panic.

Some people who have lived their entire lives in Paris routinely take elaborate detours to avoid the traffic black hole that is L'Etoile. But here I was, two minutes into scooter ownership, about to be sucked into the massive roundabout. I felt like a canoeist being drawn irrevocably toward the lip of a massive waterfall, soon to disappear without a trace. The mob of cars that engulfed me on either side had created a momentum I was powerless to resist. And so, with a deep breath, a hurried prayer to a long-neglected God, and thirty years' worth of life experiences flashing before me, I entered the fray and hoped for the best.

Cars flew at me from every direction. The only rule that seemed to apply was that of survival of the most aggressive. Brakes were squealing, engines revving, horns blaring, and tempers flaring. I fixed my gaze on Avenue Marceau and dared not look back, reasoning that what I couldn't see wouldn't hurt me. I hurtled in a blind panic toward the relative calm of one of the huge roundabout's many axes. Motion, and the fluid continuation of it at all times, was, I would soon learn, the scooter rider's best ally. Acceleration and maneuverability were the only weapons you had in your on-road armory—and all that stood between you and daily brushes with certain death. If you didn't go hard, mastering just the right balance of fearlessness, aggression, and prudence, you were on a fast track to splatsville. It was a lesson I learned in those brief, horrifying twenty seconds on L'Etoile and one that I was to carefully heed thereafter.

Several weeks into my relationship with Mojito, I had gotten used to blending seamlessly into the manic morass that is Paris traffic—and I had grown to love my newfound sense of freedom. Not only had I been permanently liberated from the Métro and its stench, but every corner of Paris was now only a short, occasionally hair-raising, but always-exhilarating bike ride away. Pockets of the city that I never knew existed revealed themselves to me. The location of one part of town relative to another—which had hitherto been confused by a modular Métro map—fell together like pieces of a jigsaw.

My new vantage point transformed familiar perspectives of well-known Parisian panoramas. Driving by the Eiffel Tower at night, I would crane my head backward to catch sight of the floodlit, ornate spiderweb of crisscrossing steel. Sailing along the quai past the Musée d'Orsay, through the cypress trees I would glimpse staccato flashes of its bulbous, backlit, oversize clock faces.

And as I burst out of the underground tunnel next to the Seine, just in front of the Louvre, on a midnight midsummer ride, the view would never fail to take my breath away. The pepper-pot turrets of the floodlit Conciergerie reflected on the glassy surface of the river. The arches of Pont Neuf perfectly framing the illuminated spans of a succession of bridges beyond it, all of them glowing golden yellow. The white light of elaborate lampposts refracted through glass and skimmed across the river's skin. The ghostly white towers of Notre Dame standing silent sentinel. On nights like these the Seine seemed not to move at all, as if awestruck by the beauty it was passing. The warm, still air of the hot Parisian day just gone caressed my naked arms. The road, by virtue of the hour, was deserted. It felt like this remarkable city belonged exclusively to me. And it was good.

Less good were the winter months, when the purchase of a goose-down, superstrength, waterproof puffer jacket was the only thing that prevented me from freezing to death. Also a little troubling was my growing tendency to leave the smallest possible margin of time between important appointments and actually leaving the house. Because the scooter made every corner of the city accessible in under ten thrill-packed minutes, I found I left my departure to the absolute last minute, ensuring a mad scramble to make any rendezvous. At times like these, no surface was safe. Sidewalks, bike paths, bus lanes, alleys, one-ways, squares, and even public parks were driven over, through, or across with willful abandon. If it was flat and it happened to be in a straight line between me and my destination, it was fair game.

I soon became a card-carrying member of the pesky scooter brigade. The curse of all car-driving Parisians, scooter drivers are morally obliged to drive with no respect whatsoever for road rules or traffic signals. Like one among a noisy swarm of locusts, I would swoop altogether too fast into a traffic jam, then squirm my way past stationary cars to the front. Near-misses and sideswipes were a daily occurrence. No side-view mirror was safe as long as I was on the road, and bumpers would quake in fear as I approached.

And woe betide any car driver who didn't yield to my aggressive antics. A well-rehearsed stream of broad-accented Aussie invective would be rained upon them, and occasionally a well-aimed boot would come thudding into their passenger door. I learned quickly to deal with Frenchies on the road as I had learned to deal with them in person. Use aggression as a default position, go in hard with border-line hysteria as an opening gambit, and be prepared to climb down as and when the occasion required. When the appropriate words of French abuse failed me (as they often did), I would let rip with a stream of choice English obscenities. I figured what they didn't pick up in actual meaning, they would surely divine from the tone. No doubt the police had a permanent arrest warrant out for a blond-haired scooter rider, terrorizing Parisian roads with aggressive driving tactics and maniacal streams of Aussie abuse.

It didn't take long for scooter fever to grip the other guys in the Paris Posse. Jules, true to his French roots, had long ago been a scooter convert and had encouraged me to buy mine. Will was the next to fall under the Vespa spell, opting for a stylish retro model. In keeping with his commitment to form over function, his cream and alloy affair looked beautiful but kept breaking down. Then finally James succumbed, purchasing an Aprilia 125, which I disdainfully referred to as "the postman's bike." And that was the thing with scooters. Much as competing alpha males in other parts of the world try to outdo one another with the rims or spoilers on their Monaros, Thunderbirds, or Ford Escorts, in Paris, respect between males was afforded according to how cool one's Vespa was. Engine size (perhaps unsurprisingly) was crucial. Anything less than 125cc was considered a girl's bike. Color was also important. To step outside the safety of black, gray, or blue was a brave and potentially dangerous move, raising questions about one's manliness. Windshields were for losers, and specially fitted scooter blankets, while extremely practical—especially in the dead of winter— were very definitely for sissies only.

More than anything else, scooter ownership afforded a certain street cred. And it always went down a storm with the ladies. Rolling up to a rendezvous with a maiden, chucking her a helmet, and inviting her to climb aboard for a thrill-packed ride through the streets of Paris was always a surefire way to start a date. As well as giving a girl a bit of a buzz, causing her to cling to my back in fear and exhilaration, taking a female pillion passenger was a great way to tell whether or not a girl fancied me. If she rode sitting upright and clinging to the railings under the seat, chances were it was going to be a dead-end date. If, on the contrary, she wrapped her arms around my waist and pressed herself into my back, there was no telling where, how, or at whose apartment the evening would end.

My only regret about welcoming Mojito into my Paris life was that I hadn't done it earlier. Atop my trusty steed, I had the city at my feet. She was beautiful, reliable, and gutsy. But as I was soon to discover, enthusiasm for my two-wheeled friend was far from universal.

Chapter 23

Sticker Bitch

I F I WAS IN LOVE with my new set of wheels, it soon became apparent that it was a sentiment not shared by everyone. The courtyard fascists in my building prohibited the parking of any vehicle on the property, so Mojito had to spend her days and nights parked outside on the street. At first I worried that thieves would be attracted to her obvious beauty and snatch her away in the night. As it turned out, thieves were the least of my worries. A more sinister threat lurked in the shadows of Rue Sainte Croix, and it wasted no time showing its face.

Mojito was one of several bikes that were habitually parked on a wide stretch of sidewalk just outside the Love Pad. Designated, city council–ordained parking spaces for two-wheeled contraptions could be found at the end of my street, but to use them would have meant walking twenty yards out of my way. And if there was one thing no self-respecting scooter driver ever did, it was to walk more than was strictly necessary. It contravened the code. It has to be said that, perched on the path, Mojito and her friends did take up a large portion of the thoroughfare. But this was Paris. Scooters litter the sidewalks with almost the same frequency as dog shit—and as with the little piles of poo, the residents of Paris had simply learned to step around them.

Not so Sticker Bitch.

Sticker Bitch was an aging crone whose life had been reduced to a daily, one-woman battle against the scooters of Paris. For reasons that were never clear to me, she was so offended by the presence of Vespas on her sidewalk, she launched a stealth campaign of harassment and vandalism to rid her rue of the sidewalk-hogging scooter scum. At what I can only assume was considerable personal expense, Sticker Bitch had printed a variety of fluorescent yellow, orange, and green stickers with cartoon figures of humans pushing baby carriages and the battle cry: RENDEZ LES TROTTOIRS AUX PIETONS!—GIVE THE SIDEWALKS BACK TO PEDESTRIANS!

Every other morning I would bounce out of my apartment only to discover that the Mojito had been defaced again. Contrasting against her shiny black lacquer would be a sticker urging me to give the pavement back to pedestrians. Scratching at it would only remove the sticker partially, leaving behind a telltale streak of gummy white paper. Wherever I drove in the city, I could tell if a bike belonged to one of my neighbors, covered as it was with familiar fluorescent protests. And while some of my scootering comrades were apparently content to let the old dear wreak her daily brand of urban terrorism, I was incensed. To my mind, this was out-and-out vandalism. A gross violation of my private property and a cowardly campaign of neighborly intimidation and harassment. Sticker Bitch had declared war. She had thrown down the fluorescent gauntlet. And I was not about to shrink from the challenge.

The thing about guerrilla warfare of the type practiced by Sticker Bitch is that its attacks are purposefully random. So crafty was she that she never struck on the same day each week, never launched her assaults on consecutive days, and regularly changed the time of day when she would swoop. I only knew she was a she—and an elderly one at that—because friends of mine who owned the graphic design agency in front of which Mojito was regularly parked watched in awe one day as a wizened figure dragged a shopping caddy up the street in one hand while dispensing stickers onto unsuspecting scooters with the other. According to my eyewitness, the mischievous old harpy moved with a stealth and speed that belied her years. And despite my grudging respect for the lengths to which she went to wage her private war, I made it my mission to discover her and punish her for her infuriating brand of vigilante vandalism.

I had it all worked out. Instead of confronting her on the street, I was going to lie in wait, watch her ply her hateful trade, and then discreetly follow her back to her house. I would then take note of exactly which apartment she lived in and return to it in the dead of night with a can of spray paint and a mind bent on vengeance. I had kept a stash of the stickers she had rudely applied to my bike. I planned to cover her door with the stickers (so she would know she had been discovered), then let loose with the spray paint. VANDALISM IS A CRIME or HOW DO YOU LIKE IT? were two of the messages I dreamed of smearing on her door. HERE LIVES A VANDAL was another. I had consulted French dictionaries and conferred with perplexed French friends to make sure I had the grammar correct. I then planned to return to the street and leave a note on all of the other bikes, belonging to similarly terrorized scooter owners, informing them of Sticker Bitch's address, should they wish to enact their own revenge.

One morning I even stayed home from work for the express purpose of sitting on a stoop opposite my parked bike, pretending to read a paper while lying in ambush. For three hours I sat and waited, but to no avail. If Sticker Bitch was going to be caught, it was going to take more than a three-hour stakeout. I began to realize I was dealing with a major criminal mind and therefore would have to box a little more cleverly.

Remarkably, at no stage did I stop for a minute to consider the absurdity of my commitment to the cause of catching Sticker Bitch. A bit of sticker on my scooter every now and then was hardly the end of the world, yet capturing the perpetrator became my singular obsession. More than anything else, I was offended that she was beating me—annoyed that she was eluding and outsmarting me.

In a major change of campaign tactics, I decided to take the "winning hearts and minds" approach; I would recruit-by-association my friendly neighborhood business folk. I took to sneaking around at night, peeling stickers off my own and similarly defaced bikes, and pasting them on the display windows of surrounding shops and cafés. If I could piss off the proprietors by polluting their property with Sticker Bitch's stickers, I reasoned, they would be motivated to confront her the next time she plied her evil trade. Make a public enemy of the old dear, I figured, and watch the neighborhood turn against her. If that didn't work, Plan B involved me taking a sticker to every printer in the quartier until I found the one who produced them. I then planned to tell the printer I was the old lady's nephew and that she wanted me to reorder a new batch and hand-deliver them to her address—whereupon I would say I had forgotten where she lived, and did he have it on record?

Again, at no stage during my nightly midnight stealth missions and concerted efforts to research every printer in a five-mile radius did I pause to wonder if I wasn't perhaps overreacting just a little. Friends, on the other hand, found the obsession entirely disturbing. Suddenly afforded a glimpse of a darker side of my personality, they began to whisper among themselves that I was starting to lose it. It was when I recounted my plans over a dinner table full of usually supportive friends—only to be met with stares of shock, bemusement, and fear—that I began to wonder if I should let it go.

Certainly one of my neighbors and fellow scooterees had done exactly that. Whether out of sheer laziness or as a deft psychological counterattack, he had allowed the stickers to build up on his bike to the point where it was difficult to discern the vehicle's original color. On a Vespa festooned with fluorescent greens, yellows, and oranges, he would putter down the street, no doubt safe in the knowledge that he didn't have to worry about not being seen by other drivers on the road. But that kind of passive resistance was not an option for me. Not only was it contrary to my spiteful personality, it would have meant surrendering the sleek appearance of my lovely Mojito—which was, after all, the main reason I bought her.

Then one day, just as abruptly as the campaign had begun, it stopped. Whether Sticker Bitch had exhausted her life savings on fluorescent sticky paper or had dropped dead, I never knew. A more likely explanation was that she simply lost interest in this cause and moved on to a new one. Because if the French are good at anything, it is turning their hand to protest—anytime, anywhere, and for pretty much any cause.

Chapter 24

The Autumn, Winter, and Spring of Their Discontent

I F I HAD TO DO MY TIME in France all over again and I wanted to make a bucketful of euros in the process, there's little doubt I would go straight into the helium business. I can't think of another gas in France that is in as much demand as helium, thanks largely to the French propensity to protest. As anyone who monitors international news will attest, a strike or major protest takes place in Paris pretty much every other week, especially during the portion of each year from September to May.

On the other hand, the June-to-August stretch is notoriously quiet on the protest and strike front. When the weather warms up and the sun comes out, the protesters pack up their placards and head south, to take their places on the beach alongside their fellow disgruntled comrades for a well-earned break from the hard work of avoiding work.

But in the prime protest period of autumn, winter, and spring, the mobs are just itching to hit the rues and express their collective discontent—and always, rather bemusingly, under the shadow of a large collection of enormous balloons. Whether they are workers opposed to government labor reform, students opposed to government plans to change unemployment benefits, old people opposed to government plans for pension reform, they all have balloons, and they're not afraid to inflate them.

Place de la République, in the tenth arrondissement, is the favored kick-off point for two out of every three Paris protests, often attracting crowds by the thousands. In my more entrepreneurial moments, I used to imagine owning a café on the Place de la République and offering a whole host of revolutionary specials. Che Guevara Croque-Monsieurs, Trotsky Tarte Tatins, and Vladimir Illyich Lenin Limonades would be among the fare for which I would charge top dollar, gravely informing my clients that all proceeds were going to "the cause."

During the morning of every protest or strike, the Place de la République was devoid of traffic yet a hive of activity. With an air of weary familiarity, the police would cordon off all roads leading to the place, letting through only the battered white vans of Communist Party activists and the open-sided trucks of hot-dog vendors. By midday the crowd would have swelled, and the place would have taken on a circuslike atmosphere. Che Guevara T-shirts appeared at every turn, and while Workers' Party delegates frantically inflated massive balloons, their colleagues unfurled placards of Lenin, raised posters of hammers and sickles, and dusted off well-worn effigies of Karl Marx. Exactly which part of the last fifty years of history these people had slept through, I was never sure. Crusty old Communists—their brittle, nicotine-stained mustaches twirled to stereotypical French man perfection—would mill among the masses, handing out manifestos for long-discredited political causes. Right-on DJ's would set up massive sound systems atop flatbed trucks to play folksy protest music (think Tracy Chapman, Bob Marley, and anything by Bob Dylan). Protest leaders in bright yellow T-shirts wielded megaphones and did their best to whip the crowd into an indignant frenzy. And if it was a student protest, there would be more Yassir Arafat–inspired black-and-white kaffiyeh headscarves per square yard than on your average day in Ramallah.

Meanwhile on the periphery of the protest mums and dads pushed strollers adorned with flags and banners, the faces of their long-suffering children painted with the battle cry du jour. Parent and child alike appeared blissfully ignorant of the cause they were protesting. For in France the point never seemed to be that you take to the streets to enact political change but rather, that you do so because it's a great day out. Just as it is an innate French reflex to treat all Americans with contempt, so it is an automatic gesture to join a protest march no matter what the cause. While Australians derive a sense of community by watching sports or speculating about the marriage prospects of Brad and Angelina, French people tap into their essential Frenchness by going on strike or joining a protest march.

As the crowds build on the ground, the sky overhead darkens with a growing armada of massive, multicolored helium balloons. So numerous and so ubiquitous are these bobbing blobs of disgruntlement, I can only assume that there is a whole phalanx of Frenchies who describe their occupation as "balloon wrangler" when filling out their tax returns. Such is the system in France, I wouldn't be the least bit surprised if half of them have compensation claims lodged with the government for repetitive strain injuries sustained while opposing its policies.

When Baron Haussmann was drawing up blueprints for the Paris that exists today, his boss, Napoleon III, requested that he create lots of long, wide, straight boulevards. History maintains that Napoleon figured the best way to avoid a repeat of the French Revolution was to create effective sight lines for his troops, when the occasion arose, so they could quell any signs of rebellion from the masses. But such was the civic planner's foresight, I wouldn't be surprised if he also anticipated the need for wide boulevards to accommodate the balloons of a thousand protest marches.

Coming as I do from a country of relative political apathy, it is certainly heartening to see a population that firmly believes it can change the minds of its leaders simply by taking to the streets. Drawing for inspiration on that quintessential people's uprising, the French Revolution of 1789, the French truly believe it is their god-given right to stop traffic, shout slogans, and inflate as many helium balloons as they goddamn please. That would be fine, if they weren't doing it every other week. Indeed, the protests come with such monotonous regularity, they have started to lose their oomph. It's all gone a little bit "boy who cried wolf."

During one memorable period of student protests during my Paris sojourn, the unrest went on for so long there were eventually protests against the protests. Kids who were tired of the month-long stand-off between their peers and the government took to the streets to demand an end to protesting. And I remember with particular fondness a train driver's strike on the Métro one year. The entire public transportation system in Paris ground to a halt because the city government was threatening to revoke a centuries-old, five percent "coal handling" loading—a throwback to the days of steam trains. But my favorite annual protest was easily the one staged by the Association of French Circus Performers. Each year a motley crew of jugglers, trapeze artists, and dwarves would take to the streets to protest the precarious nature of their industry. Only in France do you find people who have dedicated themselves to the itinerant life of a circus performer demanding job security.

All of it in a country that seems to have more public holidays than any other in the world. Through a clever melding of the Christian and Socialist calendars, the entire month of May is one long public holiday in France. When you are not spending the day off work celebrating the Pentecost or Assumption (whatever they may be), you find yourself kicking back and enjoying the public holiday afforded by the strict observance of May Day. This month-long holiday phenomenon is only compounded by the French propensity to *faire le pont,* or "make the bridge." If a public holiday falls on a Thursday, it is widely accepted that everyone will "make a bridge" and take a four-day weekend.

It may just be pure coincidence, but strikes in France have a strange habit of taking place on either the Tuesday following or Thursday prior to a public holiday, thus maximizing the potential for strikers to make an extra-long weekend of their political consciousness-raising exercise. Because after all, it's important to supplement your industrial action with a bout of reflection by the Brittany seaside.

Not that the French need any more time off work.

A mandatory thirty-five-hour week means the average Frenchie is at work for seven hours a day. Each worker is entitled to a one-hour lunch break, which is itself subsidized by the employer to the tune of eight euros per day. "Ticket restaurants," as they are known, are the lunch vouchers distributed by all employers to their workers to ensure they get a good boeuf bourgignon at lunchtime.

Even with such cushy working conditions, unemployment was still a highly sought-after state of being in France. And why not? If you got sacked from your job, the state undertook to pay you up to 80 percent of your salary for a period of two years. It was no accident then that thousands of twenty-something French people struck deals with their employers to get sacked, then disappeared overseas on taxpayer-paid two-year travel odysseys. Spend a few weekdays in Paris, and you will be struck by the number of able-bodied young Frenchies who are cluttering up the thousands of cafés in the middle of the day. They are the professionally unemployed—and they work hard at it.

I watched with alarm as the longer I was exposed to the *liberté, egalité, fraternité* manifesto that is the ideological underpinning of the French republic, the more I began to resemble Attila the Hun. Far from celebrating the workers' paradise that France was apparently striving to be, I found myself becoming disdainful of a government that point-blank refused to face up to a few very basic realities of the international economy. I was scornful of a generation of young people who preferred a job for life to an economy characterized by entrepreneurship. And in the process I began to feel my long-harbored left leanings shifting inexorably to the right. It scared me. But then I assured myself it was probably just a phase—and certainly nothing that ownership of a balloon wouldn't have sorted out.

Chapter 25

Square Peg, Round Hole

ONTRARY TO POPULAR PERCEPTION at the time, my life in Paris wasn't all rock concerts and late-night carousing. When the sun came up, I still had rent to pay, bar tabs to honor, and weekend minibreaks to Ibiza to afford. There was, in short, a living to be made and hence a serious side to my life in Paris. A professional yin to my leisure-time yang. A gig that paid the bills. In the few waking hours that I didn't commit to the pointless pursuit of pop superstardom, game shows, French women, and drunkenness, I was almost wholly dedicated to my job.

So dedicated, in fact, that I would even occasionally show up before ten a.m. Leading a double life was not easy, low-flying corporate executive by day, permanently high professional party boy at night.

"You want to be careful," my mother would intone over the line from Australia as I complained that I was coming down with yet another case of the flu. "All this burning the candle at both ends, it can't be good for you." But I was a graduate of the devil-may-care, live-fast-die-young school of reckless abandon. Besides, I had come to Paris for life experience, not career advancement.

The ICC, as a business lobby group, was inextricably intertwined with the practices of modern big business. It therefore held many pointless meetings, formed a raft of useless committees, created and enforced a comprehensive series of anti–productivity-oriented work practices, and did its very best to become so large and unwieldy as to be completely sclerotic and ineffectual. And try as I had done to fit in, I was now almost four years into the job and I still couldn't seem to make any sense of the corporate world. More than anything else, the jargon that was bandied about on a daily basis left me baffled.

"We need to increase our outreach efforts in line with the key objectives as identified in the Q1 strategy appraisal," a colleague would tell me in all seriousness.

You what?

"It is imperative we enhance the transparency and accountability of our community-based operations in line with local expectations and with respect to specific cultural idiosyncrasies," I would be told by an earnest oil company executive.

Come again?

My newspaper training had taught me to be a critical listener and reader. If words were used incorrectly or gratuitously, it would usually cause me to wince. I found I spent a lot of time wincing at work.

"We are committed to creating and implementing meaningful solutions" was a sentence I heard more times than I care to remember—and that always struck me as employing more verbs than were strictly necessary. I used to sit and wonder what the point was of creating something if you weren't going to implement it. And why were people going around creating solutions if they didn't *mean* anything?

And then there was the mysterious, all-consuming corporate-world obsession with concrete. Whether they worked for oil companies, insurance companies, law firms, the transportation industry, pharmaceutical companies, or in banking and finance, every businessperson I encountered during my time at ICC had an enduring love affair with concrete. Be it "concrete action" or "concrete solutions," nothing was considered worthy by these people unless it was coated in the thick, heavy gray stuff.

And everything but everything in the heady world of business was "key." And if it wasn't key, it wasn't worth discussing. Key outcomes, key figures, key factors, key roles. The air was thick with keys. I used to wonder how something came to be classified as key. Because as far as I could determine, there was no internationally recognized Scale of Keyness. Things were never "key" according to a universally acknowledged empirical measurement—rather they were "key" because some bloke in a tie, making a Powerpoint presentation at the front of the room, said they were.

Whatever this business double-speak disease was, it appeared to be contagious. It didn't seem to matter which country a businessperson came from, they all spoke the same impenetrable language.

"Make sure you PDA through your vitals when you are wheels down in Jo'burg," was one memorable instruction from a power-suited PR flack from America with whom I was to rendezvous in South Africa some two days later for a United Nations summit. I thought she was being fresh until I discovered she was simply asking me to send her my contact details as soon as my plane landed in Johannesburg.

The more I was exposed to this corporate world, the less I was able to convince myself that I fitted in. Rather than getting caught up in its mysterious workings and becoming a convert to its duplicitous double-speak, I was repelled by it. Here I was in a job that I could perform easily enough, but with which I had no affinity whatsoever and in which I had only a passing interest. It had served a purpose by allowing me to live in Paris, but ultimately I felt like I was cheating myself. I couldn't shake the nagging feeling that every day I spent in this job was another day of betraying whatever professional interests or talents I otherwise had.

And yet if I wanted to stay in Paris, my choices were relatively limited. Visa restrictions on foreigners working in France meant that if I wanted to continue to enjoy *la vie française,* I needed a company or organization like the ICC to sponsor me. Objectively, as my friends were wont to point out, I really had nothing to complain about. Odd though it undoubtedly was, my job gave me a ringside seat at international summits and meetings deliberating some of the biggest questions of our time.

During a UN summit in Monterrey, Mexico, I sat enthralled in a plenary hall as a wizened yet fiery Fidel Castro took the podium and delivered one of his trademark, fifty-minute tirades on the evils of capitalism. Later that same day, at a meeting convened by the ICC, I met and shook hands with the UN secretary-general, Kofi Annan. Soft skin, firm grip, wise eyes, and a voice like honey. But as I sat in the meeting room, taking notes for a press release that I would issue later that day to widespread indifference, the incongruousness of it all suddenly struck me. Here I was, some schmuck from suburban Sydney, a former gossip columnist no less, sitting in a meeting room, nodding sagely at the secretary-general of the United Nations as he enumerated the steps that needed to be taken to eradicate global poverty, yet all I could hear was the shrill squeal of "FRAUD!" echoing inside my head.

For four years now I had lived with the daily expectation that at some point someone official would sidle up to me, tap me on the shoulder, and whisper quietly in my ear: "I'm terribly sorry, Mr. Corbett, but the game is up. We know you're a fraud. Just come with us quietly. There's no need to make a fuss." And I knew that when that moment came, I *would* go with them quietly. I would shrug my shoulders, count my blessings that I had had such a good run, pack my laptop into my bag, smile apologetically at Kofi, and walk quietly away.

"But you have a secure job. Why would you leave it?" my mother would ask whenever I raised the specter of chucking it all in. "I don't understand your generation."

And how could she? She came from a generation that took on and held down jobs for life. My father worked for forty years in the same middle-management position in the same company. And so busy was he, paying a mortgage and putting three children through school, that pausing to ponder whether or not he was satisfied in his work was a luxury he couldn't afford.

But I was of the MTV generation. Our notoriously short attention spans, combined with the belief that jobs not only have to pay the bills but also must be personally fulfilling, constantly stimulating, and continually evolving, meant that I was becoming restless. For it's not enough for my generation to do a job because it pays the rent—we are cursed with the need to be *passionate* about it too.

The seeds of grass-is-greener-ism were starting to germinate. It would be only a matter of time before the first shoots poked up through the ground and demanded my attention.

Chapter 26

Lesson in French Love 3: Stop Laughing, This Is Serious

GIVEN THAT IT HAD BEEN a good twelve months since my last attempt to date a French woman—and apparently in the mood for another bout of self-flagellation—I found my love-radar once again tilting French-ward. The object of my affection this time was a Cameroonian princess called Angélique. I use the word *princess* here in its literal sense, as her father, a prominent Cameroonian politician in exile in France, was also the chief of the tribe from which he hailed. I first encountered Angélique at a party, where our eyes met across a crowded, smoke-filled, drunken room. She was exotic, attractive, and mysterious. I was drunk, loud, and obnoxious. The mutual attraction was immediate.

Whether sufficiently intrigued by my exotic Australianness, or dared by her friends, Angélique agreed to give me her telephone number. I emerged from the party quietly chuffed. A beautiful French maiden—short black hair in tiny dreadlocks, deep brown eyes, an electric smile, and skin the color and texture of velvet—had opened the door to another close encounter of the French female kind.

A few weeks of text-flirting ensued, and then a couple of dates saw us enter that gray zone known to all singles as a "sort of" an item. I say "sort of" for, as with most other things, when it came to my relationship with Angélique, I only ever understood every second word she said and hence was never really sure what was going on.

Despite four years in the country, the level of my ability to speak French had reached a depressing plateau. Due to a simple lack of sustained daily exposure to French-speaking people, I had not progressed much beyond what I liked to call Dinner Party French, a level that allows you to hold your own at a bar, restaurant, or dinner party. With Dinner Party French you could appear to be a halfway interesting human being as opposed to a monosyllabic idiot. Dinner Party French did not require an extensive vocabulary. It was a proficiency with the language that was directly proportional to the amount of wine you had imbibed. You can always tell when someone is fluent in Dinner Party French. When asked a question they do not understand, they will laugh out loud, emit a sotto voce *"ahh oui, oui, exactement,"* then quickly change the topic.

I was very good at Dinner Party French. Armed with this remarkable linguistic talent, I would spend hours with Angélique at bars or restaurants, talking about life, the universe, and everything. (At least I think that's what we talked about.) No subject was too random, no train of thought too disconnected, no desperate change of subject too obvious. In spite of—or perhaps because of—the nightly conversation gymnastics I would perform each time we met, the young Angélique obviously found the whole scenario entertaining enough to keep coming back for more.

Whether it was a social experiment on her part, to see how long one human being could talk without really knowing what he was saying, or whether it was basic relief at not having to sit opposite a cardigan-sporting, halitosis-ridden French man, Angélique consented to several enjoyable evenings out on the town. I often found her laughing at something I had said—despite the fact that I had not intended it to be funny. I was, if truth be told, never certain if I was being properly understood—which was disconcerting, but in a not altogether unpleasant way. As far as I was concerned, it was all a bit of a lark. A mutual fumble-about in the cross-cultural dark. A chance for a bit of fun and a few laughs.

And therein lay the problem. The laughs.

Now, I had often been told that I had what can only be described as a hearty laugh. Most times, it was an observation meant to flatter. In most countries, a good, loud laugh is infectious. It speaks of a jovial nature, a propensity for good humor and a warmth of character. Not in France. And especially not in restaurants in France. Whenever we would dine out together, Angélique would plead that I "stop laughing so loudly."

"Everyone is looking at us," she would explain, while quietly sinking into her chair, mortified. For if there is one thing the French hate, it is making a public spectacle of themselves. It is partially for this reason that they rarely get drunk. Control, and the personal maintenance of it at all times, is very important to the average French person. Loud outbursts of any nature, ostentatious displays of spontaneity, and the unpredictability of drunkenness are anathema to the French. Indeed, the thought that people might be looking at you, that you had momentarily abandoned the studied cool of essential Frenchness, could send a Frenchie into paroxysms of embarrassment.

It was a lesson I had learned well, having been shooshed on many occasions by waiters keen to quell the robust behavior of a table of noisy expatriate diners, of which I was often a member. Buoyed by alcohol—in that manner so tragically typical of Anglo-Saxons—we were an island of bawdiness in a sea of French restraint. Obnoxious? Undoubtedly. Having fun? Definitely. The inevitable remonstrations of fellow diners always seemed to contain a conflicting mixture of envy and contempt. You sensed that they wanted to participate, to go a bit wild, but centuries of buttoned-up French culture prevented it. The French had plenty of hair, especially the men, but no idea whatsoever how to let it down.

This was never so true as when applied to French stag and hen's nights, which are, without question, the most joyless events you are ever likely to witness. I have attended funerals that were more fun than the smile-free zones that constitute a French bachelor or bachelorette party. And while I would be the last to hold up as a shining model the Anglo versions of these occasions (marked as they inevitably are by strippers, stupid outfits, and a strict drink-till-you-vomit principle), the French sure could learn a thing from them about having a good time.

Your average French bachelorette night takes place at about two in the afternoon—the simple inability to get the time of day right perhaps indicative of a deeper misunderstanding of the wider concept. It usually requires the bride-to-be to don a silly outfit, a zebra-print dress, a set of pigtails, a wacky pair of stockings, and always, but always, a veil. With the other hens in tow, she then walks listlessly around the streets of Paris, possessed of the mistaken notion that just looking stupid will be a barrel of laughs. She will occasionally be encouraged to interact with random members of the public, usually in a sheepish and painfully forced manner, while her friends stand back and watch in horrified embarrassment. There is no laughter and no giggling, barely even a titter. Perhaps crucially, there is no alcohol. The entire enterprise is entered into with a maximum of seriousness, as if this walk on the flippant side is as vital a rite of passage for an aspiring bride as buying the dress and choosing the church hymns.

One Saturday afternoon I sat in a park behind my apartment in the Marais and watched with fascination as one such scene played out before me. The bride-to-be, dressed as some appropriation of a Pippy Longstocking character and bearing a basket filled with different cordials, walked from one park bench to the other offering complete strangers a glass of milk with—wait for it—their choice of mint or raspberry flavoring. The hilarity was so striking, it was all I could do not to split my sides with amusement. Her girlfriends, meanwhile, all stood back in a cringing huddle of humiliation-by-association, looking at their watches, whispering among themselves, and willing the entire, awful experience to be over.

French bachelor parties are no better. Sticking the groom-to-be in a wig and a dress, and sending him out onto the streets in broad daylight, seemed to be preferred modus operandi among young French males. It was called *"l'enterrement de la vie d'un garçon"*—or "the burial of the life of a boy"—and looked about as much fun. A listless gaggle of bored twenty-something men trooped about the city in jeans and sneakers, participating in a joke that they weren't convinced was funny. You wanted to march up to them and force each of them to shotgun a beer or three. You wanted to tell them to wait until the sun went down, when the cover of night would make their japes funnier. You wanted to grab the groom and tie him naked to a traffic light. Something, anything to relieve them (and those of us forced to watch them cringe) of the ordeal they were reluctantly enduring.

Maybe they were having fun. Maybe they would look back on that day twenty years hence and reflect on how madcap they had been in their youth. Maybe wanting to force fun down their throats was the worst form of cultural imperialism. But watching them traipse about the city, dying of self-consciousness, you just wanted to put them out of their misery. It was like watching a helpless animal in pain, their eyes haunted with torment and confusion. You wanted to tell them to take off the wig, slip back into something conservative, and pop into the relative anonymity of a smoky café and assume their preferred position of happy, contemplative philosophical discussion. And you just knew nothing would have made them happier.

THE SAME HUMOR DEFICIT that separated me from the greater French population was now playing havoc with my budding relationship with young Angélique. A lack of mutual laughs made proceedings strained, but it was the chasm in dating etiquette into which our fledgling relationship finally, fatally stumbled.

In a last-ditch attempt to breathe life into the fun-free zone that constituted our liaison, I suggested a Sunday evening at the movies. What could be more simple and uncomplicated, I reasoned, than a guy and a girl going off to a movie together, just as guys and girls had on Sunday evenings for as long as celluloid existed? I phoned Sunday morning to fix the date for later that night, then went about my day. One hour before our scheduled rendezvous, the phone rang. It was Angélique.

"Something has come up, and I cannot make it tonight. I'm really sorry," she said.

"Oh," I replied, somewhat taken aback. "Oh. Okay. Well, I hope everything is all right. I'll call you later in the week." And with that the phone call ended.

Not wanting to waste a perfectly good moviegoing opportunity, I immediately phoned Julien, and we arranged to meet at the cinema in forty-five minutes. As I was standing in the ticket line at the cinema barely an hour later, chatting to Jules, the cell phone shrilled again. It was Angélique.

"What happened?" she demanded, sounding genuinely confused.

"I'm sorry?" I replied. "I don't follow. What do you mean, what happened?"

"You didn't call me back," she retorted, this time with a tone of indignation.

"But you told me something had come up and that you couldn't make the movie. Why would I have called you back?"

"If you really wanted to see me, you would have called me back and insisted I come to the movies. Convinced me I had to come to the movies with you," she explained tersely.

I was struck dumb.

"Ummm, okay," I replied. "Look, I've got to go. I'll call you later."

"Who was that?" asked Julien, noticing the look of utter bemusement on my face.

I explained what had happened and professed I hadn't a clue what it all meant.

"*Mon vieux,* this is the French woman. You must ask her three times if you want her to come out with you. She will say no twice before she says yes. They want to feel as though you really want to be with them."

But I was officially done with game-playing. I was but a simple Aussie lad, from a country where a spade is emphatically a spade. If a girl wanted to come out with you, she would say yes, and no further correspondence would be entered into.

No, I decided, this was definitely the unfathomable French female antic to break the back of all my efforts to date French women. From now on, unless she was exceptional and had lived for a sustained period overseas and thus had the rougher edges of French femaleness rubbed off, I was officially not interested.

Chapter 27

Why French Women Don't Get Fat

AILING AS I DO from the monoseasonal Antipodes—where the weather oscillates between mildly warm and stinking hot—living in France was a revelation. For the better part of my childhood and early adult life, I was blissfully unaware that such things as seasons actually existed. Certainly, there were times at school in Sydney when everyone would don long trousers and sport itchy woolen sweaters over their mint-green cotton short-sleeve shirts, but the mercury never dipped much below 68 degrees Fahrenheit. Yet here in Paris, in the upper latitudes of the northern hemisphere, there were suddenly four distinct seasons. Who knew?

Summer in Paris is month after glorious month of languid nights spent sipping Sancerre in outdoor cafés. It's dramatic sunsets, daylight until eleven p.m., and Rollerblading at midnight in the court of the Louvre. When autumn comes, it transforms the city into a vivid palette of reds, yellows, and oranges. It's a stroll along the Seine beside cypress trees shimmering yellow, a walk through the Jardin du Luxembourg with the fallen leaves of the plane tree crunching underfoot. Winter, by stark comparison, is one interminably long gray day. Only the occasional flurry of snow or flash of tepid sunshine breaks the cold monotony. Winter is the season that seems to have no end. In the run-up to Christmas and New Year's the cold and rain and darkness are all a bit of a novelty, but thereafter the remaining winter months are a painful plod under a sky of perpetual gray.

And then, just when one more sunless day is going to send you over the edge, the miracle of spring arrives. Trees that have been skeletal all winter start to sprout leaves. The first daffodils push through the sodden earth like the advance guard of an army of flowers just waiting to bloom in their wake. As the weather warms, girls who have been buried in layers of clothing for months don sundresses. And the silent cue is given for the start of a most remarkable French tradition—the flirting season.

Responding to primal instincts that you only otherwise ever see displayed on the Discovery Channel, the French come out of their winter hibernation in a state of heightened arousal. If you are a woman in Paris, spring marks the start of six months of fending off horny French men, ignoring unsolicited declarations of undying love, and rejecting spontaneous offers of marriage. For French men, spring means tapping your inner caveman and comporting yourself like a dog in heat. To the untrained eye it may look like unsuspecting women are being set upon by a salivating pack of libido-crazed men, but it's all part of a finely tuned choreography, honed over generations. In fact, contrary to appearances, there's a wonderful sense of complicity when it comes to flirting in France. Men and women practice it with the same level of gusto. And rather than being the means to any particular end, it is a veritable pastime itself. People in Paris don't flirt just because they want to end up in bed together. They flirt because it is a vital part of being Parisian. A sensual energy envelops the city in spring, a heady friction fed by countless stolen glances, coquettish smiles, and subtle acknowledgments of mutual attraction.

To make eye contact with a French woman in a bar, on the Métro, or on the street is not to say "I want to shag you senseless." Rather, it is to say "You have made an effort to look good today, I acknowledge that effort, I find you attractive, I will now entertain naughty thoughts about what you look like naked, have a nice day." If, for whatever reason, you do end up in bed, that is simply a fringe benefit.

Far from being offended at being checked out on the street, most French women enjoy it. After all, the alternative is to be ignored and unremarkable—a fate too horrible for any French woman to contemplate.

The reason that chairs in outdoor cafés in Paris all face outward is not because the French are too busy pouting to actually talk to each other; it is to facilitate the gentle art of flirting. Flirting can be as simple as holding a woman's gaze across a crowded room or sending a glass of Champagne to her table with your compliments. It's engaging her in witty chat or philosophical discussion, complimenting her on her clothes, hair, or eyes. It's the gentle, accidental brush of two skins, and the frisson it invariably creates.

On trips home to Australia, armed with a new arsenal of European flirting techniques, I was able to chat easily with the ranks of attractive young things who were otherwise standing listlessly in bars, dressed to the nines, desperately trying to compete with the rugby league telecast in the corner. In Australia the closest a male comes to flirting is asking a woman to pass him his schooner of beer.

My Paris sojourn had taught me a great deal about relations between the sexes. Living with French women had been a wonderful experience. More than anything else, it was a joy to live in a city surrounded by them. Always elegant and always stylish, it wasn't so much what they wore or how they wore it that was appealing, but more the way they carried themselves. Their poise was alluring. It spoke of a deep understanding of what it is to be feminine, and what it takes to catch the eye of the opposite sex. And yet there was still so much about the French woman that I found unfathomable. And apparently I wasn't the only one.

Several years into my Paris experience, bookstores and bedside tables the world over were heaving under the weight of a nonfiction best-seller titled *French Women Don't Get Fat.* Penned by a French matron whose breadth of experience appeared to have been confined to the haughty salons of Paris's exclusive sixteenth arrondissement—populated as they are by minted dowagers with too much hair spray, too much time on their finely manicured hands, and complexions like preserved fruit—the book purported to account for the mystery as to why there are very few obese women in France. The author advanced all manner of fanciful theories: they never snack, they have three square meals a day, they eat good-quality produce, and—my personal favorite—they don't rush their food at mealtimes but savor every mouthful. Certainly these theories go some way to accounting for the fact that unlike many of its Western city counterparts, Paris is home to very few obese women (or for that matter men). During my stay in the City of Light, I had certainly seen my fair share of the city's women and had come to appreciate the effort they made to keep themselves trim.

But rather than attributing this national slimness to particular eating habits or the relative quality of French foodstuffs, my own theory about why French women don't get fat can be explained in two simple words: *nervous energy.* More than in any other country in the world, French women are forced to spend their lives in a state of almost permanent angst, worrying about whether their husbands are cheating on them. So ingrained is the concept of infidelity in the French popular consciousness, I used to wonder if it was taught as a mandatory course at school. Watch any French film, examine the lives of any of the country's public figures, and you will see infidelity celebrated as a national sport. From former presidents to pop stars, heads of companies to market vendors. French men even have a widely used term for the mistress they meet between leaving work and returning home for dinner with the family: the *cinq à sept,* or "five to seven." It is even quite common for many richer Lotharios to have secret studio apartments in Paris, bought especially for the purpose of conducting these early evening affairs.

You would also be forgiven for thinking that the French film industry exists solely to eulogize infidelity—and invariably that variation that involves older men copping off with nubile young Lolitas. Predominantly made by men in their fifties, French cinema offers up an endless parade of paunchy Pierres being lustily pursued by pert teens just dying to be ravished by men old enough to be their grandfathers. Midlife crisis, anyone? It's certainly no accident that Woody Allen films are perennially popular in France.

And so it is, in this pressure-cooker environment, that French women's waistlines remain stubbornly slim. Never mind three square meals a day. A packet of Marlboro Lights and a couple of Xanax are more like it.

As a direct result, French women, especially those in their mid- to late twenties, can never be close friends. They are either in constant competition to steal one another's partners or are locked in fierce battles with their sisters to snare an eligible member of the opposite sex. Unlike in Anglo-Saxon cultures, where bands of females can regularly be seen out on the town engaging in such admirable sisterhood activities as whooping it up in a restaurant or drinking themselves into a stupor at a bar, you never see large groups of French women out together. They're too busy at home plotting to steal their girlfriend's husband or imagining the affairs being pursued by their partners.

All of which makes for a dream scenario for the average French male. Women on tap, emaciated from the nervous energy required to be a *femme française,* and constantly struggling to win your affection. On balance, it's a pretty good deal. Consequently, the French man doesn't need to try very hard to make himself attractive to the fairer sex. Which could go some way to explaining why most of them are about as sexy as a garden gnome and laid-back to the point of being horizontal. They are awful dressers for whom the height of fashion is a pair of boat shoes and a pastel sweater tied around the neck. And their hair seems to be kept according to the Samson principle of more equals virile.

And it certainly doesn't help matters that to complement their monopoly on local women, a ready supply of gullible female sex tourists passes through Paris determined to nab themselves a little famed French loving. Susceptibility to a thick French accent and a litany of insincere declarations of love is not, it seems, restricted to one nationality.

American, British, Australian—you name it. They come, they hear, they swoon. Perfectly sensible female friends of mine, rational in all other facets of their lives, melt in the face of a few strategically uttered platitudes. "I have never felt this way before" and "you are the most beautiful woman I have ever seen" might sound to most rational mortals like the cheesiest lines ever invented. But deliver them in a French accent, with bad breath, wearing a shockingly awful outfit, and standing five-foot nothing—and you are guaranteed to get lucky.

Perhaps unsurprisingly, relations between the sexes in France border on the Neanderthal. You would be hard-pressed to find a French man who believed he could be "just friends" with a woman without at some point wanting to jump her bones.

So if the French woman appears always distant, aloof, and mysterious, it's because she believes the only way to keep a man interested is to create—and doggedly maintain—a sense of mystery. Working on the principle that men want only what they cannot have, French women work hard to keep their men constantly guessing—eternally on edge, always off-kilter, forever on their toes. All of which makes for a minefield for the expatriate who innocently decides to delve into the French dating world.

On the few occasions when I decided to throw caution to the wind and "go French," I stumbled at the first hurdle, confounded by a set of rules I didn't know and confused by behavior I didn't recognize.

Asking a French woman out on a simple date was an exercise in strategic mind games. Any initial overture from me, whether it was an invitation to dinner or a suggestion of a Sunday stroll in the park, would be met by a carefully cultivated coolness on her part. If finally she relented and deigned to let me take her for dinner, I would invariably find myself seated opposite a shadow of the vibrant, interesting woman who had initially caught my eye. All monosyllabic responses and moodiness, it made for an excruciating couple of hours.

My experience with Angélique had taught me that when it came to French women, *no* often meant *maybe,* *yes* could mean *no,* and *maybe* sometimes meant *yes*—and there was no way of telling which was which. And thanks largely to this sliding scale of consent, perfected by French women over generations and practiced to widespread effect, the male of the French species is invariably left disoriented, uncertain, and very, very tetchy.

As far as I could fathom, French dating lore required the man to doggedly pursue the woman, no matter how many knock-backs and obstacles were thrown his way. Not to do so indicated a lack of proper intent—and, in my case at least, complete ignorance of the established rituals of Gallic male-female interaction refined over thousands of years. It certainly went some way to explaining an experience I had had, post Angélique, when I foolishly decided to dip my toe back into the French dating world and invited a lovely young French woman out on a dinner date.

While I tap-danced my way through the three courses of one-sided conversation, she sat there silently, appearing bored and smothering any chance of real human interaction with her studied aloofness. Yes, it is entirely possible she simply wasn't interested in me, but why come out on the date in the first place? And why subsequently tell a mutual friend that she was mystified when I never called her again?

Later, I would reflect on the confused fumblings that passed for my repeated attempts at dating the locals and wonder if I shouldn't have played them at their own game. Would it really have killed me to undertake a bit of role-playing, profess undying love for women I barely knew, and then prove that love by submitting myself to a series of humiliating putdowns and faux rejections? I decided that yes, it most definitely would have killed me. And I was determined not to do it. It would have felt contrived. Basic dignity dictated that there were depths to which I refused to sink to take a lover. A simple reluctance to profess sentiments I did not possess did not, in my eyes, make me unromantic, but rather honest and practical—surely two more enduring traits in a potential partner.

Nope. The French could keep their complicated courting customs. That it appeared to work for them was great, but I needed something simpler, more straightforward. In short, I needed the comfort of something familiar. But where to find it?

Chapter 28

Creatures of the Night

THE AUSTRALIAN EMBASSY is something of an architectural anomaly in the City of Light. A great, gray, Harry Seidler–designed blob of concrete squatting beside the Seine, in the shadow of the Eiffel Tower, it looks for all the world as if it had been dropped into the otherwise elegant cityscape from another architectural galaxy. Built on a patch of land that (some say appropriately) was once a riverside rubbish dump, the embassy and its staff regularly play host to visiting exhibitions of Aboriginal art, stage receptions for touring Aussie rugby teams, and throw an occasional summer party for Aussie expats and Oz-friendly Frenchies.

Under the patronage of a former Australian ambassador to France, William Fisher, these parties were the highlight of the Parisian diplomatic calendar. The Brits would stage a stuffy tea party on the queen's birthday, and the Yanks would throw a sterile reception for the Fourth of July, but it was the Australian Embassy's annual summer party to which everyone coveted an invite. There was a barbecue in the gardens, free-flowing Fosters, and often even an expatriate Aussie band entertaining the crowd. People talked, drank, ate, and danced. The parties were loud, rambunctious assertions of Australianness in the shadow of the Eiffel Tower.

They were also, as I was happily to discover at the summer party of 2003, a chance to cross paths with fellow expat Australians from infinitely more exotic walks of life. Like, for example, Lido dancers. The Lido de Paris, for the sadly uninitiated, is a world-famous cabaret show, situated a stone's throw from the Arc de Triomphe on the Champs Elysées. A more sophisticated version of its better-known cabaret cousin, the Moulin Rouge, the Lido presents a nightly confection of stunning costumes, breathtaking sets, and seminaked, long-legged dancers. When it first opened in 1946, the Lido represented the height of French sophistication. Attended nightly by a glittering array of besuited and bejeweled members of the international jet set, it justly laid claim to the title of "the world's most famous nightclub." Shirley MacLaine, Frank Sinatra, and Sammy Davis Jr. were just some of the visiting American stars who "played" the Lido. But the main attraction at the Lido had always been its signature lineup of scantily clad beauties.

Draped in jewels and adorned with feathers, Lido dancers had entertained and enthralled generations of visitors to Paris. Performing for up to two thousand people a night, the sixty-five Lido dancers were the world's best at what they did. They were renowned for being extremely tall, for having legs that ran up to their shoulder blades, and perhaps not surprisingly, for the fact that many of them danced topless. And whether the Lido's impressively numerous clientele came away from their evening of cabaret on the Champs Elysées impressed by the costumes, wowed by the sets, or mesmerized by the carefully choreographed parade of beautiful women, a night at the Lido was an experience not easily forgotten.

Gracing the embassy with their presence on this particular night were two Lido dancers, both of them down-home Aussie girls who had been performing on the Paris stage for more than ten years between them. If you laid them end to end, Shay Stafford and Lisa Norman would measure an impressive twelve feet one inch. As it was, the statuesque duo were standing upright on this particular night, smack bang in the center of a four-hundred-strong party crowd. They couldn't have been more obvious.

Shay had striking blue eyes and a figure that curved in all the right places. Lisa was a dark-eyed beauty with long brown hair and softly tanned skin. Both were wearing figure-hugging jeans and designer tops. Even from my vantage point a good twenty yards away, I could sense glamour oozing from their every pore.

They tried for all the world to blend in with the crowd, to not draw attention to themselves—a task rendered fruitless by their towering stature and otherworldly beauty. Two creatures of the night, straight from a fragrant heaven. A pair of ethereal beauties alighting briefly on this seething scene of plebeian drunkenness before floating off again to take the stage of the Lido and become objects of fantasy for two thousand eager paying customers.

Every male in the room was either subconsciously aware of their presence or outright staring. By the time I arrived, a brave posse of sacrificial lambs had already formed a competitive circle around the girls, throwing humility to the winds and trying to make an impression with desperately rendered attempts at witty repartee. If you stood and watched for long enough, you could see the gaggle of suitors take turns to line the girls up, fix them in their crosshairs, deliver a volley of pickup lines, then ultimately nose-dive into a spectacular crash and burn. Bodies were strewn in a growing pile around the girls, a harbinger to those, like me, who despite the odds were still prepared to try to make an impression on the lovely young ladies.

Spying my opportunity to strike, I moved in.

James, a hulking redheaded friend who worked at the embassy and had once played representative rugby for Australia, was playing chaperone to the showgirls. Known in our circle as "Aussie James" to differentiate him from "Posse James," he was a friend of Shay's brother, and whether out of loyalty to his friend or for the purposes of maintaining a few basic Embassy hygiene standards, he was doing a decent job of keeping the drooling parade of men at bay. I cunningly selected the two best-looking men around me—Will and Dr. Steve (a visiting

Australian bowel surgeon, I kid you not)—to be my wingmen. My reasoning was simple: between looking in the mirror and showing up to work, the showgirls would be so tired of being exposed to physical perfection they would dismiss my wingmen out of hand and be fascinated instead with me—the quirky, funny-looking one.

And so I made my approach. Employing the most transparent ploy in the book, I made straight for James.

"James! Mate!" I said, bowling up to the chaperone and slapping him on the back. "How are you, buddy? Long time no see!" I looked across at his glamorous charges. "Good evening, ladies."

James took one look at me, took in the wingmen, shook his head, and started laughing. "Bryce Corbett. What a surprise," he replied. "I wondered how long it was going to take you. And I see you've come with backup."

After a reluctantly proffered introduction, I segued straight into my pitch. I knew that if I was going to hit my mark, I had to act quickly. Out of the corner of my eye I was aware of the squadron of eager suitors buzzing around our intimate little group, all lining up to make their own approaches. I needed to give it everything I had—and fast. Flying straight in, I hit the ladies with a concerted volley of humorous strafing fire, designed to throw them off their guard. I then followed through by lobbing a couple of mortars of pure wit. I parried and lunged. I danced, I ducked, and I dived. At the end of my performance, I could all but hear them thinking: *Who is this odd little man? And why won't he stop talking?* But if I was destined to crash and burn, at least I would do it in good company. After all, I wasn't the only one making an abject fool of myself.

"I'm a doctor," Dr. Steve volunteered, apropos of nothing in particular. The girls nodded indulgently. *Damn!* I thought to myself. *He's playing his trump card early.* I had to act fast.

"He's a bowel surgeon, actually," I riposted. The girls' faces fell.

Then it was Will's turn: "So, can I get either of you girls another Tim Tam?" *Cunning,* I thought to myself. *Appeal to their nostalgic side, feign interest in their culture despite knowing nothing about it— not bad.*

"Ha! Tim Tam! He's English!" I blurted out. "He wouldn't know a Tim Tam if he fell over one. So anyway, tell me more about the Lido. I work as a journalist, and I would be really interested in writing an article about you." It was admittedly a cheap shot, and I could feel the engine of my Tiger Moth faltering, its nose dipping southward. The girls, to their credit, were extremely affable. Far from being fazed by the flurry of attention, they weathered it with a remarkable patience—benevolent, almost pitying smiles pasted on their lovely faces.

And so the encounter went: twenty long minutes of three otherwise lucid, intelligent men falling on their arses. Glancing at their watches and mustering what almost passed for genuine disappointment, the girls announced they had a show to put on. They made their excuses and left. The room was heaving with the noise of drunken freeloaders, but as they retreated, I could have sworn I heard peals of showgirl laughter.

"Can you believe that hyperactive little one actually pulled that journalist line?" was among the remarks I imagined were being thrown from one Lido dancer to the other as they took flight back to the land of ethereal, from whence they came.

IT WAS NO small surprise, then, that when I stumbled across the showgirls at another embassy function a month later, they deigned to speak to me. It was Bastille Day, and the Australian ambassador was hosting a barbecue on his seventh-floor outdoor terrace for a handful of prominent Australians in Paris to watch the traditional Bastille Day fireworks. For reasons still unclear to me, I was on the invitation list and so happily joined a small crowd sipping Champagne and watching the sun set behind the Eiffel Tower. The view across the Seine, above the rooftops of Paris, and onto the Eiffel Tower from the ambassador's residence was just magical. The last of the day's sun had turned the gray-topped, limestone buildings lining the Seine and Champ de Mars a golden honeycomb color.

As we shucked oysters and feasted on fine barbecue fare, basking in the warmth of the summer evening, I mustered the courage to once again throw myself prostrate at the feet of the showgirls. Tonight, flanked by a more classic, staid embassy crowd, they were in need of party allies, and I was only too happy to step up to the plate.

"Hi," I ventured, sauntering up to Shay. "We met at the party here the other week."

A faint smile of amusement crept across her face. "Oh yes, I remember. The journalist, right? Dying to write an article about Australian dancers at the Lido."

She held herself with such composure. Every part of her sublime body seemed effortlessly poised. Back straight, shoulders pulled back, and head held high. It was a dancer's posture, imbued with a haughty, impenetrable dignity. It was extremely sexy. She took a sip from her Champagne and looked at me expectantly for a response.

"Hmmm?" I uttered, jolted from a moment's private reverie and suddenly aware that I had been staring. "Right, of course. The story. Well, you know, we should maybe get together sometime over coffee, and you can tell me a little bit about what it's like to be a Lido dancer. Or we could get together for a drink. You know. Or a dinner. Depending on whether you get any. Dinners, that is. Whether you get any dinners, what with your work schedule and all. Not whether you get any—because that's not really any of my business."

I was babbling again. She looked out across the view. The smile had crept back onto her face. "I'd like that," she said. "To get together over dinner, that is."

Now it was my turn to laugh. Mostly out of pure relief.

As the night crept on, the sky turned a stunning orange, then a deep red, before finally succumbing to the rich indigo of a typical Parisian midsummer night.

Shay and I chatted and laughed. With my initial clumsy attempts at communication behind us, conversation came easily. We talked in a kind of familiar shorthand, a product of two strikingly similar cultural and family backgrounds and two senses of humor perfectly attuned to each other. She was beautiful, she was clever, she was witty and fun. I am sure there were other people at the party, but I don't remember any of them. All I remember was a pair of sparkling eyes, a laugh that was infectious, and a warmth of spirit that made you feel good just being around.

I wasn't aware of it then, but I had already developed a crush. It had been a long time since I was in love, but that night, with Paris at my feet and a showgirl by my side, something stirred in my long-dormant heart.

And then the fireworks started.

Chapter 29

C'est Pas Possible!

COMING UP TO THE END of my fourth year in France, it was time, I decided, to take stock. I resolved to try something novel for the occasion and hence opted for a night in with a home-cooked meal. Outside the street was slicked black from a recent burst of ice-cold rain. Autumn had taken hold of the city. People wrapped in heavy coats rushed down the rue outside my window, huddled against the chill and running to escape the rain. I cracked open a bottle of Talisker whiskey, cranked up the heat, lit a few candles, and sat in my orange-walled womb, reflecting on how much I had penetrated the city in the last four years and exactly how far my assimilation as an honorary Parisian had progressed.

I was still known as *le kangarou* to my neighbors and most of the store and café owners in the street. It was clear I was never going to be a fully integrated Frenchie, but I had nonetheless done a reasonable job getting my head around many of the country's unique cultural quirks. Even so, there were many mysteries about the French that I would never fathom. So time-honored, so steeped in history, and so much a part of the cultural fabric of the nation were they, I could never hope to make sense of them.

Why, for instance, did many old Parisian apartments have the shower cubicle in the kitchen? Was it a plumbing issue, requiring that all water pipes in an apartment pass through the same room? Was it a peculiarly French time-saving device, allowing people to incorporate the washing of dirty dishes with their daily ablutions? And when and where did it become a good idea to encourage the wide distribution of electric toilets? During the last four years I had had occasion to use an electric toilet more times than I cared to remember. And while they might have been great for conserving water, there was always something unnerving about squatting over what is essentially an industrial-sized blender.

And why was Johnny Hallyday, a 1950s teen idol, still the most popular recording artist in France? Come to think of it, what was with the French predilection for all things 1950s? Especially rock-and-roll dancing? Why was it that no matter what music was playing, be it swing, a waltz, jazz, heavy metal, or techno, the French would always find a way to dance Le Roc to it? Was the jive taught to them at school along with their times tables? Were they honestly so blinkered as to believe that the rest of the world was also still jitterbugging and twisting, fifty years after the music's birth? Elvis was dead, so why was this nation still stuck in a collective dance time warp?

These French conundrums consumed me as I sipped thoughtfully on my tumbler of Talisker. No matter how long I stayed, I concluded, I was destined never to properly work them out. But my stay in *la belle France* hadn't been a complete waste of time. With some contentment I sat back and reflected on the marrow I had sucked out of life since arriving in Paris. And with no small amount of pride I enumerated the cultural idiosyncrasies that I had managed to unravel.

One revelation, which had come admittedly later in my Paris existence than was strictly desirable, was the discovery of the "Two Nos Before a Yes" principle. This is the unwritten law underpinning the entire service industry in France. A rule unknown to tourists and recently arrived expats, it states that for every request you make of a sales assistant, bank clerk, Métro ticket-seller, or bureaucrat—anyone, that is, who you might mistakenly think exists to provide you with a service— you will receive two negative responses before you get an affirmative one. It's a rule that can be applied no matter what the scenario. Need to change a train ticket? Steel yourself for two emphatic denials before you see any cooperation. Want to seek an extension on payment of your tax bill? Prepare to weather a double barrage of emphatic *nons* before a *oui, d'accord* miraculously appears. Want to convince a French woman to sleep with you? Pay no attention whatsoever to the first two rejections, safe in the knowledge that acquiescence is but one more attempt away. True, in the process of learning to dance this elaborate social tango, your average newcomer to France loses a lot of time and money. But it was a rite of passage, I now understood, and once you were in the club, a whole world of possibilities eventually opened up to you. Yes, I thought as I watched a gaggle of boys tramp down the street in clothing patently unsuitable for the plunging temperatures, grasping the Two Nos Before a Yes principle had made my life in Paris remarkably easier.

If only I had had a similar level of success penetrating that great cornerstone of the French system—the *c'est pas possible, c'est toujours comme ça* conundrum. Spend a reasonable amount of time in the country, and you cannot help but come to the conclusion that everything in France starts from the default position of impossible. *"C'est pas possible!"* is a refrain you hear from the *boulangerie* to the presidency. It's the knee-jerk response to any and every question. The *c'est pas possible* assertion is neatly complemented by the *c'est toujours comme ça* explanation. The first states the absolute impossibility of something coming to pass; the second buttresses the initial statement with an explanation against which there is no rational argument. *What you are asking of me is not possible because it has always been like that.*

It's an impenetrable circle of negativism, a perfectly self-contained circular argument that frustrates French people, expats, and tourists alike on a daily basis. And don't bother pointing out the illogicality of it all. Your argument will be met only with a Gallic shrug, a prototypical pursing of the lips, and the sharp exhalation of air. Together these two seemingly innocent expressions encapsulate all that is infuriating about the French. A reluctance to change. A complete aversion to the notion of customer service. And a smugness that asserts that *la méthode française* is the only way ever to do anything.

Take, for example, ordering a steak in a Paris restaurant. French chefs are justifiably proud of the extremely high quality of their country's cuisine. Chances are they know better than 90 percent of their clientele exactly how to cook a steak to make it taste best. But if a customer has a penchant for rump burnt to a crisp, then surely they can expect to receive their steak appropriately well done.

"Do you suppose the chef could cook this steak really well?" a customer might reasonably ask of his waiter. "I mean really well—black on the outside, no blood on the inside.

"Non monsieur," comes the inevitable reply. *"C'est pas possible."*

"Um, why not?"

"Parce que c'est toujours comme ça." Argue your way around that one.

The tide in the Talisker bottle was fast retreating. While outside a light rain had started to fall, inside, the list of timeless French imponderables was growing.

The Two Nos Before a Yes principle and the *Pas possible—toujours comme ça* conundrum were certainly annoying, I thought to myself, but neither of them held a candle to the great French *normalement* phenomenon. Translated literally, *normalement* means "normally" or "usually." Coming from the mouth of a French person, especially one whose job it supposedly is to provide you with a customer service, it has the power to make your blood bubble with rage. The word is employed to give a level of vagueness to proceedings, a noncommittal answer to a specific question. Rather frustratingly, I most often encountered the word used by people in the transportation industry.

"I wonder if you could tell me if there is a train this afternoon for Marseille?" you might ask a ticket vendor.

"Normalement" would come the reply.

"Do you mean normally yes, or normally no?"

"I mean normally there is a train this afternoon to Marseille. Whether the one scheduled to run this afternoon actually does, well, I couldn't tell you."

Setting aside the fact that the vendor was technically correct, his statement was unhelpful in that manner that French people have perfected over centuries—and was therefore infuriating. After all, it wasn't as if you were asking for a cast-iron guarantee. In the event the train did not run because of unforeseeable circumstances—an act of God, say, or a derailment—you were hardly likely to hunt down the ticket vendor and beat him to a pulp. And yet he refused to give a definitive answer, for to do so would be to assume responsibility and possibly invite blame should his pronouncement not come to pass. Better to shirk responsibility with a noncommittal response. That way, nothing would ever be his fault.

Yes, there were things that I had no hope of ever understanding, cultural chasms that would never be breached. But after four years, all things considered, I figured I was doing okay. I had a great network of friends, a cushy, well-paid job, an overactive social life, and a six-month-a-year travel itinerary that was as full as it was interesting. On the personal-life front, things were starting to look up too. I had just met a lovely Australian showgirl to whom, over a period of some months, I was starting to become closer. Shay's nocturnal work schedule, which sat at complete odds to my nine-to-five responsibilities, meant that we only seemed to enjoy semiregular phone contact and the occasional crossing of paths at dinners and parties thrown by mutual friends. But even so, there was definite love-interest potential there. What's more, Paris had just started to feel very much like home. *Un kangarou* I might well have been, but one with a stripy shirt, a curled mustache, and a beret.

With the whiskey warming my belly, I switched on my laptop to check my e-mails before turning in for the night. A message from the human resources manager at work caught my attention.

Please come and see me first thing in the morning, it read. *There is a very serious problem with your residency status. According to our records you have been working and living in France illegally for the past four years. This situation cannot continue.*

Chapter 30

I Have Gas, Therefore I Am

THE MOST IMPORTANT DOCUMENT you will ever possess in France is a gas bill. It's not much to look at, just your run-of-the-mill utilities bill—blue header across the top of a white page, boring government-inspired utilities logo in one corner, large boldface font enumerating how much you owe in the other corner. Yet gas bills in France are gold dust. Get yourself on the receiving end of one of these babies, and the rest of your French existence is pretty much assured. For the entire French system is built on the premise that once a person is connected to—and presumably consuming—gas, they are a fully functioning human being and a worthy member of French society. Until such time as a person is gassed up, they simply do not exist.

As any new arrival in France knows only too well, you cannot get a bank account without a gas bill, yet you cannot get a gas bill unless you have a bank account. Similarly, you cannot get an apartment without a gas bill, but you cannot get a gas bill until you have an apartment to which to connect gas. Most people decry this organizational catch-22 as another example of illogical French bureaucracy. But I preferred to give the Frogs the benefit of the doubt, seeing it as a canny immigration-control mechanism, a hidden test of a person's intelligence, enterprise, and cunning. If you aren't clever or conniving enough to wheedle your way around the system to get a gas bill—if you can't work out the riddle—you have no business being in France.

Clever and conniving had never been much of a problem for me. As a result, I had managed to get a gas bill within weeks of arriving in France. But law-abiding and regulation-heeding were apparently two areas in which I needed a bit of work. As a result, what I seemed *not* to possess, as my human resources manager was carefully explaining to me now as I sat in her office, was a valid residency permit.

"So when you say I am illegal, what exactly do you mean?" I asked, assuming that this being France, there were bound to be shades of legality.

"I mean you are illegal," she replied matter-of-factly. "You are not supposed to be living here in France. We are not supposed to be employing you. It seems we have been employing you illegally for the past four years. You were supposed to renew your residency card every year, and you apparently didn't. If the French government finds out, you will be deported, and we will be in big, big trouble."

Right, I thought to myself. *Not much in the way of shade there then.*

To say that I didn't know I had been an illegal alien in France for four years would be to stretch the truth—but just a little. It wasn't so much that I was acutely, cunningly aware that my status as a foreigner in France was what the authorities like to call *irrégulière*; it was more a case of me sort of knowing it, but preferring not to dwell upon it. The situation, when you looked at it, was quite absurd. Here I was, the holder of a relatively senior executive position at a respected international organization whose relations with the French government went to the highest level, and I had been an illegal alien for the past four years. It was a situation born less out of shrewd design than out of abject laziness. For to renew my so-called *carte de séjour* (or residency card) each year would have required me to visit the *préfecture de police* at least once every twelve months, take my place in the line-with-no-end and lose at least a day and a half of my life to inefficient French bureaucracy.

I could never be bothered, was never apprised by my employer of the seriousness of this oversight, and therefore had no reason to think that lacking a valid *carte de séjour* was any kind of serious problem. God knows I had been in and out of the country almost fifty times in that four-year period and had never been questioned about my vastly out-of-date residency permit.

As I walked back to my desk, a little freaked out, I began to ponder the options before me. They weren't numerous, as far as I could see. I could throw my hands up, admit defeat, and slink back to Australia, never to return. I could stay in France illegally and continue to live under the radar, but that would mean holding my breath each time I crossed the French border, not knowing whether I would be allowed back in. Or I could throw myself at the mercy of the French immigration officials, plead ignorance, and work on getting my papers properly sorted. This latter option, while the most sensible, had one major drawback. It would mean jumping headfirst into a world of bureaucracy that I had hitherto been carefully avoiding.

Being of the firm opinion that rules and regulations were for everyone but me, I had, until this point, led a relatively stress-free existence in France by simply avoiding anything that looked vaguely official.

Among the hard and fast rules I had developed to evade the system were:

- Never answer the door to strange men bearing clipboards.
- Never answer in the affirmative if someone calls the home phone and asks, in French, "Is this Monsieur Corbett?"
- Never, but never pick up registered mail from the post office.

I had learned from painful experience that the only time French people bother to register mail is when they want to entrap you. They have a vested interest, usually legal, in proving that they have notified you of something unpleasant. Better not to know, I always maintained. Then at least, if they ever caught up with you (which they rarely did), you could plead ignorance with absolute honesty.

I lost count of the number of times I would sit in my living room, reading a book or watching television, as the postman knocked fruit-lessly on my door, brandishing a registered letter for which he wanted my signature. He knew I was home, I knew he was outside the door, but no way was I crossing my threshold and stepping into whatever trap some nasty bureaucrat had set for me. The postman would eventually give up and slide a yellow slip under my door, informing me that there was a registered package with my name on it at the nearby post office. So it was that I developed an almost weekly dance with my local post office. I would appear at the window brandishing my registered mail slip and wait to see whether the letter looked official; if it did, I would turn on my heel and run. Many was the time I was unsure of the contents of my registered correspondence, but I always figured it was better to err on the side of caution, declining to sign and leaving the letter to rot in the unclaimed bin at the back of the post office or to be returned to its sender.

Every so often my mother would phone to inquire whether I had received a letter about my Australian pension fund or the Visa card PIN number notification she had thoughtfully forwarded by registered mail from Australia. I would tell her I hadn't, express dismay, and tut loudly about the inefficiency of the French postal system. It was, I admit, a rather haphazard, head-in-the-sand approach to surviving French bureaucracy, but it seemed to work for me. Until now.

THE PROSPECT of joblessness and potential deportation, while certainly worrying, didn't stir nearly as much angst in me as it appeared to stir in my friends.

"But what about your job?" "You'll be thrown out of the country!" "You'll be tossed into jail!" were among the grim predictions they kindly offered.

As far as the job was concerned, I didn't much care. I was finished with the often-tedious world of international organization public relations. I had only taken the job so I could live in Paris; perhaps this was the push I needed to shuck off the golden handcuffs. And as for the deportation doomsday scenarios, I dismissed them out of hand, figuring that as a blond-haired, blue-eyed, distinctly Caucasian Australian, chances were I wasn't on the top of the French immigration department's most-wanted list.

Besides, as grim as the prospects of jail and deportation were, nothing could come close to the *préfecture* in terms of pure terror. The *préfecture de police,* a grand edifice on the Ile de la Cité, is the sclerotic heart of the slow-moving French bureaucratic system. Situated across the street from Notre Dame, it is a high chapel of inefficiency, a shrine to incompetence. It is the lumpen, useless cornerstone of the French republic, the place where hopes and dreams go to die.

It was a place I didn't much like.

The French immigration system is overseen by the administrative arm of the national police force. When you arrive in the country on a visit, it is the *préfecture de police* that allows you into the country. When you come to France to live, it is the *préfecture de police* that grants you the right to stay. The *préfecture's* headquarters in the heart of Paris once played host to a crucial battle between the French Resistance and the occupying Nazis, at the close of the Second World War. Now it stood as the country's last line of defense in the face of hopeful immigrants hankering to get a taste of *la belle vie française.*

Every day a line of several hundred people formed outside the *préfecture.* Those in the line looked as if they hailed from all corners of the earth. There were Asians, Africans, Arabs, and me. We bore little in common beyond a desire for French residency and the haunted, drawn expression of a *préfecture* repeat visitor.

Because the *préfecture* worked on a first-come, first-served basis, you had to take your place in the line early in the morning to get inside the building. The wait could take up to two hours. Once inside you had to navigate a labyrinth of crisscrossing hallways to find the correct room. Once you had found the right room, you had to take a number and wait an eternity to be called. Once called—and sometimes it would take longer for your number to be called than the prefecture was actually open, requiring you to go home and try again the next day—you had to present your dossier to a bored public servant who would give it a desultory scan, decide that the photocopies of your parents' birth certificates were not clear enough, and send you away to start all over again. And that was supposing you were in the correct branch of the *préfecture de police* in the first place. Several times I endured a four- or five-hour wait at the Ile de la Cité headquarters and finally presented myself to the counter, only to be informed that I was at the wrong police station and needed to repeat the exercise all over again on the other side of town.

The entire system relied on assigning a paper file to each and every residency applicant. Nothing was filed on computer. Everything you were, had been, or ever aspired to be was contained in a series of loose-leaf sheafs in a grotty manila folder. I used to sit horrified as gray, cardigan-sporting bureaucrats shuffled about the office letting documents spill to the floor, no doubt condemning some poor soul to a permanent immigration limbo. They called the process "normalizing" your status, as if your entire existence were abnormal until such time as a bitter civil servant with an inadequacy complex deigned to endow your dossier with a rubber stamp. They wanted originals and triplicates of everything. They wanted parents' original birth certificates, criminal records, high school report cards, and more gas bills than any human could reasonably accrue in a lifetime. Some documents absolutely had to be translated into French, but only by one of the twenty *préfecture*-approved translators. That these translators seemed to be permanently on vacation (no doubt spending the riches they'd accrued by being on the receiving end of government-ordained kickbacks) was not the *préfecture*'s concern.

Aspiring residents from Eastern Europe had to go to Hall F on Staircase B, unless you were from Moldova, Armenia, or Albania, in which case you needed to be in Hall D on Staircase A. Residency applicants from Asia and Oceania were requested to report to Hall B on Staircase C, or Hall C on Staircase B, depending on which countries were being serviced in which hall on any particular day—which you couldn't know until you went there and checked for yourself.

It was a Kafka novel come to life. A trip to the depths of absurdity and an exercise in patience that only the most stoic could survive. It was also a daily parade of the dispossessed. Done up in national costume and arriving at the *préfecture* with all the hope and optimism of new migrants, a colorful parade of people from all corners of the world would take their number, sit in the waiting room, and watch their lives slowly slip away. During one of my many visits to the *préfecture,* I sat next to a man from Chad. He was perhaps sixty years old, dressed in traditional garb, and seemed to be puzzling over the form he had been given to fill out.

I asked if he needed help.

"I cannot read or write," he said apologetically, in heavy-accented French. It was his fifth straight day at the *préfecture,* and he was apparently no closer to being "normalized" than the day he arrived.

I offered to help him fill out the form. "It asks here for the name of your wife," I said, pen poised and ready to write.

"Loana," he replied.

"Okay," I said, scribbling a phonetic interpretation of his wife's name. "Now here it asks for the name of your daughter."

"Loana," the old man said again.

"No, not your wife, your daughter," I repeated.

"Yes," he said. "Loana."

"Same name?" I asked.

"No," he replied. "Same person."

I thought for a moment about his chances of being awarded residency with a spot of incest in his dossier and decided they weren't great.

"Perhaps we'll just write Alice in here instead," I said, quickly scribbling the name and handing him back the form.

Aiding me in this venture into the mysterious world of the *préfecture,* this edifying journey into the incredibly inefficient depths of his own country's system, was my trusted friend and advocate Julien. He had very kindly put together an enormous file on my life in France for the edification and reading pleasure of the *préfecture* bureaucrats. Called a dossier, it was packed to overflowing with gas bills, rental records, tax receipts, and character references, a carefully itemized, ringbound account of the last four years of my life. As far as Jules was concerned, the dossier was so utterly complete, so blindingly convincing, there was no way the *préfecture* would not cede upon sighting it and grant me residency on the spot. Crucial to the case Jules had painstakingly compiled was a pile of affidavits from friends and associates in Paris, attesting to the fact that in my four years in France I had not only assimilated seamlessly but had become an integral part of modern-day Parisian society.

According to the rules set out under Section D, Subsection F of the Hoops Which Must Be Jumped Through in Order to Stay in the Country Act, a residency applicant was to be favorably considered if he/she were able to prove that Paris would be a poorer place for their absence. There was little doubt that a collection of bars in the Marais would have been poorer places if I hadn't been in the city for the past four years, but to say the dynamic metropolis of Paris would have been infinitely less sparkling without my presence was more of a stretch.

Nevertheless my friends loyally put pen to paper, tapped their respective inner bullshit artists, and extolled (in two hundred words or less, as that was all the official form allowed) my myriad virtues. The result, carefully annotated by my faithful attorney, was a pile of florid prose about an individual whom I had difficulty recognizing.

The experience of reading through these overblown statements was immensely gratifying but also distinctly odd, like being present at your own funeral, listening to heartfelt eulogies from loved ones. Even more disturbing was the fact that, according to those who knew me best, the overriding reason why the French authorities should grant me leave to stay in their country was that—and I quote—"he's kind of fun to have around." Instead of affidavits attesting to my dedication to the French language, my adoration of French culture, and my commitment to the ideals of the Republic, I had a pile of statements variously declaring that I knew a lot of good bars, organized lots of fun soirées, and was great value at dinner parties.

Had there been a special clause in the Immigration Act that made special residency provision for "people who know how to have a good time," I would have been a shoo-in.

As it was, the cardigan brigade at the *préfecture* considered my application, took a cursory glance through my megadossier, and finally pronounced themselves singularly unimpressed. After I had spent eight weeks constantly shuttling back and forth between one *préfecture* and another, a verdict was finally reached in the case of *Corbett v. The Republic of France*. No, it would not be possible to normalize my papers while I was in France. I would have to return to Australia and try from there.

Jules was devastated. All those Post-it notes and plastic dividers for nothing. I was pleasantly surprised, relieved even. The fact that I had escaped prosecution, jail, or even a rudimentary rap over the knuckles was nothing short of a miracle. Testament, I was able to conclude, to the overwhelmed state of the French immigration system and the complete inefficiency with which it was run. It wasn't quite a deportation, but it was the next best thing. I was being told in no uncertain terms by my good friends at the *préfecture* (some of whom I knew by name, so frequent had been my visits) that if I ever wanted to be legal again in France, I would have to return to Australia and start the application process anew.

And so my compass swung southward.

I may have had to concede round one to the Republic, I thought to myself as I stormed out of the *préfecture* en route to planning an impromptu trip home, but there was a bit of cunning in the old dog yet. I was down but far from out.

Chapter 31

In Transit

'VE ALWAYS CONSIDERED long-distance plane travel to be a very odd thing. Four hundred people crammed into a tin can, hurtling through space at several hundred miles per hour. All breathing, snoring, and drooling on one another. It's a sustained period of forced intimacy between complete strangers during which normal rules of social interaction are suspended. Personal space is routinely violated, all rules of basic hygiene are dismissed, and behavior that would otherwise cause outrage is somehow tolerated. On any given long-distance flight, it's not uncommon to wake with your head on a stranger's shoulder—a small wet patch on their shirt testament to how deeply you have been sleeping. Long-distance flights are also an opportunity to be exposed, at disturbingly close range, to fellow humans who consider such basics as cutlery and coming up for air between mouthfuls to be unnecessary to the eating process. Long-distance air travel is also a great way to get to know the bladder capacity, or lack thereof, of whoever is sitting beside you.

Whenever I am about to board a long-distance flight, I sense a kind of war-effort mentality among my fellow passengers. As we stand there at the boarding gate, checking each other out, dreading the ordeal ahead of us, we silently acknowledge that survival is going to be assured only if everybody is prepared to sacrifice a little bit of the personal for greater good of the group. A mile-high mucking-in.

As I stood at Charles de Gaulle airport, a ticket for Sydney in hand, wondering apprehensively if I was to have the distinct pleasure of sharing my personal space for the next twenty-four hours with the extremely overweight man near the ticket counter or the mother juggling screaming twins by the window, I paused to reflect on what had been a frantic couple of weeks.

During the barely twenty days since my *carte de séjour* application was rejected at the *préfecture,* I had been a busy little illegal immigrant. On the work front, I had negotiated a deal with the ICC. Since the screw-up with my working papers was partly their fault, and thanks to the existence in France of a labor tribunal that is famously workers'-rights-oriented, the good folks at ICC saw fit to offer me a relatively lucrative six-month contract to work for them as a "media consultant." Whatever that was. They had a series of conferences and events on their near horizon, and with no obvious candidate to replace me in my job, they decided the devil they knew was better than no devil at all. On the work papers front, I had also been busy. Thanks to the trickle of freelance writing I had been doing since arriving in France, it transpired that I was technically eligible for a journalist's visa. All I had to do was go home and apply for it. And on the personal front, I had had a similarly good result. I had crossed paths again with the Showgirl. It was only a brief encounter—me leaving a dinner party just as she was arriving—but it was enough to reinforce the mutual attraction. At least that was the impression *I* got.

And so Sydney beckoned. After you've survived the Europe-to-Australia flight ordeal a couple of times, you start to develop a system, a series of airborne habits to make the experience less painful. For some, it is a low-carb, high-liquid diet and a glass of wine with dinner to help them nod off to sleep. For others it is an uninterrupted schedule of in-flight movies. For me, it was a cocktail of drugs—sleeping pills and muscle relaxants—and as much water as I could force into my system.

I performed my long-haul flight ritual as the plane rumbled toward Central Asia, drifting off to sleep somewhere over Turkey. Some six hours later I was roused by rumblings from the two young Australian guys sharing my row of seats. I turned on my TV screen and looked at the in-flight map, noting that our plane was hovering somewhere over Burma—the way flights from Paris to Australia seem interminably to do.

When finally we touched down in Sydney, it was with no small amount of relief that I peeled myself out of my seat and poured myself into the waiting arms of my hometown. Yes, I had official visa-seeking duties to perform there, but for the most part, the trip was going to be a great chance to see my family and catch up with friends. What I expected, perhaps naïvely, was to pick up where I had left off—late nights out on the town in seedy bars, carousing with old work buddies. What I got was a whole lot of dinner parties and nights out at restaurants at which the conversation always seemed to turn to cladding.

I was also invited to the occasional trip to the pub. But none of these social engagements ever went beyond eleven p.m., lest they interfere with a sunrise yoga class or a personal trainer appointment the following morning. At each dinner party I would listen politely to explanations of where the jarrah wood was sourced for the upstairs extension, or how an architect had cleverly managed to incorporate the old gum tree into the plans for the back deck. Living as I did in the heart of Paris, in a building constructed in the seventeenth century (a fact to which my regular plumbing bills bore painful witness), in a tiny bachelor pad that was paid for each month by dropping off a rent check to the little old lady proprietor up the street, my interest in back decks and house extensions was minimal. But back in Australia I couldn't turn around without tripping over a home renovation, either from peers waxing lyrical about their negative gearing, or from preening TV presenters grinning stupidly as they explained the finer points of cement rendering.

Back in the golden age of television, prerequisites for TV stardom included a quick wit, an engaging personality, and sometimes even an ability to sing. These days, it appeared that all you needed to have your own prime-time program in Australia was proficiency with a paint-brush and a full set of drill bits. Retreating home at midnight, all renovated out, I would plunk myself down in front of late-night Australian TV. During one of these edifying late night TV sessions, it occurred to me that you can tell a lot about the social life of a country by the quality of the television it produces.

In France, the TV is universally awful. The few hours of daily programming not taken up by mindless game shows or ponderous documentaries about obscure Polish performance artists are filled with monumentally dull talk shows. These latter invariably consist of a panel of apparently eminent persons (usually C-list celebs or crusty octogenarians) sitting in front of a studio audience holding forth on all manner of tedious trivia. The only thing more remarkable than the fact that TV executives allow this tripe to air in such quantity is the existence of a never-ending supply of gormless Frenchies willing to sit in a TV studio for an hour while it is being taped.

But rather than an indictment of French society, I concluded that the abysmal TV was a sign of how healthy the country's collective social life was. The fact that the French produce only rubbish TV is surely because so few of them actually watch it. Conversely, the reason the British produce some of the world's best television is that watching TV is pretty much all the entire nation of Great Britain does.

The French are all too busy eating in cafés, discussing politics over a pastis, comparing philosophical theories on the meaning of life, attempting to get each other into bed, or repelling the unwanted advances of drunken expat opportunists. In short, they are too busy living, being active members of a community, to watch industrial quantities of TV.

Unlike in Australia and even more so America, communal living in France meant much more than occupying a gated collection of cookie-cutter prefabricated homes. Being part of a community in Paris meant being a visible, active player in the daily (and nightly) drama that is played out on the streets, in the Métro, and in the restaurants, cafés, and bars of this thriving metropolis. Born of a rich cultural tradition in which town squares were the vital focus of communal village life, and encouraged by the fact that most apartments are the size of broom closets, this vast, heaving mass of physically interacting human beings makes for an exciting backdrop in which to play out your own life. On any night of the week, at no matter what hour, you can always find a crowded bar or café, take your place at a table, and feel as though your shuffle along this mortal coil is part of something bigger. It's massively comforting. In Paris you are never lonely.

But here in my hometown, I was struck by the silence. If I had stepped out the door of the inner-city Sydney apartment in which I was staying after nine p.m. on a weekday, the only thing I was guaranteed to encounter was a tumbleweed. Dark, desolate streets, even in otherwise lively downtown suburbs, echoed with the sound of silence. The only hint of life in the apartments and terraces in the neighborhood was the faint blue glow from the TV set in each one. Unlike in France, in Australia sense of community is largely derived from going home to your little box, shutting out the rest of the world, turning on the television, and passively staring at the same home renovation show everyone else is watching. I watch *Backyard Blitz,* therefore I am. Only by witnessing the televised transformation of a dilapidated suburban home by an amiable team of do-it-yourselfers, led by a teeth-whitened former male stripper, can you truly say you are a participating member of Australian society. Such is the fervor with which my country folk devour TV that, if someone told me that a crack team of government operatives stole into your house at night and spirited you away for a month of intensive social reeducation if you weren't up to date with who had been chucked out of the *Big Brother* house or voted off *Dancing with the Stars,* I would believe them.

Two weeks into my stay I started to feel apprehensive, worried that if I stood still for longer than five minutes, someone would either come along and renovate me or whisk me off to dress me in a sequined unitard and force me to dance the polka with Pauline Hanson.

In a topsy-turvy world such as this, a fella could turn to only one person to make sense of it all. It was time to visit Hazel.

HAZEL IS MY GRANDMOTHER, the dowager empress of the family, the keeper of the secrets, the knower of all things. Less a silent, omniscient oracle than a vociferous bundle of raw energy, at ninety-three years old she is often invoked by those who know her as a role model for the inevitable process of aging. Though some of her faculties are starting to fail, she is still sprightly. Though her eyes are affected by cataracts, they still have a twinkle, and while the step has slowed down in the last ten years, it still has a definite spring.

At Haze's age, every day is an event—and she makes sure she dresses accordingly. She loves nothing better than a day out "in town," as she calls it. And where others her age spend their days in tattered cardigans and slippers, she would rather be dead than be caught on the town in anything but a good dress and a smart pair of heels. When some women get old, they become wrinkled curmudgeons, lilac-scented, fragile little sparrows who are distinctly afraid of life. To them, every trip to the corner store is fraught with potential peril. Fed on a daily diet of fear-mongering from the tabloid media, they honestly believe a simple trip to fetch a carton of milk will result in certain mugging and rape.

But not Haze. With the days of her life counting down, every morning that she wakes up is a blessing, and she's damned if she isn't going to make the most of it. Consequently, if you try to call her anytime after nine a.m. Sydney time, she is invariably out the door—having already washed the curtains, dusted the Venetians, pruned the roses, and scrubbed the bathtub raw. It's invariably the movies—or "the pictures," as she calls them—to which she heads. Recently, as her hearing has become increasingly unreliable, she has taken to spending her mornings at the several inner-city cinemas that screen foreign films.

"I can turn off my hearing aid and read the subtitles," she tells my long-suffering mother, who plays able assistant to my grandmother's daily wrestle with mortality. As a result, Haze has seen more film noir, borderline porn, avant-garde, and esoteric cinema in the past five years than your average inner-city art student. I can only imagine what the ticket-sellers make of the old woman handing over her Seniors Card to get a discounted ticket to such recent art-house hits as the Swedish depress-fest *Fucking Amal* or the Kurt Cobain–inspired biopic *Last Days*. When I quiz her about these films afterward, her recollection of the plotlines is usually sketchy at best. I can only assume she sleeps through most of them.

For the better part of the last thirty years Haze has spent her grandchildren's inheritance on overseas trips, so she is quite worldly for a person of her generation. Until recently trips through the Alaskan wilderness, South Pacific cruises, and boat tours up the Mekong River were all a part of Haze's regular annual activities, but now no travel insurance company will touch her.

All of which has made her a relatively tolerant neighbor in the face of a complete transformation of the cultural mix in her neighborhood, Kingsgrove, in Sydney's inner-southern suburbs. Where once Mavises and Alans brought up little scamps called Bruce and Trevor, now Stavros and Anastasia occupy their multipillared, two-story, red-brick home. So do Kuan Yin and Jiang Li and their extended family. More than most people her age, my grandmother takes the multiculturalization of her neighborhood in stride. While she will occasionally drop the odd racist remark, she manages to keep an open mind to most things.

As I discovered one afternoon, when I needed a break from home-renovating tips, and I decided to take her to lunch. My journalist's visa for France had been approved the day before, and I was due to fly back to Paris in two days' time. Haze and I were in the car, returning to her house after a heavy-duty eating session at her favorite all-you-can-eat seafood buffet at Sydney's salubrious Star City casino. Years before, when I was barely old enough to carry my own dinner plate, Haze had taught me the cardinal rules of all-you-can-eat dining, namely, don't fill up on bread before going to the buffet, use a layer of overhanging lettuce leaves to make the surface area of your plate larger, and always, but *always* push your way to the front when the new tray of shrimp comes out of the kitchen. Today at lunch in the casino buffet, she watched me stuff myself to the point of explosion. Then I drove her back to the home she had built and proudly maintained for the last sixty-odd years. As we pulled into her street, we saw an elderly Chinese gentleman shuffling along the sidewalk in full Chinese peasant regalia, complete with Mao suit and conical cane hat.

"Oh, we've got them all here in the neighborhood now," Haze remarked. "Chinese, Greek, Italian, Lesbians—you name it."

"Lesbians?" I shot back, incredulous that any self-respecting dyke would choose to live ten miles outside downtown.

"Yes," came her reply. "You know, those ones from the Lebanon."

Spending time with Haze back in the homeland was always entertaining. Saying goodbye at the end of these visits is always a wrench.

Though you try not to dwell on it, you know that as you drop her off and pull away from the curb, that glimpse in the rearview mirror of the snowy-haired, shrunken little woman—refusing to stop waving until your car has turned the corner—may be the last time you see her.

It's a wrench that you only feel more keenly as you pack your bags and prepare for the journey back to Paris.

Your parents—whose support gave you the confidence to throw yourself at the mercy of the world in the first place—stand stoically at the airport departure gates, swallowing tears. Once you are in the plane and airborne, with the city slipping away beneath you, you realize you are trapped between two worlds. Paris is home, but you will never be a Parisian. Sydney is where your heart is, but you no longer feel you belong. You are torn between two countries, the inescapable fate of the expat.

Chapter 32

Crossing Over

A S ANY FORMER love interest of mine will readily attest, I am not the quickest horse out of the gate when it comes to seduction. More than most males, I am in touch with my emotions. But even so, my head usually needs a good couple of months to catch up with my heart—and then tell my arms, hands, and lips to do something about it.

Contact with Shay—or "the Showgirl" as I had begun referring to her—after our evening together atop the Australian Embassy some eight months previously had only been sporadic. We would see each other at the occasional party or hear of each other through mutual friends, but time spent in one another's company was rare. The situation had been compounded by our clashing work schedules and by my recent enforced absence in Australia.

But all that was to change now that I had returned from the homeland, officially resigned from my job, and taken on the ambiguous title of "media consultant." To my small group of clients, including my now former employer, the ICC, my working as a media consultant meant I was able to be more flexible in my dealings with them. They could take me on for short-term projects and enjoy all the benefits of having me as an employee (and yes, there are benefits to having me as an employee) without having any of the administrative hassles that employing someone full time in France entails.

For me, working as a consultant meant charging more, working less, and spending altogether more time in my pajamas, while concentrating on the serious business of becoming almost wholly nocturnal. This new, flexible working arrangement meant I rarely had to be awake before ten and almost never had to don a suit, look presentable, or be in an office. Waking with a three-day beard and a semipermanent hangover for several months was eminently doable.

My partner in late-night crime during this period was the enigmatic Badger. Luke Badger, a fellow Australian in Paris, worked at the Australian Embassy in one of those ill-defined public service jobs. It involved spreadsheets and balancing books, and apparently he was good at it. But his real talents lay in playing guitar.

The previous year Badger and I had taken a small Australian bar in Pigalle by storm with our acoustic Australian cover band, Brick Venir—a musical experiment that had followed Get 27 and just as quickly fizzled out. But we had recognized in each other a kindred spirit. Or perhaps it was just spirits, and a love of them, that we recognized in each other. Either way, we both had a lot of time on our hands and a thirst that never seemed to be quenched.

Paris by night is a wholly different place from its daytime counterpart. Though easily as beautiful, with its floodlit monuments and lights playing on the Seine, nighttime Paris has a deliciously seedy feel to it. Like Montmartre in the days of Toulouse-Lautrec or like Berlin in the 1930s, Paris by night is a city pregnant with possibility. The showfolk knew this better than anyone. Working nights and sleeping days, *their* Paris was almost exclusively populated with nightclub crawlers, late-night café dwellers, and patrons of secret drinking holes that stayed open until dawn.

Encouraged by the Showgirl, I threw myself happily into this vortex of debauchery. Within a matter of weeks my life revolved around

Pigalle and the showfolk's drinking establishments of choice. Most evenings would start around midnight at O'Sullivan's, the sprawling Irish pub on Boulevard Clichy. Perched next to the Moulin Rouge, it was within easy crawling distance for the Moulin girls and only a short cab ride from the Lido.

Arriving each night on the Mojito and pushing our way past the wave of drunken Contiki Tour kids at the front bar, Badger and I would take our place out back among the forest of Amazonian men and women. Like a herd of perfectly groomed giraffes milling about on a savannah otherwise populated by expatriate drunks and local insomniacs, the showgirls and showboys stood out by a mile. Stepping into their midst made you feel instantly small, decidedly squat, and distinctly pudgy. It was certainly no place for the weak of heart or low of self-esteem. The showfolk carried themselves with the upright posture typical of dancers. They lived out their evenings in a stratosphere far removed from the masses milling below. I spent a lot of time craning my neck just to make conversation.

As my exposure to the show freaks (as I would later affectionately call them) increased, the sensation of inadequacy gradually subsided. But at first I couldn't help but feel like a carbuncle on a flawless complexion. Still, you didn't have to scratch that complexion too hard to discover that the elegance was often only skin deep. Some of the Moulin girls in particular seemed to have cornered the market on trashiness. Though Paris had done its best to smooth some of their rougher edges, and though for four hours every night they were onstage visions of grace and refinement, many of them had mouths like troopers and appeared to drink for their nation. For many of the expatriate girls who danced at the Moulin for a living, a night at O'Sullivan's followed by a cheese crepe at the roadside kiosk next door was about as authentic as their Parisian experience would ever get. Caught on a late-night treadmill of bed-work-pub-bed, most of them blanched at the thought of ever leaving the quartier. And why would they? They had everything they needed right there in Pigalle, *and* they didn't have to speak French to get it. But I was a card-carrying honorary member of the Lido crew—renowned for being that little bit classier, though definitely no less partial to the odd ale or four. In retrospect I can safely say that while the experience did wonders for my posture, it did absolutely nothing for my liver.

For the mere mortals who happened to stumble into O'Sullivan's on a night when the showgirls were in residence, there would be hilarious scenes of unchecked gawking. A small amphitheater of slack-jawed admirers would form around the showfolk, their faces a mixture of unbridled lust and wide-eyed confusion about how exactly to cross the invisible line and breach the magic circle.

There was no such reluctance, however, the night the Australian rugby team, the Wallabies, came to town. In Paris for a match the next day against the French, the likely lads from Down Under sauntered into the bar, took in their surroundings, and made a beeline for the beauties. In between chugging competitions, dancing on tables, and leering at every woman with a pulse (doubtless part of a coach-ordained prematch preparation program), the boys tried their hardest to impress the showgirls, pulling out every trick they knew from that extensive tome, *The Australian Male's Guide to Sure-Fire Female Seduction.*

"There's a lot of pretty girls in here, but I reckon you're the most prettiest," I heard one young Wallaby say to a Lido dancer, before forcing his tongue down her throat.

It was all I could do not to burst with national pride.

On less notable evenings in Pigalle, and usually after the O'Sullivan's patrons had been sufficiently blinded by the showfolk's freakish beauty, the Posse would cross the rue to Café Oz (no further description required) or (if we were feeling really trashy) straight to Jack's, the hole-in-the-wall Irish bar a stone's throw from O'Sullivan's. Jack's was the kind of bar in which the carpet squelched underfoot. It had nicotine-stained walls and ceilings. A brutish, ugly little bar, it played bad music and served expensive drinks in mismatched glasswear. It had nothing at all going for it other than the fact that it was open until nine a.m. and thus wholly satisfied the sole Creature of the Night Bar Criterion. Since most nights at Jack's didn't begin until four a.m., I rarely partook of its unique early morning charms. Even consultants needed their beauty sleep.

But one morning—in a display of dedication to the showfolk

cause above and beyond the call of duty—I set my alarm for five a.m. in the full expectation of waking up, riding Mojito to Pigalle, and joining the party at Jack's just as it reached its crescendo. It was the morning of showgirl Lisa's twenty-sixth birthday. The same morning, as it happened, the Australian trade minister was to be guest of honor at a special business breakfast at the Australian Embassy, to which I had been invited. Roused by the early morning alarm and refreshed by a full three hours of sleep, I donned a suit for my eight a.m. power breakfast and jumped on the Mojito for my five a.m. rendezvous with Sodom and Gomorrah.

A pair of finely toned male buttocks pressed up against the bar window greeted me as I pulled up outside Jack's. Inside the bar the scene was similarly debauched. Showgirls teetered on heels, showboys made light work of pints, and as the sun crawled over the horizon outside, we all proceeded to pay noisy, drunken tribute to the gods of the fast-fading night. Descending the basement bar stairs at one point to avail myself of the facilities, I happened upon the birthday girl striking a pose that I suspect was rarely required of her on stage. Plunger in one hand, cocktail in the other, she was bent double over the toilet tending to a blocked S-bend pipe that had flooded the floor. She was resourceful as well as beautiful.

Suffice it to say, my performance before the Australian trade minister some three hours later was less than scintillating. Trying hard to focus on the floating croissants in front of me, while straining to keep track of the speech—laden as it was with fiscal this and deficit that— I kept the waiters busy with regular top-ups of filter coffee.

Throughout this period of late nights and drunken sunrises—and somewhat miraculously, given the drunken perma-fog that otherwise clouded our thinking—the Showgirl and I began to privately recognize a mutual attraction. A peck on the cheek here, a squeeze of the hand there, a lingering look for good measure—it was the furtive flirting of the not quite sure. The kind of courtship that was so tentative as to almost not be there at all. It was a seduction technique at which I was an unrivaled champion. Disguise your true feelings so utterly and convincingly as to render them completely unrecognizable. That ought to do it. Ah yes, a few more weeks of this, and the Showgirl was bound to become bored, confused, or indifferent. Even I had to admit I was playing this one to doomed perfection.

There was nothing else for it—I had to bring out the big guns. Through the funk of late-night carousing, I resolved to seek the counsel of the only people on the planet less qualified than me to offer seduction advice—my buddies.

It was time to convene a Steak Tartare Summit.

Chapter 33

How Not to Court a Showgirl

I T WAS, I explained to my mates as we sat around our usual lunch table at the Grand Corona, like a kind of sustained tango. Partial as we all were to talking in high-falutin' metaphors, I had chosen the sensual dance of the Argentinian proletariat to depict my current situation with the Showgirl.

"You know how the tango is the most sensual dance in the world?" I began. "Two partners, moving as one about the dance floor, gliding effortlessly across the parquet, their bodies aligned, in tune and together, but never touching? All of that beauty and sensuality and sexual tension caught in the empty space between their frantically beating hearts."

It was lunchtime on a Thursday. The Grand Corona brasserie and café on the Place d'Alma was packed with a mixture of office workers, Eiffel Tower tourists, and ladies who lunch. It was the chosen venue for most of our biweekly Steak Tartare Summits, mostly because it was conveniently located near James's, Will's, and Julien's offices, but also because it served a mean *tartare aller-retour*—a hunk of seasoned raw meat, lightly braised on both sides. Perfect food to aid the contemplation of life's big ponderables that these male-only lunches comprised. James took in my tango metaphor, nodded agreement, and splashed his steak tartare with Worcestershire sauce.

"Just get her pissed and shag her," he offered as he tucked into his fries. "I don't understand what you're waiting for. If it's a gold-embossed invitation you want, you're not going to get it. Get in there, and get on with it." Undeniably his advice had merit. It was simple, straightforward, and held out the promise of quickly deciding things between me and the Showgirl, one way or the other. But short of assuming the mannerisms of, or being able to momentarily channel, a gruff northerner from Yorkshire, the strategy was beyond me.

"What you want to do, mate, is take her for a dinner," offered Julien. "Somewhere intimistic." It was one of his oft-used, made-up Franglais words. "Somewhere romantique. Tell her that you have never felt like this before, that you cannot eat, you cannot sleep, you cannot look at the moon without thinking of her." I looked at him waiting for the punch line, then remembered he was French. He actually believed this shit.

"She's Australian, Jules," I replied. "She'll either laugh or barf. Either way it's not going to work."

"Why don't you write her a letter?" said Will, divulging one of his own preferred methods of seduction. "Or an e-mail. You're good with words. Write it down, keep it light, keep it witty, and see what happens."

I blanched at the thought of committing all my feelings to paper. What if the sentiment wasn't mutual? What if I had been imagining it all this time? How would I bear the indignity of rejection and cope with the knowledge that the physical, printed evidence of my folly was being kept for eternity in one of those girly keepsake boxes with other quaint Paris mementos, brought out every now and then for a laugh? No, much better to stick to my current strategy: follow her around like a lovesick puppy, entertain her with my jokes, wow her with my wit, and generally stand around at her Lido dancer soirées like a little kid with his nose pressed up against a candy-store window.

Anyway, I told my lunch companions, the Showgirl and I were actually much closer and much better friends than we had been three months ago. Surely that counted for something.

"Bad news" came the reply from Will. "You let this gradual drift continue, and you can forget any idea of anything ever happening between you. Unless you do something soon, you are in mortal danger of becoming a *good friend.*" I felt a shudder pass through me. He was of course right.

Unless I took evasive action soon, I was on a one-way trip into territory from which there was no return: the Land of Just Good Friends. It's a place in which countless thousands of hopeless men linger. The no-man's-land between friendship and relationship. A barren, windswept place reserved exclusively for that unfortunate slice of the brotherhood who, instead of making a move on the object of their desire, choose instead to become a really good male friend. Painfully close to the woman they are dying to jump but never allowed to touch.

Teetering as I was on the edge of the precipice, I realized my situation had been brought on in large part by the Showgirl's current emotional predicament. Having just endured a particularly nasty, drawn-out breakup with a French man, she was in no mood—or emotional head space—to embark upon another relationship. The fact that after three years together the French man had refused to accept the breakup and hence had launched a concerted stalking campaign only complicated matters further.

By virtue of our strengthening friendship, I heard more and more from the Showgirl about the freaky ex and his increasingly disturbing behavior: making phone calls at all hours of the day and night, standing outside her apartment at two a.m. waiting for her to return from work, hacking into her e-mail account to keep track of her movements. Most countries call it stalking and have laws to prevent it. But in France it was apparently all a part of the melodrama of being in love. And in my attempt to provide support and advice, I had drifted dangerously close to the border of Just Good Friends Land. If I didn't make a move soon, or discontinue the sympathetic-shoulder-to-cry-on routine, I was doomed.

As useful as the lads' counsel had been, especially that of James, I needed a fourth, and crucially female, opinion. Someone straight-talking, no nonsense and eminently sensible. Melinda was the obvious choice. As fellow Australians in Paris, Melinda and I had formed a fast friendship since meeting two years previously. Though she had arrived in France with the stated aim of avoiding all contact with fellow Antipodeans, she was prepared to make an exception for me.

"Because you like red wine as much as I do and you seem to neither know nor care about Australian football."

Following through on a year-old promise to research a newspaper story about Australian showgirls on the Paris stage, I organized a couple of tickets through the Lido press office and asked Melinda to join me for the show. As we took our seats, it struck me that I was about to see the object of my affection as close to naked as she could possibly be. Though swathed in feathers and sequins throughout the hour-and-a-half performance, the Showgirl was one of sixteen so-called "nude" dancers at the Lido, meaning she spent much of the show in a state of semiundress. I was careful to ostentatiously maintain eye contact with her each time she strode on stage.

At the end of the show, and with a few bottles of complimentary Champagne coursing through our systems, Melinda and I arranged to meet the Showgirl at the stage door, where we invited her to join us for a postperformance drink. The three of us sat in a bar off the Champs Elysées. Over a carafe of wine, the Showgirl and I listened attentively as Melinda explained in impressive detail her upcoming wedding: the choice of venue, the choice of menu, the importance of making sure the placecards matched the napkins and the best man's tie. Now in our early thirties, this was a conversation both the Showgirl and I had heard from many different friends, many times over. We exchanged knowing looks.

Somewhere in between a lengthy description of the wedding dress and a verbal treatise on the timely demise of sugared almonds as bonbonniere, the Showgirl managed to establish an easy rapport with Melinda. So much so that later, after we had all bid one another goodnight, I received a text message from Mel giving the Showgirl an enthusiastic thumbs-up. We convened a follow-up session of wine and cigarettes for the following night to discuss next steps.

We met, as we habitually did, at the Bar des Artistes, near the apartment Melinda shared with her English carpenter boyfriend, Conrad, in the down-at-heel tenth arrondissement. We ordered a pichet of Bordeaux and lit up a couple of Marlboro Lights. We only ever smoked in each other's company, an illicit indulgence we reserved for the express purpose of better integrating with our wildly puffing Parisian counterparts.

"I'm not being funny," said Melinda, employing the clause with which she started any sentence containing a potentially harsh personal judgment. "But you're acting like a spineless idiot. I cannot believe you can be so extroverted in every other part of your life and yet incapable of expressing yourself when it really matters. If you're waiting for divine intervention, it isn't going to come."

She was right, of course. The time had come for me to push the boat out, throw caution to the wind, and tell the Showgirl how I really felt. I resolved to get her alone in the coming days and make my feelings known.

As it turned out, intervention did in fact come. But it was neither divine nor desirable.

"Where are you going?" I asked the Showgirl, as we stood together one night at the bar of Café Oz in Chatelet.

She had just received a text message and, after quickly replying, was gathering her things and preparing to leave.

"Hmm? Oh, I have to go and meet someone," she replied. She was looking typically gorgeous. Her short-cropped auburn hair framed her elegant neck. Pale skin, blue eyes, and expertly chiseled cheekbones: I was staring again.

"But it's just getting interesting here," I ventured. "The entertainment is just beginning." As indeed it was. The visiting ranks of Australian football's finest, the touring Kangaroo rugby league team, had only just trooped into Café Oz and were setting about making embarrassing spectacles of themselves. Despite having to play against the

French national side the next day, they were off on a bender, drinking industrial quantities of beer and employing some of the worst pick-up lines ever employed to woo French women.

"Does that actually work where you're from?" I overheard one unimpressed young French woman say to a leering twenty-two-year-old from Sydney whose attempt at a pickup had included a crude compliment on her hair color and a boast that he had once drunk twelve schooners of beer in a one-hour period "and not even chucked."

"I'm going to have to leave you to show those Kangaroos how it's done," said the Showgirl before disappearing out the door. I watched her leave, felt my heart sink again, and launched into a now familiar round of quiet self-flagellation. *Idiot! Idiot! Idiot!* I silently scolded myself. *Why didn't you say something? Do something?*

Hours later, when I met up with Lisa at another bar, I asked her about the Showgirl's disappearing act.

"Oh, that will be Guillaume," Lisa replied.

"Who's Guillaume?" I asked, knowing I was not going to like the answer.

"Guillaume Canet. The French actor. He was in that movie *The Beach* with Leonardo DiCaprio—little fella, kind of cute, but small in that French way. They've been having this on-again, off-again fling for a while. He calls her up whenever he's in town, and if she's in the mood to see him, they hook up." Cue sound of heart crushing.

"Oh right," I managed to respond, oblivious to the scream of panic welling inside me. "She's seeing a French movie star, of course." Bloody perfect. Not only was I now competing with a French man, on his turf, but he was a goddamned famous one at that, whose cheeky Gallic grin graced the walls of lusty teen girls' rooms all over the country. Performing a mental checklist, I concluded that the only two things I had over him were height and a comprehensive knowledge of Australian TV commercial jingles from the late 1970s and 1980s. The prognosis was not great. Height was something the Showgirl could have any night of the week at the Lido, and there is only so much entertainment you can squeeze out of Rita the Eta Eater.

Lisa went on to explain that the Showgirl had come across this randy little celluloid Frog some months previously at the Paris premiere of the Leonardo DiCaprio film *Gangs of New York*. Invited to the postpremiere party at Queen nightclub by a promoter wanting to pepper the place with appropriately stunning women, Lisa and the Showgirl had duly attended, been spotted by Leo and Guillaume, and were invited back to the lads' Plaza Athénée hotel suite for some VIP party action. En route the Showgirl—apparently in a state of high inebriation—had tripped on the stairs leading out of Queen and cut open her finger, deeply and seriously. We're talking to-the-bone and severed tendons. There was, according to Lisa, a lot of blood. But determined not to let a dangerously dangling digit stand between her and a Leonardo DiCaprio/Plaza Athénée in-suite bash, she had simply wrapped the offending appendage in a makeshift bandage and soldiered on.

Wow, I thought to myself. *She puts parties with movie stars in luxury hotel suites and all-night drinking ahead of personal health and safety.* I felt myself fall in love all over again.

Once they were in the suite and milling drunkenly with the other DiCaprio–ordained VIPs, the Showgirl's enthusiastic dance-floor twirling and blood-soaked-bandage-wielding apparently brought her to the attention of the party's high-profile hosts. Sensing either a media or a diplomatic incident on their hands, they asked security to politely escort the "two tall girls" out of the room, down to the lobby, and into a taxicab bound for the nearest hospital. But before they left, the wily Monsieur Canet had nabbed the Showgirl's cell number. *Et voilà*—instant illicit, mutually beneficial affair. The bastard. I decided on the spot that I hated him.

But then, who was I kidding anyway? Here she was, the toast of Paris, an object of desire, fantasy, and envy for several thousand people each night—why would she be interested in a schmuck like me? I was kind of funny, perhaps. Amusing to have around, certainly. But not serious boyfriend material. As we spun around the floor of our mutual attraction, engaged in our very own wholly enjoyable albeit slightly confusing tango, I had been cut in on. And by a short-arsed Frog, to boot. I turned to the bottom of my trusty pint glass for comfort and proceeded to get very drunk.

And so the weeks passed. The Showgirl conducted an illicit affair with a French movie star while I dedicated a whole lot of effort to the serious business of appearing to be indifferent. I suppose, in retrospect, I should have made more of a stand. If I was serious about my obsession with the Showgirl, I ought to have risen gallantly to the challenge: looked with scorn at the child-size gauntlet thrown down to me by this height-challenged French film star and beaten him at his own game.

But I didn't. Instead, I spent more and more time with the Showgirl during daylight hours, allowing myself to be sucked ever closer to the border of Just Good Friends Land. The flexible hours of my new working arrangement and her nocturnal work schedule meant that days had become a new staging ground for our budding friendship.

We would meet for picnics on the Champ de Mars and sprawl on the lawn in the spring sunshine under the span of the Eiffel Tower. We would meet for coffee in the cafés near the Love Pad whenever the Showgirl was visiting the Marais from her apartment in the seventeenth arrondissement. One day, in a cunning change of my trademark seduction tactics (i.e., so subtle as to be barely noticeable), I even tried to get to the Showgirl via her beloved cat, Willy.

Willy was a blue-gray Chartreux. As a youngster, he was reputedly a very handsome cat. Now six years old and recently neutered, Willy had developed a definite weight problem. He was, not to put too fine a point on it, a very fat cat. Willy was a house cat, which in Parisian terms means an apartment cat. He had lived out his entire six-year existence within the four hundred square feet that constituted the Showgirl's tiny apartment. In an attempt to show Shay how much I was into animals, I took it upon myself to educate Willy about the wide world outside her living room and bought him a leash to take him on a daytime excursion. His first outing was to Parc Monceau, a beautiful public park just minutes from where the Showgirl lived. The three of us trooped down to the park.

I carried, or rather lugged, Willy in his cat carrying bag. Upon arrival in the garden, I set the bag down on the ground and urged him to step forth and finally taste the forbidden fruits of freedom. But he was having none of it. He point-blank refused to budge. All the trees, grass, sky, and open space were too much for his little brain to process.

He sat resolutely inside his bag, head down, mewing in distress. I attached him to the leash and tried to walk him across a stretch of lawn. He hunkered low into the ground and went heavy. The only movement he would concede was to make a beeline for my Vespa helmet and attempt to crawl inside. Paris's only agoraphobic cat—just my luck.

We decided to abandon the cat experiment and retreated to the Showgirl's apartment. I spent the afternoon sitting in her kitchen as she prepared cupcakes and biscuits for a dressing-room party. We whiled away the time making small talk and chatting in that easy way we had.

Willy, fully recovered from his outdoor ordeal and back in the domain of which he was the undisputed king, sat opposite me in the kitchen, laughing at me with his iridescent green eyes. If the Showgirl was none the wiser about the crush I had developed on her, Willy certainly seemed to know all about it, flashing occasional looks of disdain in my direction.

As if! he seemed to be saying to me. *Loser! Move on! Next!*

Paris was over for her, the Showgirl told me. A disastrous end to a long-term relationship, a level of exhaustion at having to keep up a grueling nightly work schedule, and a desire to return to the homeland in which she hadn't lived for almost eight years were all pointing her in the direction of Brisbane, Australia.

"What is there to keep me here anyway?" she asked me. "Other than Willy, I don't have any ties." She would give it another six months, she said, then it would be *au revoir, Paris.*

I sat there and nodded my head in agreement, hoping she couldn't tell my stomach was churning.

But before packing up and leaving Paris for good, she said, she would return to Australia for a three-week vacation. Back to Brisbane, to the cradle of family, to the sunshine and surf.

When she left, I would miss her.

Chapter 34

And So, to a Pool in Marrakesh

THE SHRILL BEEP of a text message jolted my phone into action and woke me from my slumber. I sat bolt upright and glimpsed the time on the digital clock embedded in my three-star hotel room bed head. In the early morning Marrakesh heat and through the funk of a Heineken hangover, I realized I was already late for work. As I fumbled on the bedside table for my phone while simultaneously vaulting toward the shower, the contents of the message stopped me in my tracks. *At travel agent. Have swapped nights off. Fares to Marrakesh for 140 euros. Should I come down?*

It was the Showgirl. Recently returned from Australia, she was taking me up on my invitation to join me for a few days in Morocco, where I was at a work conference. She had drifted into a travel agency.

Sure! Of course! Get thee on a plane! I replied, choosing to ignore the rising panic welling inside me. What did it mean? Was she coming all the way to Marrakesh from Paris for a forty-eight-hour jaunt because she liked me, or did she simply have a yen to do a bit of shopping in the bazaar? Was I going to make an abject fool of myself by assuming that her moment of travel madness had been inspired by a desperate desire to see me? Or—worse—was I about to overlook the bleeding obvious, ignore her unmistakable overture, and miss a golden opportunity to show her how I felt in return?

True, during her time in Australia we had spoken almost every other day. Long phone calls about nothing in particular. Also true, our ill-defined relationship had gravitated to the forefront of the Showgirl's mind. Yet even so I couldn't be sure what this gesture meant. In the often-tricky, high-stakes game of budding attraction, nothing is ever clear.

It was with no small amount of impatience and anxiety, then, that I worked through the end of the conference. Ostensibly convened by my high-paying client the ICC as a "coming together of world business and political leaders," it was really just a big-business mutual back-slapping fest—and, by association, a chance for the decidedly shady Moroccan government to briefly assume the guise of respectability. For four days, in the heat of early summer, the great and the good of the business and political worlds converged on Marrakesh to exchange platitudes and max out expense accounts.

When finally the corporate hot-air convention was over, I was able to concentrate on the imminent arrival of the Showgirl and hone the art of appearing nonchalant on the outside while freaking out on the inside.

When she arrived, having had barely two hours of sleep between finishing at the Lido and boarding a flight to Morocco, she reacted with a predictable lack of enthusiasm to my suggestion that we jump straight into a taxi and drive 125 miles across the desert to the seaside resort of Essaouira. In consultation with a small posse of work confidants, I had decided that a romantic drive across the desert, followed by a couple of languid nights by the sea in the famed Moroccan coastal town, would set the perfect tone for my grand seduction. It sounded fine, until you factored into the equation the fact that said work colleagues were also planning to make the same trip. In my eagerness not to presume that anything was going to pass between the Showgirl and me on this little Moroccan weekend, I had signed us both up for a group outing, believing it was better to play it safe than to make sweeping assumptions about her intentions and book a romantic weekend for two. It was the first of many unfortunate decisions.

My second error of judgment was to invite the otherwise eminently entertaining Mary G. to share a taxi with us across the desert. Mary G., or Mary from the Island as I liked to call her, was an ICC colleague and fellow Australian. Hailing from Townsville, she had spent the better part of her early adult years living on Magnetic Island, a tiny speck of land off the northeastern coast of Australia, in the same stretch of Coral Sea that played host to the Great Barrier Reef. A thriving metropolis it definitely wasn't.

In a previous professional life Mary had worked at one of Townsville's local councils, as its PR and events manager. Among the highlights of the local council's cultural calendar for which Mary was responsible was the annual Guinea Pig Look-alike Competition, requiring owners to dress up their guinea pigs as famous historical figures. The year Mary presided over the proceedings, the John Lennon guinea pig was the victor (complete, I am told, with wire-rimmed glasses and long dark hair); a bridal guinea pig and a Hawaiian guinea pig shared a closely fought second place. I know, because she told me about it several times. At length. Possessed of that tendency peculiar to people who spend a large amount of their lives in remote areas, she was constantly telling stories about people you had never heard of but whom she assumed you knew intimately. The stories were always offered unsolicited and came packaged in a stream of consciousness.

"You know Jase," she would state, not ask, apropos of nothing in particular. "He used to spend days on end in his Jason recliner in our house on Olympus Crescent, stoned off his brain. There was this one time when he was so stoned, and his Jason recliner reclined too far, and he went backward onto the floor arse over tit."

Other recurring characters in the Mary's island-inspired monologues included a ferry-service operator, who also wrote the gossip column for the local rag and once had a mishap docking the ferry after a big night on the mainland; and the one I never tired of hearing about, the island's resident artist who collected cane toad roadkill, stuck the unfortunate amphibians to a canvas, and painted large tropical tableaux for sale to tourists. All of which was eminently entertaining (a) if you knew Mary and (b) if you hadn't just gotten off a three-hour flight after two hours of sleep to arrive in a random Third World country to meet a guy you thought you might be interested in.

Shell-shocked from the journey and jointly assailed by the heat and Mary's Magnetic Island tales, the Showgirl sat silently in the back of the taxi as we sped across the barren landscape. We arrived two hours later in Essaouira where things immediately took a nosedive for the worse.

Contrary to the lyrical tourist-brochure evocations of a Moroccan paradise by the sea, Essaouira was a dive. A whitewashed-stone fortified seaside township, it was hemmed in on one side by a dingy fishermen's port and on the other by a series of garish Sofitel-style chain hotels. The much-vaunted beach was a windswept stretch of gray-black sand. At low tide the water receded, revealing black, oily sand flats, punctuated here and there by the occasional tire or other piece of industrial refuse. The romance register took an immediate plummet.

A rousing lunch of freshly caught seafood by the port might turn things around, I thought. But the fact that we were made to sit at a filthy bench table, drink water from glasses of dubious cleanliness, and wait for our fish to be grilled while stray cats fought over the guts at our feet took something away from the moment. The Showgirl was uncharacteristically quiet. Inside I was quietly dying. I knew it—of course she hadn't come to Morocco to throw herself at me. And even if she had been contemplating it, surely the pungent aroma of fish guts baking in the afternoon sun was quickly changing her mind. What a presumptuous fool I had been to instruct the advance members of our party to book a double room for us in the local *pensione.* What a disaster to arrive in said room and discover that not only were the walls paper thin (I could hear my travel companions whispering next door) but that all the furniture in the room had been freshly varnished that morning, ensuring headspins and nausea for anyone who dared spend more than ten consecutive minutes inside. If the gods of fate were trying to send me a message, it couldn't have been more loud or clear.

So a sleepless night passed, with the Showgirl and me stretched alongside each other, listening to the hacking snore of our neighbors while gasping for fresh air. Both of us did a fairly convincing job of feigning sleep, but at least one of us spent a good part of the night staring at the ceiling and wondering what the hell she had been thinking, coming all the way to Morocco for this. For my part, I lay in bed with my back to the Showgirl, staring at the wall and rueing the decision to come to Essaouira. I should have taken the initiative, booked a lovely hotel in Marrakesh, and used the privacy and anonymity afforded by a couple of days in a foreign city to weave its magic. Lying there listening to my colleagues turn over in bed, hoping morning would arrive before asphyxiation did, and lamenting my uselessness as a seducer of women, I found myself wishing the bed would simply open up and swallow me.

But with a new day came hope—and a new resolve on my part to take the proverbial bull by the horns. Determined to move away from patently jinxed Essaouira, I bundled up the Showgirl and her belongings and threw her into the back of another taxi. For another two-hour cab ride. Across the same featureless desert. Back to Marrakesh, where she had started her journey the day before. But this time it was different. There was no Mary, no tales of Tropical Phil. There would be no rotting fish guts or hotel rooms that smelled of paint thinner. It was just her and me and the prospect of the two of us alone in an exotic new city. It was, I told myself over and over, now or never.

Once back in Marrakesh I selected the cheesiest five-star hotel I could find. It looked for all the world as if the Love Boat had become somehow marooned in the desert of central Morocco. It had all the charm of a 1970s Miami megahotel smack dab in the middle of Marrakesh. There were brass fittings at every turn, macramé wall hangings, and bellboys dressed in ill-fitting, dirty white tunics. Our room, a pastiche of pastels and floral design, had been thoughtfully decorated with only a passing regard for anything resembling good taste. It was perfect.

"Will that be a double room or a twin room, sir?" came the inquiry of the mustachioed man checking us in.

"A double will be fine," I responded, without missing a beat. I stared intently at the guest register, not daring to make eye contact with the Showgirl. She tactfully looked away, pretending not to have heard.

We moved our bags to the room, made a few jokes about the awful interior design, and pointedly refused to acknowledge the large queen-size bed—the proverbial elephant in the room. We quickly donned swimsuits and headed for the pool.

Down at the pool, we stretched out on sun beds. Pale imitations of proper cocktails were ceremoniously delivered to us by a team of six eager-to-please waiters. The ignominy of the previous night slowly fell away. We were beginning to relax now, starting to feel comfortable in each other's exclusive company, unwatched and unmonitored by others. I felt free and daring.

Later in the afternoon we trekked off to the city center for a couple of hours, shopping in the sprawling souk, a shady labyrinth inside the Marrakesh medina, filled with tourist pap of every hue and variety. A late-afternoon downpour of rain suddenly rendered the souk a muddy, dripping maze. Rivulets of dirty water coarsed through the darkened alleys while heavy globules of rainwater dripped from the tattered canopy overhead. We darted from stall to stall, dodging patches of rain and holding hands so as not to lose each other in the market's mad cacophony. Drenched and laughing, we picked our way out of the souk, pausing occasionally to take refuge in a textile merchant's shop or under the awning of a pottery merchant's makeshift stall.

Once back at the hotel, we set about cleaning ourselves up for dinner. I sat politely on the large bed, feigning interest in the room service menu while the Showgirl got ready for dinner. Just as I was fumbling in my suitcase near the bathroom door, she stepped out of the bathroom in a towel. We performed the time-honored dance of the slightly embarrassed, both stepping left, then both stepping right, before one of us ceded passage to the other. All the while I did my best Hugh Grant impression, apologizing profusely for nothing in particular.

For dinner I chose a secluded little Moroccan restaurant. It was a

cavernous, candlelit room beyond a secret door tucked down a dark al-
ley. A man dressed in traditional *djellaba,* holding aloft a flame torch,
led us to the restaurant's entrance. Stepping off the pitch-black back-
street on which the restaurant was located, we found ourselves in an
open-air courtyard. A small fountain tinkled in the center, its waters
scattered with rose petals. The dining room was a massive, high-
ceilinged room, decorated with Moorish tiles. We were the only two
in the restaurant, our easy conversation interrupted only by the gentle
gurgle of another rose-petal-filled fountain and a traditional Moroccan
musical trio warbling gently. I couldn't believe my luck. The setting
was perfect. Off the back of an eminently pleasant afternoon in the romantic setting of the Marrakesh medina, I now found myself filling
the Showgirl's wine glass in a candlelit Arabian cavern for two.

From an Essaouira-inspired disaster, a Marrakesh miracle had
sprung. All that was needed now was a hearty Moroccan meal, a bottle or two of the local red to loosen up proceedings, and a subtle up-
ping of the flirting ante.

Arriving back at the hotel some three hours later, a little tipsy and
basking in the two-person bubble we had happily created, we decided
a midnight dip in the pool was in order. Sneaking past the night
watchman in the foyer, we slid into the glassy waters of the swimming
pool, still warm from a day spent under the Moroccan sun. Palm tree
fronds were silhouetted against a full moon. The water caressed our
suntanned limbs. The soporific effect of two bottles of Moroccan wine
took hold of our heads. The lilt of the Showgirl's laugh, the way the
hotel lights reflected off the water and played in her eyes, had me cap-
tivated. I moved slowly toward her. There was a smile of recognition,
a coquettish tilt of the head. And then we kissed.

Chapter 35

Life Is a Cabaret

AS NEWS OF my budding new relationship with the Showgirl spread, many who knew me were bemused that someone as elegant, accomplished, and downright beautiful as the Showgirl would be interested in the likes of me. How, they would wonder—often out loud and with more genuine incredulity than I cared for—did a geek like me land a class act like her? It was a question I heard often, most commonly from mates wishing to emulate my form, and in response I invariably shrugged and hinted at an animal magnetism that made me irresistible to all women.

The truth, though, was a whole lot more pedestrian. The science of Showgirl seduction was in fact deceptively simple. These girls are uniformly strikingly good-looking. Each night they take to the stage and become visions of exquisite feminine beauty. But because of the hours they work and the men to whom they are most commonly exposed, finding a decent fella is, for the average female cabaret dancer, nigh on impossible. Starting work at eight p.m., when most people are preparing to go out, and finishing at two a.m., when most people are preparing to go to sleep, means the sample of eligible bachelors whom the average showgirl meets is relatively small. The only men with whom they spend any real time are male cabaret dancers, a good 60 percent of whom are gay. Taken together, you have what dating experts might call a captive audience.

The secret to nabbing a showgirl, as I discovered, is actually quite simple. You just have to be able to hold your drink well enough to be still standing at five a.m., be relatively presentable, and have enough self-esteem and self-possession that you don't mind feeling like the short, ugly kid at every one of their gatherings. Once you master that, life truly is a cabaret.

Courting a showgirl, I discovered, has many fringe benefits. Apart from the obvious, it affords an entrée into a most remarkable world. For it takes a special kind of person to become a cabaret dancer. First of all, you need to be unusually accomplished in the coordination stakes. A streak of physical beauty never hurts; nor does a natural tendency for performance and drama. But the most crucial prerequisite for anyone wishing to make it as a Parisian cabaret dancer is a casual relationship with reality.

Lizzy, one of the Showgirl's dancing colleagues from the U.K., had that quality in spades. Unfailingly pleasant and possessed of a genuinely good heart, she had been dancing professionally since the age of fifteen, when she joined Julio Iglesias's European tour as one of the crooner's backup dancers. By virtue of Lizzy's relative youth at the time and the extreme lifestyle into which she had been thrust, Julio reputedly took the young charge under his wing, calling her "my little baybeee" and taking a genuine paternal interest in her subsequent career. Life for Lizzy post-Julio had been a succession of dance contracts with various cabaret theaters before she landed the gig at the Lido, aged twenty-one.

She was a very attractive young woman, the sort whose height and beauty could cause an entire restaurant to fall silent when she entered. The problem was, she was acutely aware of her appearance, and Lizzy's looks, as a result, were not so much a part of her persona as they *were* her persona. Worryingly, she had not only assumed the nickname

"Barbie" within the ranks of the Lido dancers, but she actively encouraged people to refer to her using the less-than-flattering nickname.

The only thing more certain than Lizzy being late for work every day was that her tardiness would have invariably been caused by a melodrama of epic proportions. Lizzy was partial to the odd pet, a kitten here, a puppy there. They were usually named after her fashion designer of choice at the time. Hence Louis the puppy and Chanel the cat entered Lizzy's life for brief but typically dramatic periods. One evening, as the Showgirl sat quietly in her dressing room applying makeup in preparation for the evening's show, Lizzy came rushing in with tears streaming down her face.

"Shay," she managed between sobs, "do you have a shovel I could borrow?"

In her thirteen years in showbiz, the Showgirl had been exposed to some interesting characters and had seen and heard pretty much everything. But this was a new one. Intrigued, she paused in the middle of applying enormous fake lashes to her eyelids and asked, "Now why would you need a shovel, Lizzy?"

"Louis has died," Lizzy announced through tears. "I want to give him a proper burial. I want to bury him in Parc Monceau." Parc Monceau is one of the city's more refined public spaces. It is an oasis of calm, a carefully maintained, extremely proper French garden in the heart of one of Paris's most exclusive neighborhoods.

"You can't just bury a dog in a public park," the Showgirl replied, doing her best not to laugh. "There are laws against that. Besides, what are you going to do? Carry him up there in a plastic bag and dig a hole when no one is watching?"

As well as being one of the senior dancers in the Lido troupe, the Showgirl—by virtue of her age, experience, and healthy relationship with common sense—was something of a den mother to the dysfunctional younger show sprites who surrounded her. It was to her that they turned when they couldn't connect their phone, fill out their tax forms, or fathom the mysterious workings of French bureaucracy. Or, as it now seemed, when they needed to dig a hole in a public park to dispose of a dead pug. Eventually the Showgirl convinced Lizzy of the foolishness of scaling the twelve-foot-high wrought-iron fences of Parc Monceau by night to stage a midnight interment. Lizzy finally opted for a cremation of the unfortunate pooch. To this day the ashes of Lizzy's much-loved canine (the same one for which she was prepared to scale a fence and break the law) are still sitting on a shelf in a vet's office in Paris's west, waiting to be collected.

Louis's exposure to the mad world of Lizzy was at least mercifully short, but Chanel the kitten had to endure a longer sentence as her mistress's pet. When one afternoon the ordeal apparently became too much, Chanel found a quiet corner of Lizzy's apartment and hid out. The hysteria that ensued included a good half hour of Lizzy riding up and down her street on her small rhinestone-embossed metal scooter, calling her cat's name and telling the ladies of the night (who used Lizzy's street as a staging ground for their activities) that she had *"perdu ma chatte."*

"Elle est grande, comme ça!" Lizzy explained to them earnestly, indicating with her hands the approximate size of her "lost pussy"— blissfully unaware she was using the French slang term for a woman's privates. Exactly what they made of the toweringly tall young English girl scootering up and down their street, telling all and sundry she had lost her pussy, which was "about this big," can only be imagined.

But if Lizzy was a constant source of amusing anecdotes from the Lido, she had no monopoly on eccentric behavior. Among the boys there was twenty-one-year-old Ross—or Diana, as he was known to his castmates. Among his many other interesting attributes (including the fact that his surname was Parker-Carr), Ross had pectoral implants. As a result, every shirt he owned featured a plunging neckline to maximize chest exposure—and those that didn't were soon cut into compliance with a trusty pair of scissors. Ross liked to accentuate his newly (and expensively) acquired assets by massaging baby oil into his beloved chest. He also liked to share it with others. Many others. Often. Even sometimes at the same time. On any given evening he would rush into work after a night and day spent handcuffed to a strange bed for the S&M pleasure of a random stranger or three.

"Oh my god, sorry I'm late," he would exclaim to the Showgirl, rushing into the dressing room. "I was with these three guys last night, and one of them was really into—"

"Okay, enough, Ross, spare me the details," the Showgirl would interrupt, lest she be showered with gruesome details of her silicon-enhanced colleague's less-than-conventional extracurricular activities. Ross, also from England, appeared to single-handedly keep the French fake tan industry in business.

He would often choose midperformance to make wry observations to the Showgirl. "I don't believe in short people," he once informed her, apropos of nothing in particular. On another occasion, while the pair of them were waiting backstage to make their entrance, he stared thoughtfully at her bare breasts before announcing that a colleague with whom he had worked the previous year in Monaco had also once worked with the Showgirl and was convinced that her breasts were not real. (Such, apparently, was the level of conversation backstage at the Lido.) Barely pausing to register the absurdity of standing seminaked in a showgirl costume while a gay man dressed as a bird of paradise questioned the provenance of her breasts, the Showgirl insisted they were just as God had given them to her and invited him to check for himself. Several counts before he "flew" on stage, he gave a perfunctory squeeze. Satisfied that they were the genuine article, he expressed his admiration, then disappeared toward the spotlight in a flurry of lycra and feathers.

Just another day at the office for the Showgirl.

Also from England, and also doing his bit to enhance the reputation of showfolk everywhere, was Luke. A natural redhead, Luke dyed his hair and eyebrows black each month in an intricate home-dye procedure involving tin foil and toothpaste. He also had a razor-sharp wit and a penchant for gossip—if you wanted something spread about the Lido in the fastest, most efficient way possible, all you had to do was tell Luke. And he had developed a series of unpaid debts at various corner stores in his neighborhood, such that being with him and needing to pop into a shop to buy a drink became a precarious undertaking.

"Can't go in that one. It's a Fraud Shop," he would advise, referring to a scene of one of his petty crimes.

Others were truly charming, if a little crazy. Tobias "the human toothpaste commercial" Larsson was a freakishly tall Swede with a heart as big as his smile was bright. He traveled in a pack of fellow Swedes, all of whom were models and so impossibly good-looking you wanted to hate them—except that they were infuriatingly nice. Foremost among his gaggle of unfeasibly good-looking friends were Jan and Jon (pronounced *yaan* and *yoon*). I could never manage the subtleties to properly pronounce their names and hence referred to them as the Swedish Wonder Twins. One had blond hair, blue eyes, and a jawline to make Brad Pitt jealous. The other was dark-haired and brooding and seemed to always be in some exotic location shooting Chanel campaigns.

For his part Tobias had been a juggler, a tightrope walker, a firebreather, an importer of Moroccan smoking pipes, and a free postcard entrepreneur and had even "done time" in Sweden for drunk driving. All by the age of twenty-three. Now he was earning a living wearing elephant masks and g-strings on the stage of the world's most famous cabaret—the absurdity of which was completely, and endearingly, lost on him.

When summer rolled around, Tobias would talk incessantly of the beauty of his homeland, eventually convincing a troupe of us—including the Showgirl and me—to travel to the Swedish countryside, where his parents had a cabin. Jointly owned by his father Kent and his uncle Bent, the cabin was spectacularly located by a lake in a picture-postcard Scandinavian pine forest. Tobias had thoughtfully invited the Swedish Wonder Twins, plus two Brazilian male models with whom he happened to be sharing his apartment that month, plus their Australian male model friend. Suffice it to say, when it came time to strip down and swim in the lake, I feigned an earache and opted to stay safely clothed on shore.

Complementing the troupe of Lido male dancers were a handful of taciturn Russians. Direct from the Kirov Ballet, they had come to dance cabaret in Paris because it paid better and offered an official escape route from the dreariness of life in the former Soviet Union. The Russian boys were uniformly mute and would utter only a monosyllabic *da* in response to any question. Except for Alexei, who hailed from the Black Sea. Alexei loved to talk, and though he had a heart of gold, he had the memory of a goldfish. He was especially bad at remembering names and hence called everyone "darling"—which, delivered in a thick Russian accent, was actually quite charming.

Upon arriving in Paris, Alexei and his partner Michael had bought a cat. When their feline started to develop mobility problems, they took him to the vet.

"And wouldn't you know it, darling," he later explained to the Showgirl. "It turns out our little Plushka has acute arthritis, kidney failure, two hips which do not work, and as if this isn't bad enough, is a hermaphrodite. Apparently he has both sets of sex organs. And his knees they bend to the side, darling!" Suffice it to say, with so much stacked against him/her, Plushka gave up the ghost early in his/her life. Small mercies, and all that.

Part of this heady backstage mix were a few intracast relationships, one of which saw a male Lido dancer dump his Moulin Rouge boyfriend to start dating a Lido showgirl. There was never a dull moment. That the Showgirl managed to survive eight years in Paris (four at the Moulin and now four at the Lido) without becoming a complete freak was testament to the fact that underneath the sequins and feathers, a sensible head sat atop her lovely shoulders.

My budding relationship with the Showgirl, and the fact that I had met many of the crew that made up the Lido cast during long evenings of extracurricular drinking, made me an honorary member of the Lido family. While waiting for the Showgirl at the stage door, postperformance, I would chirrup my hellos and dispense French-style double-cheek kisses to what seemed like a constant flow of beauties. Russians, Americans, English, Australians, French, and Dutch—they would pour out the door, greet me with a smile of recognition, and peck me on the cheek before being spirited off into the night by a waiting taxi, husband, or boyfriend. That I could barely tell one from the other, so tall and uniformly striking were they, seemed not to register with them. By cunningly employing a rolling series of noncommittal greetings—including "Hey, how are you!" and "Good to see you—did you have a good show?"—I was usually able to bluff my way out of most potentially embarrassing situations.

One night I stood at the stage door with a male buddy who was keen to meet a Creature of the Night of his very own. He hovered expectantly at my ear as the parade of air-kissing began.

"Who was that?" he would whisper insistently after another beauty fielded my inane "Have a good show?" inquiry before disappearing into the night.

"Absolutely no idea," I would respond.

"And that one? What's her name?" he would ask, after I had spent five minutes discussing in detail a tall blond dancer's imminent plan to leave the Lido to perform on a cruise ship.

"Couldn't tell you."

But if the family into which I had been happily drawn was a sprawling and relatively dysfunctional one, and though its members were difficult to tell apart, there was no denying that it was a family in which everyone truly looked out for one another. Thrust as they all were into a topsy-turvy lifestyle, most of which was played out at night, and forced to spend most of their waking hours in one another's company, the dancers enjoyed a distinct camaraderie. Together they weathered one another's ups and downs, celebrated special occasions, and helped each other navigate the maze of daily life in Paris. Their network of mutual support spread beyond the dressing room of the Lido and into their daily lives.

What that meant, among other things, was that if a showgirl went away on vacation, she could expect her plants to be watered, her mail to be collected, and her pets to be minded. Even if that pet happened to be Harry.

Chapter 36

There's Something About Harry

Harry—or Satan With Fur, as I liked to call him—was the world's most evil dog. A short-arsed little rat of a thing, with a serious case of Small Dog Syndrome, he was a yappy, snappy, uptight bundle of bitterness. His bite was at least as bad as his bark, as I knew from repeated exposure to it, and the chip he carried on his tiny Yorkshire terrier shoulders was at least twice as big as he was.

Harry belonged to Lisa, a good friend of mine and an even better friend of the Showgirl. Lisa was possessed of a wholly unnatural attachment to her dog, as well as a deluded idea that it was both sweet and adorable. The Showgirl would constantly tell me I was imagining it, but I used to swear Harry had an overactive hatred gland, filled with pure bile, which he only tapped whenever I was in the room. I used to tell her that if Linda Blair's character in *The Exorcist* (spinning head, projectile vomiting) had a canine equivalent, Harry was definitely it.

It's fair to say that Harry hated a lot of things in life. He hated Rollerbladers, detested motor scooters, and went apoplectic at the sight of a cyclist. Sit with him at an outdoor café, and he was territorial to the point of obnoxious, growling at passersby and snapping at their heels. But perhaps his most antisocial attribute was his apparent dislike of black people. At the very sight of a black person, he would launch into a barking, snarling frenzy—a trait that made a reluctant racist of you each time you walked him down the street. Harry also hated most males, especially those who had any kind of relationship with his owner. He seemed to take as a personal affront any friendship Lisa developed with any member of the opposite sex.

It has to be said that I'm not great about being unloved. Not to put too fine a point on it, I can't imagine why anyone would not love me and want to constantly be around me. To therefore encounter a canine—allegedly man's best friend—that would whip itself into a foaming, shivering frenzy every time I entered the room left me bemused. Any normal person would simply accept that the dog and they were just never fated to get on, but it left me distressed. Determined to make the goddamned thing love me, I would force the issue, backing it into corners to smother it with affection. That ploy, unsurprisingly, only served to make matters worse. And so eventually I gave up on him, choosing instead to quietly detest him and glaring at him with contempt whenever Lisa's back was turned.

Whenever Lisa traveled, the Showgirl and I would take care of Harry. What this amounted to, at least in my case, was locking Harry in the living room of the Love Pad (where Shay had taken to staying most nights) and occasionally flicking open the door to throw food at him. I reasoned that the less time he and I actually spent in each other's company, the better off we both would be. But the funny thing about Harry was that while he apparently hated me, he couldn't stand not being in the same room as me. Whether it was to keep an eye on me lest I mount a rearguard attack, or simply because beneath his gruff exterior there was a scared little doggy just wanting to be loved, the little horror would follow the Showgirl and me from room to room. Normally we didn't mind. As long as we remembered to put on our shin guards to counter his regular, unprovoked nips at the ankle, we were generally happy for the company (schizophrenic though it was).

But one night his need to be near us proved a little too much.

As anyone who has ever owned a dog will attest, man's best friend is occasionally privy to scenes of household nudity and bedroom intimacy that, as a discerning, decent human being, you would never expose to any other living creature (unless you are Pamela Anderson or Paris Hilton). A naked dash from the shower here, a nude wander about the living room there, a bit of afternoon delight between consenting adults for good measure—it's all part of the daily experience of being a dog. On this particular night Harry the pint-size pervert decided to take a ringside seat to a rather energetic bout of lovemaking. Now, quite apart from the moral and hygienic arguments for keeping a canine at bay during the making of the love, there are also performance issues to consider. It's difficult to maintain focus, for example, when you feel a pair of beady brown eyes trained on your alabaster buttocks.

But on this particular night Harry's penchant for peeping turned out to be the least of our problems. A much more pressing problem was his habit of ingesting anything that passed his snout. It was just after three a.m. on a warm August midweek evening. Having just enjoyed a spot of intrarelationship intimacy, the Showgirl and I were lying back and drifting off to sleep, listening to the city slumber around us.

Suddenly, out of the darkness and breaking the silence, we heard the sound of Harry chewing. I roused myself from my state of semisleep, lifted my head, and puzzled over the unusual noise.

"What could he possibly be eating here in the bedroom?" I said to the Showgirl. "There's nothing on the floor except—*Oh my god!*"

It was one of those horrible realizations that hit you like a freight train, a conclusion so terrifying in its inevitability that you are momentarily paralyzed. I sat bolt upright and scrambled for the light.

After a split-second the Showgirl registered the truth. "Oh no, please tell me he hasn't," she said, jumping to her feet and racing across the room to Harry. "Please tell me the condom is still there on the floor."

It wasn't. We could only conclude it was halfway down a canine gullet, making its slow but steady passage through a doggy esophagus toward a doggy stomach, doubtless hell-bent on becoming permanently lodged in a doggy intestine.

I lurched for Harry's mouth, attempting to force my fingers down his throat in a desperate attempt to retrieve the offending article. To no avail. The pooch sat and looked back at me with what I swear was pure defiance. As if to underline his disdain, he took a final, contemptuous gulp and proudly licked his chops.

"This is *not* happening!" the Showgirl exclaimed, hands on head, imagining being slowly killed by an irate best friend. "Oh god, no—this *cannot* be happening!"

"Are you kidding?" I responded, beginning to see the humor in the situation. "This is *hilarious*! He just chowed down a condom!"

It was a moment of pure, ill-timed blokery, of the kind that men the world over have perfected over eons of intersex miscommunication. It earned me a lightning rebuke.

"You are *not* helping, and this is *not* funny!" the Showgirl shot back. "If anything happens to this dog, Lisa is going to kill us. Both of us. Painfully and slowly. Now get online and find a vet, *fast*!"

Suitably chastened, I hopped out of bed and turned on the computer. As Shay tried to talk Harry into a voluntary vomit, which he was having none of, I scanned the online yellow pages for a nearby emergency vet.

"Here's one," I said, passing the phone to the Showgirl. "He's in the quartier, and he does twenty-four-hour visits. You better call. Your French is better than mine. And I'm not sure I can speak to him without laughing."

A withering look wiped the smirk off my face.

"*Bonjour?*" the Showgirl began, as the vet roused from his slumber to answer the phone. "*Oui. Excusez moi de vous déranger, monsieur, mais nous avons un petit problème avec notre chien.*"

I stifled a guffaw, knowing what was coming next.

"*Il a mangé un préservatif,*" she continued.

Apparently the vet was not the slightest bit fazed by this revelation. "It will probably pass naturally," he informed the Showgirl, without missing a beat. "But if you wanted, I could give him an injection to make him vomit. That way you will get your *préservatif* back."

It was a worrying response on several counts. First, what kind of people did he think we were to want to retrieve (and presumably reuse) a prophylactic that had been half-ingested by a dog? And second, given the reflexive and apparently routine nature of his response, did he receive a lot of calls in the dead of the night from people who wanted to have a condom removed from their dog's innards? Before I had time to properly reflect on the depths to which modern society had sunk, we were hastily donning clothes and setting off for the vet clinic.

As he trotted happily through the deserted streets of the Marais, Harry looked like he hadn't a care in the world. Head held high and tail erect, he sniffed excitedly at every car tire and lamppost we passed. For him this emergency dash to the twenty-four-hour vet was an unscheduled pee and poo walk. We stood outside the clinic, watching the first light of dawn turn the sky cobalt gray. Before long a disheveled figure shuffled into view. Hair tousled and shirt untucked, wearing what looked suspiciously like a pair of pajama bottoms, the vet—a young guy in his early thirties—beckoned us inside the clinic and invited us into the operating theater.

"Let's have a look then," he said. "How long ago did he eat it?"

"About half an hour ago," said the Showgirl, impressively maintaining composure. The compact had been established. We would talk of the condom currently lodged in Harry's gut as if it were anything else—a marble, a pen lid, a plastic bag. Anything but what it actually was, the carelessly discarded prophylactic of two now sheepish, formerly horny Australians. I looked steadfastly at my feet, certain that I would burst out laughing if I made eye contact with anyone.

"And you'd like me to induce him to vomit then?" the vet asked. "All it will take is an injection, and he should bring it straight back up."

"I think it's probably for the best," the Showgirl replied. "He's only a little dog, I don't want to take the risk of it lodging in his intestine." What she really meant was: *I don't want him passing a condom in two days' time when we will have given him back to his owner.*

The vet took a syringe and administered the injection.

For a full five minutes nothing happened. Harry pottered happily about the clinic, his little claws clicking on the tiles. Then suddenly he stopped dead in his tracks, threw me a wide-eyed *what have you done to me?* look, and started heaving. His tiny body convulsed, and then, with a cough, a sputter, and an unholy retch, Harry delivered the goods. Keen to dispose of the evidence as swiftly as possible, I swooped in quickly with a handful of paper towels, mopped up the vomit, and ditched the soggy mess into the vet's garbage bin.

By the time we left the vet clinic, Harry with an empty stomach and the Showgirl with an empty purse (having forked out a fortune for emergency vet services), the sun was starting to come up. Though distinctly woozy on his little feet, Harry picked up where he had left off a half hour before, sniffing, pissing, and scampering his way up the deserted street.

"Do you think we should tell Lisa?" the Showgirl asked.

"Are you mad?" I replied. "The dog is fine, nobody needs to know. Some things are better left unsaid. Let's keep it a secret."

And so we did.

Chapter 37

Allez, Allez Lido!

As the black curtain draws back and the band strikes up, she floats down a set of mirrored stairs, swathed in an 18,000-euro ostrich-feather coat. A tall, stylized crown of diamanté sits atop her head and glitters under the spotlight. Striding center stage, she pulls open the coat and, with arms outstretched, glides toward the audience. A necklace of jewels cascades over perfectly formed breasts. A belt of tiny white rhinestones spills over hourglass hips. Legs that seem to go forever lead up to that smile, that wonderful, infectious smile. She is infused with the joy of dance. Her body moves with effortless grace. Each movement is a fluid, sensual celebration of the human form, of music and beauty.

I sit in the darkened auditorium, my eyes glued to her. To watch her on stage is truly inspirational. The auditorium is full tonight, and the audience is breathless, mesmerized by her every move.

The music builds to a crescendo, and massive pieces of elaborate set pull back to reveal forty-five dancing girls, each sporting a barely there mirror-mosaic dress, a golden sequin-encrusted hat, impressively high heels, and a backpack with a huge spray of purple and black feathers. They move as one downstage, envelop the Showgirl with their feathers, and in a rolling series of high kicks and precision turns, spin on their heels and strike a long-legged pose. The stage is a riot of gaudy color, a heady confection of sequins, feathers, legs, and smiles. The audience is on its feet, applauding wildly. There are now sixty dancers on stage and almost a thousand people in the auditorium. But as far as I am concerned, there are only two of us in the room tonight. As the song hits its final high note, a phalanx of burly Russian male dancers thrusts her up into the air. Hovering in midair, she looks my way, catches my eye, and gives me the subtlest of winks. My heart soars.

THE LIDO DE PARIS is widely considered the most prestigious cabaret revue in the world. In the heady, albeit rarefied, sphere of international cabaret, it is the granddaddy of them all. If Paris created the revue format, the Lido has perfected it, setting the standards by which all similar shows—be they in Las Vegas, Seoul, Shanghai, or up the road at Montmartre—are measured. In years gone by the Lido was the venue *du choix* for a tuxedo- and tafetta-wearing jet set. For a good thirty years after its opening in 1946, a night spent quaffing Champagne in a candlelit booth at the Lido was considered the height of international sophistication.

These days the venue plays host mostly to French families on a special night out, middle-aged couples up from the country on a once-in-a-lifetime visit to the nation's most prestigious cabaret, Eurostarring Brits across for a night of Champs Elysées glamour, dodgy Russian businessmen with busty blondes in tow, and busload upon busload of Korean, Japanese, and Indian tourists. Though the clientele has changed over the years and the venue has become decidedly less exclusive, the Lido remains a proud part of the French national heritage. Tell a French person you work as a Lido dancer, and they will almost bend over double in reverence. Tell them you are going out with a Lido dancer, and they marvel out loud at your incredible good fortune.

"Les Bluebells," as female Lido dancers are called (after the iconic former ballet mistress, Madame Bluebell), are considered to be the quintessence of Parisian sexy chic. As a result, Lido girls enjoy a mild kind of celebrity in Paris—which they are generally happy to assume, especially when it means special service at restaurants, line-jumping at nightclubs, and rarely having to pay for a drink at a bar. Their status is certainly not hindered by the fact that most Lido dancers spend the better part of each night on stage in a state of semi-undress.

As one of several revue shows in Paris, the Lido de Paris features a line of dancing girls who perform topless. The Showgirl was among them. So I had to become accustomed to the fact that my new girl-friend made her living by dancing every night, twice a night, with her breasts exposed to a room of up to two thousand strangers. But I have never been the jealous type, and—not to put too fine a point on it— the Showgirl had spectacular breasts that frankly deserved a standing ovation every night.

Besides, in the context of the Lido spectacle, and presented as they were draped in jewels and swathed in feathers, breasts were about the least noteworthy aspect of the Lido show. Okay, perhaps that's over-stating it a little. A stage full of beautiful, leggy women with exposed breasts is noteworthy no matter what the context. But in France, where an exposed buttock and set of breasts are routinely used to ad-vertise yogurt on the sides of buses, a high-end revue at an esteemed cabaret venue on the respectable Champs Elysées in which a few women in elaborate feathered costumes just happen to have their tops off is actually considered quite tame.

Moreover, unlike people in more prurient countries, the French have always been very comfortable with the female form. They are neither offended nor threatened by the naked female body. For them, cabaret is a proud form of artistic expression, one that has been simultaneously celebrating the joy of dance and the beauty of the female physique for centuries. And as the French explain pa-tiently to the sniggering ranks of titillated tourists who come to see cabaret shows: they are breasts—more than half the world has them. Get over it.

"But doesn't it make you feel strange?" people would often ask me. "To have your girlfriend dancing topless in front of so many people every night?"

Strange, never. Proud, always. And if that sounded odd, I would defy them to watch the Showgirl dance and not be moved by the beauty of it. Her every move on stage was executed with studied poise. The tilt of her head, the flourish of her hand, the flick of her heel. The choreography seemed to start somewhere in her soul, then pass like a wave through her body before finally being released in a carefully poised extremity. One continuous, graceful movement segued smoothly into another. On stage the Showgirl would nightly make the improbable look effortless, the physically demanding appear graceful, and the excruciating seem elegant.

Excruciating it sometimes was. For make no mistake, beyond the glamour there was grind. The Lido is open 365 nights a year. The dancers perform two shows a night, six nights a week. The first show starts at 9:30, and the second starts at 11:30, finishing at 1:30 a.m. The revue in which the Showgirl danced, *Bonheur,* had cost more than nine million euros to stage. The costumes alone cost three million euros. Because of the size of this investment, *Bonheur* was scheduled to run at least five years to recoup costs.

The female dancers perform in four-inch heels, often wearing feathered backpacks weighing up to twenty pounds and headgear weighing up to ten pounds. Because they high-kick on the same leg every show, twice a night, six nights a week, they often suffer ankle and knee injuries from the repetitive strain. Backs and necks are creaky, hips and hamstrings are strained, and bodies are bruised from being lifted awkwardly by enormous Russian dance partners. Their lives—and jobs—are not unlike those of professional athletes. And like professional athletes, they expect similarly brief careers. Pushed to extreme physical limits in the execution of their daily work, suffering injuries as a matter of course, most dancers stay on stage only until their mid-thirties, when fatigue and injury force them off.

As a principal dancer and "swing," the Showgirl was one of only a handful of cast members who knew how to perform all eighteen of the different female roles in the show—and regularly did so without so much as batting a false eyelash (a fact that never ceased to amaze me). For her, each night on stage was different from the one before. One night she was the featured principal dancer; the next she was a Bluebell in the chorus line. In recognition of her seniority and star quality, she even regularly replaced the singer, striding about the stage as the star of the show.

This variety helped keep her fresh, but she and the majority of her colleagues still had to step into the spotlight each night and perform the same show, every night, twice a night, for up to five years. Their challenge was to maintain enthusiasm, to dance each night as if it were their first. The task was made all the more onerous by the sight of Korean tourists slumbering in the front row. As any showgirl will tell you, herniating the disks in one's back on a nightly basis for the entertainment of snoring Koreans can sometimes prove a little disheartening.

It wasn't that they needed a riotously applauding audience each night. They didn't need to be showered with long-stemmed roses during each curtain call. But audiences that had the courtesy to stay awake, or at the very least not snore loudly during some of the show's quieter moments, were considered infinitely more pleasant to perform for. And it wasn't as if the show was boring. All the impressive sets, fancy costumes, and energetic dance performances—not to mention breasts—gave plenty to keep audiences on the edge of their seats.

And even occasionally off the edge of their seats.

During one matinee performance near Christmas the Showgirl was distracted from her onstage exertions by the sight of four waiters carrying the slumped form of an elderly gentleman through the auditorium toward the exit. We later learned that the old fella's heart had given out midway through the Lido spectacle. He was watching the show with his wife, having received tickets from their children for their golden wedding anniversary. The couple had traveled to Paris from their tiny provincial village in southern France to realize a long-held dream, to see the Lido de Paris, and it had all proven too much. At least for the husband it proved too much. But that wasn't going to stop the wife from enjoying the show. As her partner of fifty years was extracted from the seat next to her, she sat tight in her chair, refusing to budge until the revue was over. She was later overheard telling bemused maître d's and ambulance men that after waiting all those years and traveling all that way, she was not going to miss the end of the show.

The Lido creates a little bit of quintessentially Paris magic on stage each night. For those sitting in the auditorium, it offers up a world of grace, poise, and glamour, a trip back to a gentler, more elegant age. But step backstage at the Lido during a performance (as I had the unmitigated pleasure of doing on several occasions), and you found yourself in a whole other world. Down in the dressing rooms before the show, body makeup is slapped on with a common garden-variety sponge, of the type usually reserved for car washing. Fake eyelashes are applied to eyelids using Copydex wood modeling glue, apparently the sworn favorite of showgirls and drag queens everywhere. In fact, seen close up, full showgirl makeup looks not unlike that sported by drag queens. So bright were the stage lights, the gunk had to be applied with a trowel to give the desired glamour-puss effect.

On stage, and with the spotlights upon them, showgirls are elegance personified. They perform each carefully choreographed move with grace and delicacy. The second they step out of the glare of the spotlight, however, they become instantly ungainly and rambunctious. They clump off stage like a herd of frenzied, sequined giraffes. Dressers stand ready to collect the hats, feathers, and backpacks they discard as they gallop—in four-inch heels—to the dressing rooms, where another team of dressers waits to help them into whatever outlandish costumes the show requires next.

Remarkably enough, despite the thunder of hooves and the blaring of music, each showgirl is so adapted to her environment that she is capable of maintaining an uninterrupted flow of conversation with her colleagues, whether on stage or off, from the second the curtain goes up to the minute it comes down. They talk about where they had their legs waxed that day, problems they are having with their boyfriends, advice on how to fill out a tax form, plus whatever gossip and chitchat has filtered up from the dressing rooms below. And they continue these conversations on stage, while they are performing a series of complicated dance steps.

"Did you manage to fill out your tax return?" Step, ball change.

"No, not yet. I'm going to ask François to take a look at it." Double pirouette, turn, and smile.

"Are you two still seeing each other? I thought you'd dumped him." Turn, two, three, four.

"I did. Well, I will. Once he's helped me with my tax return." Prepare, pull up, back bend, and pose.

No topic of conversation is too banal. No language is too bawdy. And since the dancers hail from more than twenty different countries, at any given moment during the show the backstage area echoes with obscenities exclaimed in four different languages.

Witnessing a stream of obscenities pour from the perfectly painted mouth of an otherworldly creature, taller than your average Amazon woman and dressed as a pink feathered pompom, is nothing short of surreal. Even more surreal is to find yourself in conversation with one of them during a lull in onstage proceedings.

During one of my backstage sorties, while researching the much-talked-about article I had finally found a magazine to commission, I was approached repeatedly by dancers whom I had met socially through Shay. Dancers, I hasten to add, who each time I had interacted with them previously had been fully clothed. As they stood there making small talk in their sequined g-string and not much else—their unusual height and four-inch heels conspiring to ensure that my eyes were exactly at breast level—it was all I could do to concentrate on the conversation at hand.

Maintain eye contact! Maintain eye contact! I thought to myself over and over, nodding politely as they explained to me where they had been on vacation the week before.

This was the thing about Paris showgirls. Because they did what they did every night, six nights a week, they saw nothing even remotely unusual about their job. They were dancers; the Lido was a regular job and a prestigious gig to boot. Some people wore suits, sat at a computer, and sent e-mails for a living. They just happened to wear sequins and feathers and high-kick their hearts out.

Down in the dressing rooms they were surprisingly unpretentious. Contrary to popular expectation, the dressing-room camaraderie among dancers was considerable. Sure the Showgirl would occasionally return home with tales of backbiting and bitchiness, but for the most part the cast comprised one big, happy, well-fed family. And while you might expect that they passed the time between shows (the *entr'acte*) touching up their makeup, replying to sacks of unsolicited love letters, or checking the number of carats in the diamond trinket sent by a love-struck Romanian prince, what they really did was eat. A lot. Indeed, despite their amazing physiques—or perhaps, infuriatingly for other women, because of the metabolisms that went with those physiques—the human species *Showgirlis heightus maximus* appeared able to eat more than most mere mortals. Every cast member's birthday was marked with a dressing-room party, for which each dancer baked or bought an edible treat. These twenty-minute eating marathons invariably involved more cakes, chips, dips, cheese, chocolates, cookies, quiches, and pastries than you could poke a size-ten waistline at. And with a cast of sixty, there was usually a birthday every week, meaning the Showgirl seemed to be constantly tripping off to work with a plate of her signature homemade, all-butter, pink-iced cupcakes. A showgirl is weighed when she starts dancing at the Lido and is thereafter contractually obliged to neither gain nor lose more than five pounds during the period of her contract, but your average dancer would rather give up breathing than go on a diet.

During the early months of our courtship, the Showgirl and I would make semiregular visits to the Cloche d'Or, an all-night eatery in Montmartre that caters to a strictly showbiz clientele. Given that it was usually around two a.m., I tended to opt for something light and easy to digest, in full expectation that I would be lying horizontal in the next two hours. If the Showgirl was feeling peckish, she'd settle for an oven-baked Camembert as her entrée, followed by a *confit du canard* with potato *dauphinois*. If she was feeling ravenous, she'd tack on a crème brûlée for dessert. At another of my favorite late-night watering holes, Le Tambour, the Showgirl would turn up after work, take her place at the table of whatever drunken reprobates I happened to be consorting with that night, and promptly order a steak frites with Roquefort sauce. I used to sit and watch her devour her food in amazed admiration. A red-meat-scarfing, red-wine-guzzling gastronome trapped inside a Paris showgirl body. What was not to love?

Somehow, between the two cabaret shows a night, the two a.m. finishes, and my nominal nine-to-five existence, our courtship continued along its merry way. It was an essentially nocturnal affair, played out under the neon lights and rain-slicked streets of early morning Paris. It was unorthodox in the extreme, but not without its own unique romance.

BACK IN THE AUDITORIUM, the show is drawing to a close. As I sit sipping Champagne, watching my beloved do her job with strength, pride, and obvious joy, it occurs to me how extraordinarily lucky I am. And then, as if reading my thoughts, and just before she makes her entrance to perform the show's signature love songs, she fires off a quick text message.

This one's for you Curly.

Minutes later I watch her make her entrance and slink slowly downstage in a figure-hugging red-sequin dress. Finding her mark, she steps into the spotlight, seeks me out in the darkness, makes eye contact, and smiles, then sings:

Amoureuse,
Je me perds dans le bleu de tes yeux,
Amoureuse de tes mains, tes cheveux
Plus je te vois, et plus je te veux
Amoureuse
Si tu m'aimes, sur les quais de la Seine à Paris
Dans tes bras jusqu'au bout de la nuit
Toi et moi ensemble pour la vie
Si tu m'aimes.

It's a song about love. About lovers in Paris, and how love found in Paris lasts forever. And I know it is a song written for the show. And I know if it were any cheesier, the Frogs would have long ago packaged it up and exported it with great success. And yet in that quiet moment in the dark, I let myself imagine that the song was written just for us. That she is singing it to me, declaring her love in a blaze of high-kitsch cabaret glory. And I feel like the luckiest man on the planet.

Chapter 38

Moving On In

"LET'S MOVE IN TOGETHER," said the Showgirl one bright summer morning. We had just woken up. We were lying in bed together, our bodies entwined, staring at the ceiling and contemplating the day ahead. She said it like she would say "Let's have croissants for breakfast" or "Let's think about a trip to New York next summer." The tone was nonchalant, breezy, conversational.

On the face of it, there was nothing at all outrageous about her suggestion. No matter how you looked at it, it was a perfectly rational proposition. After all, it's not as if she had proposed we quit Paris and move to Texas to join a cult. She didn't ask me for a kidney or anything. Yet I could hear air-raid sirens blaring in my head. I invoked the tried-and-true response that has served men down the ages—and didn't say a word. She absorbed my silence and forged on.

"We've been together for almost a year now. At some point you are going to have to acknowledge that this is a real relationship."

Tapping an instinct innate in all men, I felt the commitment gland kick into action and quickly, seamlessly changed the topic. But the

Showgirl was no fool. She knew a diversionary tactic when she saw one. And what's more, she was clever enough to let it slide, content in the knowledge that now that she had sown the seed, she could revisit the ground in a week's time and see how it was germinating.

I used the ensuing week's respite to compile a mental list of all the blindingly obvious reasons why moving in together would not be a great idea. The Love Pad had been my faithful abode of five years—I couldn't just up and leave it. It's a hassle to notify everyone of my change of address. We'd both have to give notice on our respective apartments. If we broke our leases, we might not get our deposits back. Good apartments in Paris are hard to come by. Apartment hunting, and the drama of agreeing on which quartier we will move to, are stressful. Moving itself is always such a nightmare. All those boxes and all that painful purging of the clutter you have accumulated during five years of concerted hoarding.

"Why can't we just keep things going along as they are?" I said to the Showgirl the following week, when the topic was revisited. "You have your space when you need it, I have mine. It's perfect."

"But I never use my space," she replied, not unfairly. "I have a studio apartment I only ever use to change clothes in. It's a seven-hundred-euro-a-month closet." She did have a point. It was a shrewd shifting of the argument from an emotional to an economic imperative, and, as such, a direct appeal to the male side of my brain.

I used the subsequent week to mull over the math. If we were to move in together, we *could* get a much larger apartment than either of us was currently living in, and each pay less rent per month for the privilege. The Love Pad, after five years of neglect, *was* starting to look a little tatty around the edges. And god knows, a break from the Marais would do my liver no end of good. A change of scene was as good as a vacation. It wasn't like we'd be getting *married* or anything. It was just two sensible, consenting adults making a rational, com-monsense decision. A merger, if you like, that had sound economic underpinnings and fringe benefits to boot.

"All right," I said one night out of the blue, as we lay in bed to-gether.

"All right what?" she replied.

"All right, I'll move in with you."

I stared at the ceiling with a self-satisfied grin pasted to my face, bracing myself for the flood of joy and outpouring of gratitude that were doubtless heading my way.

"Jesus!" she exclaimed. "There's no need to say it like it's an obligation, as though it's some massive sacrifice on your part." She paused to make sure I was fully aware of what an insensitive dolt I had just proven myself to be. "Are you sure you've thought it through? Checked with your mates? Made sure they approve? Are you certain it won't cramp your style too much? We wouldn't want you rushing into anything!"

It was a disaster, an unmitigated disaster. I'd committed a schoolboy error of the first order. You'd think a man of my age would know better, but I walked blindly into an emotional ambush. I skipped into the ring with my head held high and my guard down. I had been foolishly caught wrong-footed and was now floundering on the ropes, copping a hammering. She punched out a flurry of verbal jabs across the bed with all the fury of a woman slighted.

It's not that we men set out expressly to upset our female partners. It's just that our brains are wired differently. What the female brain sees as a romantic gesture and a display of commitment to the future growth of a relationship, the male sees as a practical way to save rent and not have to do his own laundry. It's just a question of perception, when you think about it.

Besides, it's a recognized scientific fact that women mature earlier than men. Women therefore see the writing on the wall sooner than do men. Perhaps because their primal radar is on constant lookout for a suitable mate to fertilize their eggs, women know instinctively, very early on, if a relationship has a chance of a future. We blokes, however, live for the moment. If it's good now and looks like it will continue to be good tomorrow, we're happy to hang around. Beyond that, all bets are off.

The Showgirl, intuitive by nature, had seen that our relationship had long-term potential a good five months before she raised the specter of us moving in together. Smart in that way women are, she also knew that I was going to take some time to catch up. But she knew too that like a tortoise to her hare, I would get there eventually.

I bought her a large bunch of flowers, wrote her a card bearing a mea culpa message, and whispered some genuinely heartfelt words of adoration in her ear.

Nothing would make me happier than moving in with you, I inscribed on the card, in a sign that after an unscheduled wobble, I was back in relationship cruise-control mode. After floundering on the turn, I was back in the race.

Within a week we had handed in notice on our respective apartments and were pounding the pavement in search of our new, shared home. It's no small thing to decide to move in with a partner. As a male, you may like to kid yourself that it is for purely commonsense reasons, but it represents a massive commitment. It wasn't as if I had been living a wild single life for the past year. Taking a leap into the realm of shared bills, bathrooms, and bed linen was going to be more of a natural progression than a jarring life change. But giving up my apartment would still put a definitive end to my bachelor days. The only consolation was that the notice period for our respective apartments was three months, so I would at least have a bit of time to get used to the idea.

Or not.

DURING A RARE meeting with clients one Thursday afternoon, I received a phone call. It was the Showgirl.

"You have to come and see this place," she whispered down the line, from the corner of the empty bedroom of an apartment she had visited on spec. "Now! You have to come now! There are three other couples here, and I swear this place will go in a minute."

I dutifully excused myself from my meeting, hopped on the Mojito, and tore across town. Pulling up at the address the Showgirl had given me—Rue Oberkampf in the eleventh arrondissement—I was underwhelmed. The street was a bustling Paris rue filled with food shops, with a fresh fruit market, a butchery or two, and a few bakeries thrown in for good measure. It was fine—a run-of-the-mill Paris street—but nothing special.

The building was an elegant, eighteenth-century stone affair. Beautifully restored, it had a commanding presence in the street. Taking the elevator to the sixth floor as instructed, I knocked on the door and waited. Footsteps approached from behind the door. A click of the lock, the door swung inward, and—wow.

Polished wooden floorboards stretched down a ten-yard hallway, leading into a huge double living room that looked out across the rooftops of eastern Paris. Directly ahead the twin spires of Saint Ambroise Church were russet against a clear blue sky.

The Showgirl stood grinning in one corner of the room.

"Come here," she beckoned, leading me back up the hallway. "Wait until you see this." We walked into the bedroom and stood at the window. I was rendered uncharacteristically speechless.

The whole of Paris was laid out before us. Looking from left to right, I could see practically every major monument in the city. The dome of the Pantheon, the towers of Notre Dame, the piped profusion of the Pompidou Center, the Arc de Triomphe—and of course, the Eiffel Tower. They sat in a neat line on the near horizon. A confusion of lead roofs and terracotta chimney pots stretched out before us. If you had asked someone to imagine the typical Parisian apartment with the quintessential Parisian view, this would be it.

By virtue of the fact we were on the sixth floor, and therefore in the roof of the building, our walls rose up from the floor and gently arched inward at ceiling level, giving a garret feel to the rooms. Because our building was at the top of a small incline, our view across the Paris rooftops was uninterrupted. What's more, the apartment boasted sky, glorious sky, as far as the eye could see. In a city in which many people live out their days and nights in tiny, airless vaults whose only window gives onto a dank courtyard, being able to look out a window and see actual sky affords a sense of space that it is impossible to put a price on. Hailing as we do from the Antipodes, where skies seem to go forever, we recognized in this apartment an antidote to the claustrophobia that a city like Paris otherwise invokes. In Paris apartment terms, we had stumbled upon a rare gem. I decided on the spot that I absolutely had to live here. We absolutely had to get the apartment.

Like many things in France, the securing of an apartment requires a dossier. The all-important gas bills must be within it, as must rental receipts from previous owners, pay slips from employers, character references, and bank account statements. You have to expose yourself shamelessly to a complete stranger, invite them to pore over every detail of your financial and personal life, then—just to make sure you have a fighting chance—employ every trick you know to gain an advantage over your fellow apartment-applicants.

Being a couple of foreigners—or *étrangers,* as the French would have it—we were at a natural disadvantage before we had even begun. But in some ways being foreigners worked in our favor. Tenancy laws in France are weighted heavily in favor of tenants: if a tenant stops paying rent, for example, the owner of the property only has a very small window each year in which to evict the troublesome lodger. So Parisian proprietors sometimes hedge their bets by taking on foreign tenants, who are more likely to leave after a certain period. They also like foreigners because we are usually blissfully ignorant of our rights and can often be charged an absolute premium in rent.

Determined to get the apartment, I launched Operation Charm Offensive with our prospective landlady, a very pleasant young fashion designer and mother of two. As the Showgirl put the finishing touches to the dossier, making sure it contained, in triplicate, every gas bill either of us had ever been sent, I slipped in a copy of the article I had written for an Australian magazine about the Showgirl dancing at the Lido. It was a shameless playing of the Lido card, an unabashed instance of pimping my girlfriend in order to secure an apartment. It worked like a charm. Within hours of submitting the dossier, we received a phone call from the landlady. In between gushes about the Lido, she told us the apartment was ours. Ten other couples, all French, had applied for the apartment, but we had won out. The Showgirl had struck again.

It meant we would both have to sublet our apartments for the upcoming three-month notice period. It meant we'd be madly packing up our lives in box- and masking-tape-frenzy much sooner than either of us had planned, but it was too good a pad to let slip by.

Three weeks later we picked up the keys from our new landlady and walked to the apartment to let ourselves in. It was early evening, just before the Showgirl had to take herself off to work. The front door creaked open to reveal gleaming floorboards. The smell of fresh paint hung heavily in the stale air. We threw open the windows to the unusually warm October night. The sound of our footsteps echoed through the rooms as we trooped excitedly from one to the other.

In the living-dining-room area, I stood for a few minutes wondering exactly what had possessed the former owners to line an entire wall and a large dividing structural support with full-length mirrors. The effect was not unlike that of a dance studio, though according to our landlady, the gay couple who previously owned the apartment installed the mirrors for another purpose completely.

"Apparently they used to have some really wild parties here," she informed us. The mind boggled. With such a brash 1970s heritage and more mirrors than your average nightclub, we decided on the spot to dub our new home Studio 54.

At our new bedroom window, we drank in the view. I popped the cork off a bottle of Champagne, and we toasted our new abode, staring across the rooftops, marveling at our good fortune. The sun was setting behind the Eiffel Tower. The sky was a burnt orange. On the bare wall behind us, the golden light of a glorious sunset cast an artful shadow of the ornate wrought-iron window railing.

I couldn't see the Love Pad or Rue Sainte Croix de la Bretonnerie from my new vantage point. Down there in the melee of central Paris, among the jumble of gray, cream, and terracotta, I could vaguely make out where they would be. Somewhere down there the boys would be preening, the bars would be heaving, my ideologically sound former neighbors would be painting protest banners, and Sticker Bitch would be prowling. But that I was no longer among it didn't matter a bit. I had Paris at my feet and the Showgirl sipping Champagne at my side. What more could a fella ask for?

Chapter 39

Rive Too Gauche

THERE IS A BIRD in Australia called the bowerbird. The male of the species is renowned in bird-watching circles for its propensity to collect shiny objects that it uses to decorate its nest, or bower, in the hope of attracting a mate.

As I sorted through the two distinct piles of boxes in the living room I now shared with the Showgirl—one pile containing all of her worldly goods, the other containing mine—it struck me that the male of the human species is not so far removed from its shiny-object-obsessed flighted friend. Brushed-steel appliances, alloy-accented furniture, and high-tech boys' toys—all in varying grades of gray, brown, and silver—sat in one corner of the room, defying integration with the Showgirl's lilac cushions, purple tulle curtains, and pink pebble lamp. Moving in together was clearly going to take some heavy-duty compromising. She would have to accept my stinky Afghan rug, I would need to agree to occasionally sleep on Laura Ashley sheets. She would have to create room in our shared closet for my enormous collection of T-shirts, and I would have to agree to share living space with Willy.

Willy had the appetite of an ox and the personality of a shrew. I've never been much for cats. If people can be divided into those who prefer dogs and those who prefer cats, I have always fallen on the side of the canines.

Ever since we had first set eyes on each other, Willy and I had enjoyed a fairly prickly relationship. I didn't much like him, and he pricked me regularly with his claws. But Willy had been a fixture in the Showgirl's life longer than I had been, and hence he had to be afforded a modicum of grudging respect. In fairness, Willy was probably no more excited about moving in with me than I was about moving in with him. During the year of my relationship with the Showgirl, Willy had been a dispassionate observer. As long as he was fed twice a day, had somewhere warm to sleep in between meals, and wasn't dragged outside on excursions to the park, he really could have cared less who was dating his mistress.

But once he was thrown into the same permanent living arrangement with that person, he apparently decided the lines needed a definite redrawing. It was claws at midnight. During the daylight hours, when the Showgirl was around, Willy and I would give the impression of being happy housemates. He would walk past me without hissing, and I would occasionally reach out to stroke him without giving him a backhander. The minute she walked out the door for work, though, the claws were sharpened and the gloves came off. Willy would purposefully seek out the armchair I liked to sit in and would move only when forcibly extracted—and even then, with a fit of hissing and spitting that would have made Linda Blair proud. For my part, and largely because my inner brat remains part of my personality I have never successfully grown out of, I would never fail to pass him in the living room without pulling his tail, holding him upside down, or chasing him with the dust-buster, of which he was unnaturally terrified. The minute the Showgirl returned from work, hostilities would immediately cease and an uneasy truce would reign. Until we were left alone again. It was a most unorthodox arrangement, but it seemed to work for us.

Thankfully, soon after we moved in together, the Showgirl and I took in another lodger: a little white fluffy dog called Polar. As in bear. It was not, it should be pointed out, a name we had selected. Polar belonged to one of the Showgirl's dancing colleagues, a fellow Aussie who had come to Paris for a one-year Lido contract and immediately purchased a dog. Apparently there was logic in there, but I was never able to see it. When said colleague then decided London was a better place to tread the boards, she hatched a plan to ply her furry friend with paracetamol, stick him in a box in the trunk of a car, and sneak him onto the ferry and into England. Wedded to reality as we rather boringly were, the Showgirl and I intervened and offered to puppy-sit Polar until his mom sorted out her shit.

Polar's passport (yes, like all dogs in France, Polar was in possession of a passport) clearly stated that he was a *bichon maltais*. Anyone who spent more than five minutes in his company would know that he was more Muppet than actual dog. He had a black button for a nose, two black currants for eyes, and a trotting gait that made it physically impossible for him to move without looking like a wind-up dog. And as if to max out the cute factor, the unruly mop of white shaggy hair that fell over his eyes gave him the look of a permanently disheveled, cheeky little schoolboy. Polar and Willy got on famously, provided Polar accepted Willy's rules of engagement: namely that the relationship was conducted entirely on Willy's terms, that Polar would be recognized only when Willy chose to acknowledge him, and that Polar would be thwacked roughly in the head twice a day when Willy was in the mood for a wrestle. Again, it was a most unorthodox arrangement, but it seemed to work for them.

Whenever I managed to drag myself away from this rooftop menagerie, I was fast discovering the joys of living in a real Parisian neighborhood. Only by moving away from the Marais did I become aware of how surreal it really was. Though I had been wholly seduced by its many charms when I first arrived in Paris, I had recently come to think of it as the most Disneyland-esque of Paris's twenty arrondissements. It was the prototypical Paris neighborhood you could imagine a Disney animator might dream up, all cobbled streets and quaintness. The Marais was so picture-postcard pretty, it sometimes felt like you were living in the Paris diorama in the It's a Small World attraction: a boiled-down, perfectly formed, so-authentic-it-must-be-a-film-set quartier of the French capital. Compounding the unreal nature of the Marais was the fact that it was almost exclusively populated by moneyed young French and expatriate professionals. It seemed to exist solely as a preening quartier for the city's gays and as a mustering point for "lifestyle stores" that did a roaring trade selling cheap, gimmicky homewares to people who found it amusing to spend forty euros on a cheese grater shaped like a Kewpie doll.

Oberkampf, by comparison, felt like a little pocket of real Paris. It had a much more diverse demographic makeup than that of the Marais. It had rich young professionals in recently converted warehouses, young families in large if dilapidated Haussmannian apartments, and a healthy smattering of old folk. There were blue-collar, white-collar, and no-collar workers. There were even black people and Arabs—somewhat of a revelation to me after the monocultural Marais.

Our new street proved in time to be a marked improvement over my old rue for its diverse range of shops. Rue Oberkampf was lined on either side with fresh food stores. A *fromagerie,* two *boucheries,* three *boulangeries,* two *pâtisseries,* and a fresh fruit *épicerie* covered all possible variations on the French-food-shop-*erie.* An Italian deli, a Greek deli, and a massive fresh food market, held every Tuesday and Friday at the end of the street, complemented the onstreet offerings and meant we wanted for nothing in the food department. By stark comparison, Rue Sainte Croix in the Marais was great if you were in the market for a tight T-shirt or suddenly found you had run out of amyl nitrate, but if you wanted a bottle of milk or a loaf of bread, it was useless.

The Showgirl and I soon became fixtures in our new arrondissement, helped largely by the presence of the Muppet-on-a-leash. I was amazed to discover, almost six years into my Paris stay, that the secret to getting Parisians to acknowledge you in the street was ownership of a cute dog. You could wander naked down a Parisian rue handing out fifty-euro notes, and no one would look twice. Step onto the street with a fluffy white dog in tow, however, and you had to beat them off with a stick. It explained why so many Parisians owned dogs. Without them, they would never actually interact with one another. The social fabric of the entire city was held together by a profusion of perpetually pooping pooches.

We soon became faithful customers of the various purveyors of fine foods in our rue and got to know the unique cast of characters that manned them. There was the Virgo fruit shop, as the Showgirl and I named it, because of the owners' habit of displaying all the produce in anally retentive rows. So perfectly was the fruit arranged, woe betide any man or woman who presumed to wander up and pluck an orange from the tray. A swift rebuke and sometimes a slap on the hand would ensure that the fruit was left undisturbed. Across the road was the Butchery We Never Visited. It was owned and operated by a dour, sallow-faced husband-and-wife duo. Despite several attempts to engage them in conversation, it was all we could do to extract a smirk out of them when ordering our *entrecôte*.

We therefore took our custom to the *boucherie* a little farther down the street. It was a large shop filled with all manner of exotic meat stuffs, manned by a group of jovial, mustachioed men with not a full set of fingers between them. My favorite feature of the shop was its rotund elderly female cashier, who sat behind her cash register and directed traffic in the store. She only ever moved to chase off the local homeless men who would occasionally help themselves to the potatoes roasting at the bottom of the chicken rotisserie outside on the street.

Next door to the butchery was the gay fishmonger. We knew he was gay because he loudly proclaimed his sexual orientation via a series of photos, posters, and flyers at the front of his store. Exactly what impact sexual orientation has on one's ability to monger fish—and therefore why he felt the need to profess his so loudly—I was never able to fathom. Then there was the cheese shop, a veritable shrine to dairy products and bacteria. The place was packed to its stinky rafters with cheeses of every hue and consistency. The stench that emanated from the store was formidable. Prerequisites for a career in cheese shop ownership, I concluded, included a completely dysfunctional sense of smell and a willingness to toil every day in the small-business equivalent of an armpit.

As different as our motley crew of *commerçants* were, common to all of them was a passion for their trade. Every day we would experience firsthand the joy of interacting with shop assistants who were passionate about their produce. More than simply running a bar code over a scanner, they performed each sale with a flourish. Each customer was a potential convert to the religion they had discovered in their produce—and they would willingly take time, no matter how long the line in their store, to explain the unique qualities of a certain cut of meat, bottle of wine, or variety of cheese.

It wasn't just the plentiful foodstuffs that made our new arrondissement so livable. Barely a ten-minute walk from our apartment lay the Canal Saint Martin. To the untrained eye, the Canal Saint Martin appeared to be nothing more spectacular than a concrete-lined puddle of stagnant water, along which canal boats would occasionally pass. If you happened to be in possession of a canal boat, and got your kicks out of traveling long distances at a snail's pace, you could navigate your way from the Seine (into which the Canal Saint Martin emptied) along a vast network of canals and locks all the way across the country to the Mediterranean. I was never tempted to take the trip myself and was instead content to use the canal for its infinitely more practical purpose: a scenic backdrop for eating, drinking, and late-night carousing.

Now, it may well be difficult to imagine a fetid stretch of algae-ridden water as scenic, but surrounded as it was by typically Parisian apartment facades, lined with trees, and featured as it had been in a key scene from the internationally successful *Amélie* movie, the Canal Saint Martin was the trendiest pocket of all Paree. In the midst of a wholesale gentrification, the quartiers surrounding the canal had recently proven fertile ground for a proliferation of groovy cafés, grungy-but-cool bars, and fashionable restaurants and boutiques. Hovering on the wrong side of respectability, the canal and its surrounds enjoyed the distinct honor of being the kind of place bourgeois Parisians from the sixteenth arrondissement would rather die than venture into—and by default, it was eminently cool. On warm summer nights barely a patch of concrete canal ledge wasn't populated by picnicking Parisian youth. Bottles of rosé, wheels of cheese, and long sticks of baguette were bandied about with abandon. Guitars were strummed, hash was openly smoked, and beer was bought in plastic cups from any of the bars lining the canal, ensuring that by ten o'clock on most summer evenings, the four-hundred-yard stretch of canal from Rue Faubourg du Temple to Rue de Lancry was heaving.

Smack bang in the middle of all the action, and doing a roaring trade because of its prime position, was Chez Prune. The café, like the canal it sat next to, was nothing special to look at. But thanks to its location and relaxed ambience, it was packed every night of the week. Across the canal was the Hôtel du Nord (immortalized in the eponymous 1938 film by Marcel Carné), whose dining room had recently been taken over by a celebrated set of Parisian restaurateur brothers and hence had been rendered *über*fashionable. Le Sporting, another chic eatery a little farther up the canal, the café-bar L'Atmosphere, the Chilean restaurant Santa Sed, and the sleek Italian pizzeria Maria et Luisa helped ensure that there was always a lively buzz to the area after dark.

Happily ensconced in the new neighborhood, and having found an interior design compromise that somehow incorporated both my Afghan rug and the Showgirl's collection of floral bed linen, we set about establishing a cohabitational rhythm. I was working from home, making occasional visits to clients or trips across town to conduct interviews for stories I had been commissioned to write. Shay was working nights, leaving home at 7:30 p.m. and returning at two a.m. It was, on the whole, a very sweet setup. With most days to ourselves, we spent a lot of time in each other's company. She would rise around eleven a.m., by which time I had done a couple of hours' work. We would run errands together, visit shops, or grab lunch at a café, all the while relishing being in Paris and loving falling in love. Studio 54 was spacious and comfortable enough that we could sometimes spend entire days indoors, slothing about in our pajamas, content to look down on Paris from our aerie built for two, rather than actually getting down amongst it. At night a key turning in the lock at two a.m. would herald the Showgirl's return from work. She would come bouncing through the door, her hair wet from her postperformance shower, still buzzing from the adrenaline of having performed two shows. I would pour a couple of glasses of red wine, and we would debrief her night at the Lido. It was unconventional, but it worked perfectly well for us.

When the Showgirl went to work, I made good use of my evenings by exploring the neighborhood for a local bar. As luck would have it, the hip Brazilian bar-restaurant Avé Maria (which had played host to many an entertaining evening in the past) now lay just outside our door. And since its bar was regularly tended by Morgan—an Australian friend who had been in Paris some twelve years—a cold beer or shot of ginger rum was only ever a too-tempting, too-short elevator ride away. Between the myriad nightly distractions on offer farther up our street (including the ever-reliable Café Charbon, a bustling bar fashioned out of a former dance hall) and the amenities that lined the canal, I had no occasion ever to leave my quartier.

Moreover, in moving from the Marais to Oberkampf, farther north of the Seine and therefore deeper into the so-called "right bank," I had become a card-carrying Rive Droite-ist. So much so that on the rare occasions when I crossed the river into the Rive Gauche, it all seemed dull and monochrome compared to the Technicolor explosion of vitality that was the Rive Droite. Where the Right Bank was gritty, colorful, and dynamic, the Left Bank was polished, staid, and conservative. Populated almost exclusively by rich Parisians—whose weekend wardrobe of choice included tasseled suede loafers, a business shirt, chinos, and a pastel sweater draped around the neck for guys, and jeans, pumps, tailored jacket, and pearl earrings for girls—the Rive Gauche served no practical purpose as far as I could tell beyond keeping tourists herded together in one part of the city so that real Parisians could enjoy the other, authentic parts of it.

You couldn't walk down a street on the Left Bank without being assailed by an American accent or being nearly mown down by hordes of Hello Kitty–sporting Japanese girls making a beeline for Café Flore.

Like its equally famous sister café, Les Deux Magots, Café Flore appeared to exist purely as a commercial and anthropological experiment to see just how much people would pay for a cup of coffee. At seven euros plus tip, it was always the one hit of caffeine I was willing to forgo. The Latin Quarter, once the home of artists and students and the cradle of a people's uprising in May '68, was now just a hoary collection of cheap restaurants offering more awful "tourist menus" than you could poke a wilted lettuce leaf at. Every night hordes of hapless tourists, clutching maps and dressed to the nines in Teva sandals and socks, would stumble into this taste-free zone. The irony of them being in one of the food capitals of the world and eating French onion soup from a can was almost too cruel to contemplate. Directed there by out-of-date guidebooks or hotel concierges, they were sucked into any one of countless identical outdoor cafés, made to sit on cheap outdoor furniture, and left to choose from a fixed menu offering lettuce with two bits of grated carrot, a greasy serving of chicken and chips, and a pallid crème caramel.

So it had come to this: almost six years into my Paris sojourn, I had become a Paris snob. The symptoms were all there. An inability to step outside the confines of my quartier, a borderline indifference to the myriad amazing cultural attractions on my doorstep, a deep and abiding dislike of tourists, and a tendency to dismiss anyone who had spent less than five years in the city as a Johnny-come-lately Paris part-timer. When had I become so jaded? It wasn't that I was tired of Paris, but rather that I needed to look at it through fresh eyes—from a new perspective.

Racing all over the city on a hell-bent mission to spend as many consecutive nights as possible in a state of high inebriation had been fine while it lasted, but if I wasn't careful, I was in danger of becoming a caricature. I was in danger of turning into my worst nightmare— one of those forty-year-old men who think that by wearing a tight T-shirt and moving awkwardly to the music in nightclubs, they can avoid looking tragic. The Marais was crawling with crusty old male expats who were clinging, like so many badly dressed, aging Peter Pans, to the notion that simply being in Paris allowed them to eschew responsibility, postpone indefinitely the process of growing up, and mince around bars smoking hand-rolled cigarettes.

I was determined not to become one of them. I needed a change of pace. I needed a new focus. I needed—quite obviously—to make an honest woman of the Showgirl.

Chapter 40

The Longest Day

BEING DISPOSED of a famously indecisive nature, I always knew the toughest, most agonizing decision I would ever have to make in my life would be deciding to ask someone to marry me. For the longest time, committing to spend the rest of your life in the company of one single person seemed to me one of the more perverse customs of our society. I used to wonder how, at the age of thirty, a person could say, hand on heart, that they would love, honor, and obey their partner fifty years hence. It all seemed a bit forced and unnatural to me. As a swinging bachelor with a short attention span, the very concept of being beguiled, sustained, and enchanted by one person for the rest of my life seemed altogether unlikely.

Even if it did come to pass, even if I was to meet someone I thought I could marry, I was certainly not going to take that decision lightly. Like all major decisions in my life, I imagined it was going to require months of deep contemplation. I would spend hours staring out my bedroom window, across the Paris rooftops, weighing the pros and cons. I would compile lists, hold intense evenings of discussion and debate with close friends and confidants, seek counsel, and duly consider opinions. I was, after all, the king of collective decision-making. It was a widely acknowledged fact among my friends that I was fundamentally incapable of making an important decision without first workshopping it with my mates.

Yet unbeknown to anyone, here I was, two years into my relationship with the Showgirl and on the eve of a planned vacation to Sicily, sitting in Cartier's flagship store on the Champs Elysées sizing up engagement rings. The decision to propose to the Showgirl had not come to me as an epiphany. It wasn't a vision I'd seen in a dream. Nor was it the result of weeks of canvassing trusted friends and relatives for their opinion or blessing. Instead, the prospect of us spending the rest of our lives together had become a happy inevitability. A fate toward which I was willingly, gladly floating. Our everyday lives had become so effortlessly intertwined, it seemed only natural that our long-term destinies should fuse as well. If this truly was to be the most important decision I made in my life, I wanted to make it alone—without a quorum, without censure or debate. I wanted it to be a decision made with conviction—even if it was on impulse.

"So have you made a decision?" asked Laeticia, the Cartier salesgirl and the only other person in the world who knew I was poised to pop the question. "Each of them is a beautiful ring. You cannot go wrong."

On the black felt tray in front of me sat three fat diamond rings. The first one looked big, the second looked bigger, and the third looked frankly ridiculous. Simultaneously representing the rest of my life and a significant potential dent in my bank account, they all caught the light and glittered at me cheekily. The science of stones—cut, clarity, and carat—had been explained to me half an hour earlier, filling me with confidence that I was about to make an informed judgment rather than execute a stab in the dark. What if it is the wrong style? What if she hates it? What if, heaven forbid, I have it all wrong and she is not the slightest bit interested in marrying me?

Outside, through the Cartier windows, the Arc de Triomphe towered above the Champs Elysées, the most famous avenue in France. One hundred yards down the Champs, the Showgirl was busy rehearsing at the Lido, a Parisian place that had featured heavily in our courtship. The setting was poignant and perfect, the timing was as good as it would ever be, and the ring was beautiful. It all felt right.

"I'll take that one," I said, ignoring the churn in my stomach and the sudden quickening of my heartbeat. Laeticia emitted a tiny squeal, clapped her hands excitedly, and busied herself with preparing my very expensive purchase. I can safely say I have never ridden the scooter home with more caution than I did that afternoon. The following day, with a suspicious bulge in my shoulder bag, we set off to the airport. The vacation, planned some four months previously, was to take in the Italian island of Sicily. My parents were visiting Paris from Sydney and would be joining us on the Sicilian sojourn, so I had factored into the proceedings a romantic little getaway for the Showgirl and myself to a resort on the Aeolian island of Salina. Three very long days stood between me and the Aeolian island where I intended to propose. Three days of laboring over the wording I would use to ask the Showgirl to become my wife, the exact location I would choose, and the time of day that would be most appropriate. Three days spent wandering the cobbled streets of the picturesque Sicilian town of Taormina, in the shadow of a steaming Mount Etna, with my parents in tow.

So paranoid was I about losing the ring before I had a chance to proffer it to my beloved, I had it safety-pinned to the inside of my trouser pocket. For three days and nights I walked with my hand in my left pocket, obsessively checking to make sure my secret package was safe. At night, when we changed clothes for dinner, I would wait until the Showgirl was in the shower, furtively unpin the ring from my shorts pocket, and repin it into whatever trousers I was wearing out that evening. When we went to the beach, I did so with a Cartier diamond engagement ring pinned to the inside of my swim trunks. The stress was exhausting. Never has something so small weighed so much.

By the time we bade adieu to my parents and boarded the ferry for Salina, the tension had become almost unbearable. I was distracted and distant. That the Showgirl had not noticed or questioned me about my strange behavior was testament to the full-time job she had been doing keeping Mum and Dad Corbett entertained. Playing to a tee the role of attentive significant other to their middle son, she had exhausted herself with my parents and could not have been more ready for a couple of days' respite.

As the ferry docked at Salina port, I looked across at the Showgirl—the wind tousling her hair, her face turned to the sun, and a smile lighting up her face. She looked at ease, relaxed, as if she had not a care in the world. A young woman on vacation with the man she loved, blissfully unaware of the colony of butterflies churning his stomach.

The night previously we had curled up together in our Taormina hotel room and watched the Italian romance film *Il Postino* on my laptop computer. I had bought the DVD in Paris, with the full intention of using it to set the scene for the impending marriage proposal. Filmed in its entirety on the island of Salina, the film tells the tale of a bumbling young postman who learns to harness the seductive power of poetry to woo the woman he loves. The majestic vista of Salina's twin verdant volcanic cones tumbling into the turquoise waters of the Mediterranean forms the stunning backdrop for much of the film. I smiled with relief as the same backdrop materialized now before us, finally confident that with this setting, the actual proposal would be a walk in the park.

I couldn't have been more wrong.

The day a man proposes is quite possibly the longest day of his life. Unless he gets it out of the way over breakfast, he has to carry around the knowledge of what he is about to do for the rest of the day. By virtue of its very nature, it's a burden he cannot share, resulting (at least in my case) in prolonged periods of nervous silence. (Not, you may have gathered, a normal state for me.)

Now comfortably ensconced in Salina's five-star Capofaro Resort, we awoke the next morning to a picture-perfect early summer day. From our private veranda and across a vineyard, we could see a plume of smoke rising from the top of the volcanic island of Stromboli. I roused, as is my custom, a good hour before the Showgirl, whose nocturnal habits tended to follow her even on vacation. For fifteen minutes I watched her slumber beside me, reveling in the knowledge of what the day had in store for her. For my part, beyond knowing that today, our only full day on Salina, was my best and only chance during this vacation to ask for her hand in marriage, I had no idea when, where, or how the proposal would unfold. But confident that the day would unfurl and the perfect moment would present itself, I hopped out of bed and started making preparations.

I removed the ring from its safety pin in my pocket and transferred it to its impressively large red and gold-gilt Cartier box. When the time came to proffer the ring, it would look infinitely more impressive in the box than on the end of a safety pin. The box was then safely stored in the bottom of my camera bag.

Having decided to explore the island on a scooter, we headed for the small port town near the resort and collected our steed for the day, a battered, incontinent, sputtering little rental scooter whose lack of alignment required you to steer approximately thirty degrees to the left of whatever direction you actually wanted to head in. As wedding proposal vehicles went, it was hardly the most luxurious. But then, the beauty of the island was such that our mode of transport would surely prove inconsequential.

We spent the morning winding our way through gorgeous scenery. The roads weaved up and down mountainsides and were framed overhead by the verdant boughs of flowering trees. Sweeping valleys spilled like folds of green velvet over sheer cliff faces into the sea. At each new crest or hairpin bend in the road, a new vista of exquisite beauty would take our breath away. The Showgirl was in raptures. The proposal was in the bag. After a lazy lunch of local pasta in the sun-drenched garden of a tiny taverna, we headed for a tiny fishing village offering a view back across the beach that had been featured in *Il Postino*.

As we spread our sarongs on a rocky outcrop some fifty yards from the water's edge and settled in for a spot of sun-worship, I rehearsed my proposal line, confident that this was the perfect spot to pop the question. To our left was a sliver of beach from the romantic flick we had watched two nights before. To our right were the glassy waters of the Mediterranean. The only other sign of life was a lone female sunbather, down by the water and spread out on the rocks beneath us. I positioned myself behind the Showgirl, spooning her from behind and encouraging her to lean back into me.

"What's all this about then?" she asked. "You're very affectionate all of a sudden."

There are several things a man wants to hear when he shows his lover a bit of impromptu affection. This is not one of them. "What do you mean 'all of a sudden'?" I replied defensively. "I'm always affectionate, aren't I?" I was thrown now, convinced she knew something was up.

"All right, all right. Keep your wig on," the Showgirl said. "Sorry I mentioned it. Keep cuddling please, it feels nice."

Nursing my wounds but determined to rescue the moment, I decided to wait a few minutes until the mood softened. In my head, I rehearsed my three proposal options over and over: *Will you marry me? Will you do me the honor of becoming my wife? I love you and want to spend the rest of my life with you. Marry me.*

I took a deep breath and extricated myself from behind the Showgirl. Moving then into a kneeling position in front of her, I took her hand, looked her in the eye, and said: "There's something I have to ask you." She looked back at me expectantly, clearly with no idea what I was about to say.

"I wanted to ask you—" I stopped midsentence, distracted by a sudden movement by the sunbather below. I found myself staring wide-eyed in her direction—mouth agape.

Apparently unaware of our presence, or simply unfazed by it, our sun-soaking companion was midway through heeding the call of nature. On her haunches by the water's edge, and with her bikini bottom pulled carefully to one side, she was busily releasing a long stream of steaming piss.

"Oh my god!" exclaimed the Showgirl. "Is she doing what I think she's doing?"

The moment was ruined. No way was I going to propose while a woman urinated next to us. Call me an old romantic, but it just didn't feel right.

"Let's move. This place is sullied," I said, silently cursing the pissing woman as we packed our things and clambered back up the hill to the scooter. "Let's go to that beach—we'll have it all to ourselves," I suggested, swinging into motion Proposal Plan B.

Ten minutes later we were sitting on the *Il Postino* beach. Behind us a sheer cliff face rose some hundred yards toward the sky, its white stone facade scored with an intricate network of lines and fissures. Before us the sea undulated toward the twin volcanic islands of Filicudi and Alicudi. The sun sank toward the horizon. The setting was perfect. We had the beach to ourselves. It was the same place the postman had seduced his would-be wife. A stunning spot, loaded with significance, it would make for the perfect "where did you get engaged" dinner party story. It was, I decided, time to strike. Having already rehearsed my moves, I prepared to execute them once again, moving in for the mandatory preproposal cuddle before shuffling around into a position from which I could get onto bended knee.

Suddenly a pair of German backpackers came crashing down onto the beach. The woman removed most of her clothing almost immediately, in that way Germans do. Then for reasons known only to Germans, she decided to pierce the silence of this idyllic stretch of beach by striding up and accosting the only other two living things upon it. She bowled up the beach and took up position between us and the water, blocking out our sun. A seminaked, middle-aged German woman wearing Teva sandals and not much else.

"Hallo there!" she bellowed loudly, despite standing directly in front of us. "Have you seen the jellyfish in the water? Did you know that if they sting you, you will die?"

Excellent, I thought to myself. *Perfect Proposal Moment Number Two ruined by the German fascination with the macabre.* I sank back down onto the sand.

"Yes, apparently it is a swift but agonizing death," continued Frau Morbid, clearly warming to her theme. "All it takes is one sting, and *pfft.*" She drew a line across her neck with her finger. "You're dead!" As the Showgirl politely feigned interest in lethal oceangoing invertebrates, I sat fuming, willing the German to leave us in peace. With the sun dipping toward the horizon, the ring was feeling heavier and heavier.

One exhaustive inventory of freakish seaside vacation deaths later, we bade *auf Wiedersehen* to our Teutonic cheer merchant and watched as she disappeared back up the cliff path with her partner.

I had to propose on this beach, I told myself. It was the perfect spot. The late afternoon sun beat down as I let the air settle, the mood change, and I readied myself for proposal attempt number three. The Showgirl was sitting between my legs, reclining into my chest. Both of us sat in contented silence, staring out to sea. I carefully reached around to the camera bag, took the ring box in my hand, and started to slowly, quietly extract it. My heart raced, my breath quickened. This was it, one of the most important moments of my life. The only sound was the gentle lap of tiny waves on pebble stones.

Then: "Did you shower this morning?"

It was the Showgirl.

"Because your armpits really stink."

I slowly slid the ring back into the bag. It was doomed. The whole beach-proposal concept was fast turning into a farce. Whatever the gods of fate had in store for me that day, it definitely did not include proposing marriage on this beach. I suggested we return to the hotel so I could tend to my apparently offensive body odor.

We packed our things and headed up the cliff path. I felt defeated and desperate, my arms pinned self-consciously to my sides. Behind us, the sun dipped below the horizon. The clock was ticking, and I was no nearer to asking the Showgirl to be my wife. We were scheduled to leave the island and meet up with my parents in just over twelve hours. I could sense the window closing.

Later that evening back at the resort, as we cleaned ourselves up for dinner, I was a nervous wreck. As the only guests left in the hotel, I had arranged for us to dine on the poolside terrace. I had it all figured out. We would have a great meal, we would drink a good bottle of wine, and when the Showgirl got up from the table to powder her nose, I would ask the waiter to take the ring to a separate table with a view across the ocean and place it there with a bottle of Champagne. Thereupon we would move over, and hey presto—surefire marriage proposal.

So it was with my armpits duly scrubbed, I escorted the Showgirl from our little cottage, through the vineyard, and toward the pool and dining area. It was a warm evening. A gentle sea breeze ruffled the leaves on the vines.

"Why are you bringing the camera bag to dinner?" the Showgirl asked, not unreasonably.

"Huh?" I replied, caught short. "Oh right, yeah, the camera bag. Um. I guess I wanted to get some footage of the pool." I realized how lame it sounded even as I was saying it. "And you know, film the meal and stuff."

"Right," she replied, not the least bit convinced.

As we sat at the table, the waiter rushed over and starting setting a third place.

"Um, what are you doing?" I asked.

"As you are the only guests in the hotel this night, the manager, Mr. Fabio, is pleased to dine with you" came the reply.

"You've got to be kidding," I retorted, altogether too forcefully. "There's no way he is eating with us. No way. Not a chance. Not possible, you understand?" Panic was rising in my voice.

"Honey!" the Showgirl interjected, shooting me a reprimanding look. "Relax! There's no need to be so rude! If the manager wants to eat with us, it's fine. We will have plenty of opportunities to dine just the two of us. It's no big deal."

"Ah, but it is a big deal," I said, packing up the silverware as fast as the waiter could lay it. "Not tonight. Not now. Not—going—to—happen." I accentuated each word by thrusting a piece of cutlery back into the bemused waiter's hand.

"Whatever," the Showgirl responded, rolling her eyes and returning to her menu. The meal was off to a rocking start. From this sterling, slightly neurotic performance, I was going to have to work doubly hard to recover.

The meal arrived, and it was delicious. The wine was plentiful, ably lubricating the proceedings. Except for the lone figure of the hotel manager dining by himself some five tables away, the dinner was perfect. But why hadn't the Showgirl gotten up to use the toilet? A ladies' room visit was crucial to my proposal plan, and while usually her bladder had the storage capacity of a thimble, tonight she was a camel. No matter how often I kept refilling her water glass, she didn't budge

Damn your uncooperative bladder! I thought to myself, glancing at the clock and watching the minutes tick away. It was just after midnight. In nine hours we would be boarding the ferry for the mainland, with my parents waiting expectantly at dockside. We would be out of our little two-person bubble, off our island getaway, and back to the joys of mediating the disputes between my parents as one drove and the other got us lost. Time was fast running out, and the Showgirl's bladder was showing no signs of relenting. I had to act, and act quickly.

"Would you like another liqueur?" asked the waiter, cleaning up the glasses from the previous three I had thrown back in a nervous gulp. If I didn't stop procrastinating, I would soon be too drunk to walk, much less pull off a marriage proposal.

"No, thank you," I replied. "But we would like two glasses of Champagne and a plate of strawberries to go please."

The Showgirl roused herself from her mildly drunken funk and sat upright in her chair. I could almost hear her thinking: *Champagne? Strawberries? My, he is pushing the boat out tonight.*

With Champagne flutes in hand, I took a lantern from the dining table, grabbed the Showgirl by the hand, and walked her slowly back through the vineyard toward our cottage. The dark outline of a long-extinct volcano could be made out against a sky that seemed to be pulsating with stars. I installed the Showgirl on the veranda with the strawberries and Champagne, then sneaked inside to transfer the ring box to my back pocket and prepare the proposal soundtrack.

Knowing this moment would require a suitable soundscape, I had burned a CD with all of our favorite, mushy songs. I had carried it with me to the restaurant and had intended to ask them to play it as she emerged from the ladies' room. It now spun on my laptop, flooding the night air with one of our favorite tunes, the Bobby Darin song "More."

"When did you make this?" the Showgirl asked, cocking her head and clearly starting to suspect something.

"Never you mind," I replied. "May I have this dance?"

We stepped barefoot out onto the lawn. I took her by the hand and pulled her close to me, and under the stars we started to dance. Her head fell onto my shoulder as we turned slowly about the lawn.

"Look up," I instructed. We drank in the night sky together, taking a deep breath to savor the moment.

"Shay," I said finally. "There's something I have to ask you." I got down on bended knee, pulled the ring box from my back pocket, opened it, and held it up to her. "Will you marry me?"

She was momentarily struck dumb. With a sharp intake of air, hands over her mouth, and eyes wide with disbelief, she emitted a short squeal and started to cry.

"I take it that's a yes?" I ventured.

"Yes! Yes! Of course yes!" she finally managed.

A canopy of stars hung above us. Beyond the pale circle of light cast by our lantern, all around us was pitch black. We felt, for the briefest moment, like the only two people on Earth.

Chapter 41

The View From Here

I LOVE SITTING UP HERE in my little aerie in the eleventh arrondissement. From my desk in the study I have fashioned out of our tiny walk-in wardrobe, I stare out the window and enjoy a quiet moment with the Paris rooftops.

It's early evening, and in the bedroom next door the Showgirl is stretched out asleep on the bed, stealing a few moments of rest before she takes to the stage on the Champs Elysées and performs her two shows. Her long limbs are folded into her, her delicate eyelids are closed, and her mouth is ever-so-slightly agape. Her breathing is slow and regular.

Summer is in full swing now, and after a day of blistering heat, the city is baking below me. Out a window thrown open to catch a hint of cross-breeze, I see clumps of orange chimney pots sprouting from gray rooftops. A terracotta army marching across an uneven patchwork of leaden fields to the near horizon.

On that horizon the Eiffel Tower stands proud, waiting patiently to perform against whatever magnificent backdrop this evening's sunset offers up. The early signs look good. To the right of the tower the sun dips below the horizon, cueing a blaze of oranges and reds. Wisps of cloud above the tower are tinged with pink. Against a sky of powder blue, swallows dip and turn, effortlessly riding the thermals of a city cooling down.

As the clock strikes seven, the tower explodes in a frenzy of flashing lights. Momentarily electrified, it shimmers, as if quivering with excitement at the prospect of presiding over another spectacular summer evening. In what looks suspiciously like unbridled joy, the world's most famous monument briefly shucks off its staid composure and severe metallic lines to become a glittering, dancing shard of light. Later in the evening, when darkness falls, the searchlight atop the tower will spin around, casting its beam across the city, sweeping across our bedroom wall as it goes.

From this vantage point I look back on the last six years of my life in this remarkable city. I came to Paris on a whim. Two years into an overseas jaunt and desperate to escape the daily reminders of a broken heart, I had hopped a train to Paris on a wing and a prayer. Like the old harlot she is, Paris took me to her bosom. She welcomed another seeker to the fold, introduced me to her myriad nightly pleasures, and set about seducing me as she had done countless times to countless chancers before me.

On the practical front, the move from London to Paris had meant making the happy transition from nuisance to novelty. From being one of half a million Australians in London to one of only five thousand in all of France, I went immediately from omnipresent to exotic the minute I crossed the Channel. Stand in a bar in France and tell a French man you are Australian, and he will almost explode with excitement. Whether he is simply relieved that you are not English or genuinely delighted at having met that most extraordinary of the human species, a real live Australian, I can never tell. Either way it is immensely gratifying.

It was an experience that only served to make me prouder of my homeland. I suddenly began to appreciate all the things I had previously taken for granted, simply because I saw them reflected in the eyes of an awestruck foreigner. And not just the obvious things like beaches, sunshine, and space, but things I had never really considered before. Things like political stability, relative wealth, a high standard of living, and most strikingly, the sense of the possible that exists in a country like Australia.

Propping up the bar on any given night in Café Charbon in Oberkampf would expose me to people from all over the world, a veritable grab bag of nationalities including Moroccans, Algerians, Tunisians, Cameroonians, Senegalese, Armenians, and Russians, to name a few. Each of them, whether first- or second-generation Parisian, seemed heavy with the disappointment of having come to a land believing that there would be streets paved with gold, only to discover that their inescapable fate was to sweep them. Together with an entire generation of students and other young people, among whom unemployment ran at a rampant 26 percent, these "new French" felt trapped by a system that seemed bent on maintaining the status quo and stifling opportunity. French attempts to resist globalization by peddling their admirable if delusional idea of "cultural exception" struck me as tantamount to trying to stop the tide from coming in.

Compared with my sunny New World homeland, the fault lines in Old World France were striking. An aversion to change, a strict adherence to "the way things are," plus a society that was (despite its constant bleating of the revolutionary war cry *Liberté, égalité, fraternité!*) essentially elitist had created a dead-end nation for the generation that was supposed to be its future. Australia was a series of sketches on a blank canvas compared to the dusty old Renaissance masterpiece that was France. The great tableau Down Under of rich ochres and ocean blues was a work in progress. There was room enough left on the blank portions of the canvas for you to feel as though you might add a splash of color of your very own.

In France, however, the lines had been drawn centuries before—and beautifully classic though the painting was, it had long ago been framed, hung, and signposted "Do not touch!" Without a doubt Paris is a perennially popular tourist destination because the city is one glorious museum. Beautiful old buildings, quaint little streets, turn-of-the-century cafés, stunning monuments—all of them are steeped in history and jealously guarded by a city council bent on milking the city's romantic appeal for all it's worth. It is a living, breathing museum in which I was usually very happy to feature.

As an exhibit in the Exotic Oceania section, I was mostly content to play my role to expatriate perfection. But much as I had come to love my adopted home, I knew deep down that I would never belong. I wasn't French and never would be. Moreover, my flight from Australia had been motivated not by a burning desire to escape its strictures, but rather by a burning desire to see what else was out there. As such, the prospect of going home was never a question of *if* so much as *when*.

The longer I stayed away from home, the more determined I became to eventually return. Paradoxically, the longer I was away, the harder and less viable that return journey became. Like thousands of expats before me, I was trapped between two worlds. The curse of the Australian expat is that what you left behind is, for many different reasons, at least as good as what you have found.

I likened my Parisian luck to the same fortune I had had in having great parents and a good childhood. While the sturdiness of the foundations from which you came made it possible for you to move away in the first place, they would also ensure you would eventually come home. But how to reconcile my longings for home with the joys I had discovered in this new place?

There are so many things I miss about Australia. I miss the light, the sense of space, and the fact that the sky seems bigger and bluer. I miss fish and chips at the beach, watching a southerly storm break out at sea, bindis in my feet, a schooner of beer, and real Thai food. I miss the purple blaze of a jacaranda in summer, the laconic sense of humor of my countryfolk, their complete inability to take themselves seriously, and the general sense of happiness. I miss it all acutely, especially on those days when living in France requires more energy than I can muster.

Whether it's a winter that seems to have no end, a day spent in line at the *préfecture*, a rude waiter, or an hour spent sitting in traffic caused by another protest march, I often find myself wondering what the hell I am doing here.

Then I am reminded of all the reasons I came to Paris in the first place—and the things that have made me want to stay. Because people go into raptures over a cut of steak and a great glass of wine—and could not care less about having a back deck or the right brand of sunglasses. Because having a modest yet comfortable lifestyle is more important than acquiring and aspiring. Because Paris is an international city with a village atmosphere—you can phone a friend and within five minutes be sipping a beer with them on a sunny terrace. Because participating in political life, reading books, and engaging in lively intellectual debate in smoke-filled bars is considered just as mighty and worthy a sport as chasing a pigskin around a paddock. Because when I wake up in the morning and go to sleep at night, I have this view—this spectacular view over the world's most beautiful city.

And while none of it, in sum total, is necessarily better than what I left behind, all of it is different. And for now, that's enough of a reason to be here.

THE SHOWGIRL STIRS in the next room. She'll soon be awake and heading off to work, and our life together will hum happily along in the comfortable groove we have carved here.

When we landed in this city all those years ago, so far from our homes, neither of us could have guessed at what fate had in store. I thought I would stay a year, while Shay thought she'd see out a twelve-month dance contract. That one year has turned to six is testament to the spell Paris is capable of casting. That I traveled to the other side of the world to meet and fall in love with someone from my homeland is a small miracle I am happy to lay at the feet of this most remarkable city and the magic it seems so effortlessly to weave.

Maybe our time here is limited. Maybe one day we'll decide to head home. We'll pack a couple of bags, give away our motley collection of some-assembly-required furniture, and bid adieu to the fascist fruiterers and fingerless butchers. I'll say a fond *au revoir* to my former neighbors, the boys, the Orthodox Jews, Xavier, and Sticker Bitch, and the Showgirl will take her final curtain call.

Then again, Paris has held us in her sway for this long, who is to say she won't continue to enchant us as we embark upon the next stage of our lives together? It is Paris, after all.

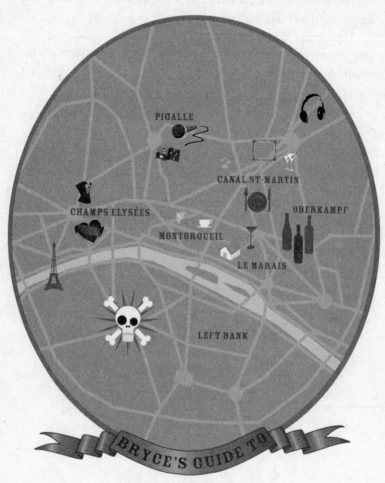

PIGALLE

CANAL ST-MARTIN

CHAMPS ELYSÉES

OBERKAMPF

MONTORGUEIL

LE MARAIS

LEFT BANK

BRYCE'S GUIDE TO

PARIS

© CHRISTABELLA DESIGNS

Bryce's Guide to Paris

Le Marais

LE CONNÉTABLE (Rue des Haudriettes, fourth arrondissement), where all good evenings go to end.

AU PETIT FER À CHEVAL (Rue Vieille du Temple, fourth arrondissement), because everyone needs a local watering hole.

ROBERT ET LOUISE (Rue Vieille du Temple, fourth arrondissement), bench tables, open fire, slabs of meat, and a hilarious octogenarian *maîtresse*.

L'AS DU FALAFEL (Rue des Rosiers, fourth arrondissement), best falafel in Paris.

LA PERLE (Rue de la Perle, third arrondissement), popular with the cool kids.

AUX TEMPLIERS (Rue Caffarelli, third arrondissement), dead cool, well-hidden watering hole.

ANDY WAHLOO (Rue des Gravilliers, third arrondissement), great mojitos, cheesy tunes, superstylish, always a winner.

Canal Saint-Martin

CHEZ PRUNE (Quai Valmy, tenth arrondissement), groovy canal-side café-bar.

LE SPORTING (Rue des Récollets, tenth arrondissement), good French fare in sleek surrounds.

MARIA ET LUISA (Rue Marie et Louise, tenth arrondissement), Italian pizzeria with style.

SANTA SED (Rue des Vinaigriers, tenth arrondissement), Chilean restaurant run by a pair of musical brothers.

FAVELA Chic (Rue du Faubourg du Temple, tenth arrondissement), caipirinha-soaked sweatbox.

LA BARAONDA (Rue René Boulanger, tenth arrondissement), Maurizio's restaurant, best pasta in town.

L'EPHÉMÈRE (Canal Saint-Martin, near Jaurés, nineteenth arrondissement), art-space-cum-bar-bum-live music venue. Popular in summer.

BAR OURCQ (Canal Saint-Martin, near Parc de la Villette, nineteenth arrondissement), Sunday afternoons in summer for boules, beer, and DJ.

Oberkampf

AVÉ MARIA (Rue Jacquard, tenth arrondissement), the Brazilian bar-restaurant where anything can happen and usually does. Beware the ginger rum.

L'AUTRE CAFÉ (Rue Jean-Pierre Timbaud, eleventh arrondissement), as good a typical French brasserie as you're likely to find in the 'hood.

CHATEAUBRIAND (Rue Parmentier, eleventh arrondissement), art deco–designed eatery popular with the fashion set.

BAR ROSSO (Rue Neuve Popincourt, eleventh arrondissement), where the cool kids hang midweek.

LE 9 BILLIARDS (Rue Saint Maur, tenth arrondissement), for Saturday-night shenanigans.

Montorgueil

LE TAMBOUR (Rue Montmartre, second arrondissement), the twenty-four-hour eatery where there is always a crowd and always a late-night freak or three.

LA CANCALE (Rue Montorgueil, second arrondissement), perfect for Sunday-morning recovery brunch.

LE COEUR FOU (Rue Montmartre, second arrondissement), hip little hole-in-the-wall bar.

Pigalle

AUX NOCTAMBULES (Boulevard Clichy, eighteenth arrondissement), sixties crooner Pierre Carré performs every night at eleven, complete with red suit and quiff. Unmissable.

O'SULLIVAN'S/THE HARP (formerly Jack's)/Corcoran's/Café Oz (Boulevard Clichy, eighteenth arrondissement), quartet of expat bars popular with Contiki Tour kids and Moulin Rouge dancers.

LA CLOCHE D'OR (Rue Mansart, ninth arrondissement), late-night eatery popular with showgirls.

MOULIN ROUGE (Boulevard Clichy, nineteenth arrondissement), can-can your heart out.

Champs Elysées

LIDO DE PARIS (Champs Elysées, sixteenth arrondissement), where magic happens nightly.

CRAZY HORSE (Avenue George V, sixteenth arrondissement), has to be seen to be believed.

Avoid the rest of the sixteenth arrondissement like the plague.

Left Bank

Nothing to see here.

Acknowledgments

Thanks are due to the many friends, family, and acquaintances whose shared experiences over the past eight years have given me fodder for this book.

I am grateful too for the invaluable copytasting efforts of Miranda Murphy and Alister McMillan. I owe a special debt of gratitude to Melinda Welton-Howard for her snappy title suggestion; to Penny Green for her sage words of advice; to the holy trinity of book cover collaborators—Carla Coulson, Arno Ferrié, and the Lido de Paris; to Nik Quaife, for providing me with a quiet corner of southwestern France in which to get the book ball rolling; and of course to my un-flappable, ever-pleasant editors, Ann Campbell and Laura Lee Mattingly, and my trusty agent, Faye Bender.

Thanks also to my long-suffering family for taking it all in the spirit in which it is intended, and to my beloved, Shay, who is a daily source of inspiration.

And finally *un grand merci* to Paris, the old seductress with the timeless charm.

we were
sorry to hear
of your loss

About the Author

BRYCE CORBETT is an Australian journalist who has been living in Paris for more than six years. He arrived in the City of Light following a two-year stint in London, where he worked as a print journalist at *The Times* and as a television producer at Sky News. A former Sydney gossip columnist, Bryce has written for a variety of international newspapers and magazines including *The Australian, People, Harper's Bazaar, Vogue,* and *Australian Gourmet Traveler,* and he has worked as a TV producer for networks in Australia and the United States. He currently lives on the Rive Droite with his wife.